What comes after you say, "I L♥VE YOU"?

What comes after you say, "I L♥VE YOU"?

BY JAMES R. HINE

WITH A FOREWORD BY DAVID R. MACE

Pacific Books, Publishers   Palo Alto, California

LIBRARY OF CONGRESS CATALOGING IN PUBLICATION DATA

Hine, James R.
    What comes after you say, "I love you"?

    Includes bibliographical references.
    1. Marriage. 2. Love. 3. Sex in marriage.
I. Title.
HQ734.H633   306.8   80-11277
ISBN 0-87015-231-9

PACIFIC BOOKS, PUBLISHERS
P.O. Box 558, Palo Alto, California 94302, U.S.A.

Foreword

I once asked a group of men, picked at random, to answer this question: "Suppose I offered you the choice between a congenial job and an unhappy home, or a happy home and an uncongenial job. Which package would you settle for?" I told them to take time to think it over before replying.

Somewhat to my surprise, the majority of them answered, in effect, "It was a tough decision to make, but give me the happy home, and I'll put up with the job." I had intended to put the same question to a group of women, but I decided there was no need to do so.

Domestic bliss is a blessing highly prized. From the age of magicians' spells down to the era of scientific research, efforts have been made to discover the secrets of successful marriage. Knowing what the secrets are could make all the difference, for multitudes of men and women, between happiness or unhappiness, fulfillment or frustration, pain or joy.

The first major research on marital happiness was published by Lewis Terman in 1938. Since then, a series of such studies has been reported—in America by Ernest Burgess, Leonard Cottrell, Clifford Kirkpatrick, Harvey Locke, Reuben Hill, and others; in Britain by Eustace Chesser; in Sweden by Georg Karlsson.

In recent years, researchers in the family field have turned in other directions. Despite our increased knowledge and skills, we have not used these resources to follow up the earlier studies of marital happiness. Marriage itself has been under direct attack, and the attention of many family specialists has been diverted to the new alternative life-styles.

There are now clear evidences, however, that the focus of attention is coming back to the marital dyad, particularly the new form Burgess described as the "companionship marriage." Promising new breakthroughs are occurring in the understanding of couple communication, in the creative use of marital conflict, in the treatment of sexual dysfunction. A swing from the remedial approach to marital disharmony to the more hopeful preventive approach, accompanied by a nationwide grassroots movement for marriage enrichment, indicates a renewal of confidence in the possibility of better and more fulfilling relationships between husband and wife.

Coming at such a time as this, Dr. Hine's book is especially welcome. Based on new and important research in a field too long neglected, it draws extensively on the best modern scholarship. Yet it is written not primarily for the experts, but for ordinary men and women, for whom it has a message of confidence and hope. Best of all, it is written by a man who is not only a highly qualified scholar and teacher, but also an experienced and sympathetic marriage counselor. To an unusual degree, Dr. Hine has mastered the rare and difficult art of taking the profound insights of the specialists and making them intelligible to the people who can put them to the best use—married couples striving to live together in love and harmony.

Books on how to succeed in marriage flow from our presses in a steady stream. Some offer little more than an assortment of pious platitudes. Some are sound in content but not easy to read, others lively in style but with little substance. From so vast a literature it is not easy to select more than a handful of books on marriage, for the reading public, that are really first-rate, and most of these, in a time when our knowledge is rapidly increasing, soon go out of date.

I would unhesitatingly give Dr. Hine's book a very high rating. I have read it with interest and with profit. I can recommend it, without hesitation, to the married and to those approaching marriage, as an authoritative, sound, and very helpful guide to the great art of living the shared life. The mastery of this art, as we are at long last coming to understand, is far from easy; it may take a lifetime. There could be no better way to begin than to study this book and assimilate the wisdom it contains.

DAVID R. MACE

Preface

My files, and those of every marriage counselor, are filled with cases of people who, at one time in their lives, said to each other, "I love you," but who later came to a place where they could no longer make this declaration or tolerate living together as husband and wife.

Did they mean it when they first said, "I love you"? Did they take love seriously at that time? Most of them thought they did. What happened? Many are apt to say, "Perhaps the love they thought they felt for each other was not the real thing." This reply raises a question about the nature of genuine love, one that we will discuss more fully later.

But I am convinced that being in love, even in the best sense of that word, does not guarantee a successful and happy marriage. So much depends on what comes after the love is felt and declared. To say that a couple "fell in love, were married, and lived happily ever after" is a simplistic, overly romanticized concept of what marriage is all about. But it is one which, unfortunately, is still entertained in the minds of thousands of young people who enter marriage with inadequate preparation, knowing little about what it takes to make a marriage succeed.

What does it take to make it succeed? An attempt to answer this question is the subject of this book. It all began several years ago, when I was reading *The Family in Search of a Future,* in which Herbert Otto said that so much was being written about the pathology of marriage and family life, when more ought to be done to discover why marriage succeeded. This statement motivated me to start a research project (which is still in process) to determine, from the experiences of a number of couples I knew, why their marriages were successful.

In the summer of 1972, I invited a number of couples I had known for many years to join my wife and me for a week in a retreat center in northern New Mexico. I explained that we would be discussing their marriages in order to discover more about marital success. I had worked with these people in marriage preparation classes of one sort or another, and had followed the progress of their marriages through the years. All but one couple (married eight years) had been married fifteen years or more. Nine couples and their families accepted the invitation and came to our session. All did advance work before coming, by preparing materials that would be useful to us in the study. During the sessions, each couple talked with the group about their marriage and later made tape recordings for our future use. Among other assignments, each couple wrote in detail about why they believed their marriage was successful. After the retreat, the couples continued to send me materials they had worked on regarding their approach to role concepts, value patterns, and religious beliefs.

In the summer of 1973, I invited nine more couples in the Tucson area to join the study. These people I either knew personally, or they were recommended to me as having well-functioning marriages. All but two couples (married five and eight years, respectively) had been married more than ten years, and one couple had been married forty-seven years. Since that time, these couples have continued to furnish me with material similar to that obtained from the first group. From material and information gathered from these eighteen couples we were able to construct an evaluation instrument consisting of thirty-nine characteristics they considered to be most important to the success of their marriages. We have received replies from all eighteen couples evaluating themselves on this instrument. We have also used this instrument to evaluate fifty-six additional couples with varying degrees of success in their marriages for comparison purposes. We have self-ratings from all 148 persons involved in the study, indicating on a scale between 0 and 100 how successful they believe their marriages to be. Our original eighteen selected couples scored 90 or above. Thirty-three additional couples scored 85 or above. Nine scored between 60 and 85. Fourteen scored below 60. All marriages scoring below 60 showed marked signs of serious problems, and some were on the verge of failure.[1]

We hope to continue this study for five more years, enlarging both our

---

[1] In June of 1976, Vicki Straub, a doctoral candidate in the field of Counseling and Guidance at the University of Arizona, sent the Locke Marital Adjustment Test to the families in our select group. Fifteen of the eighteen families responded. The "happy" range in this test is a score between 100 and 119. The "very happy" range is between 120 and 135. Nine couples scored in the "very happy" range. The other six scored in the "happy" range. One couple achieved a perfect score of 135. Thus we have three sources of agreement: the couples' evaluation of their marriages, my evaluation, and that of the Locke Marital Adjustment Test.

select and comparison groups. But we think we have enough material now to help us say something useful about what goes into a successful marriage. What is said here may not be startlingly original. Many of our conclusions are those reached by others who have studied this area before. We hope we can reinforce the time-honored principles that marriage educators and counselors have been emphasizing for years, and discuss new insights to help us.

For the young couple contemplating marriage, and for the couple already married but hoping to enrich their marriage, we hope this book will be sufficiently illuminating and practical to help bring about marriages that are individually fulfilling, socially productive, and consistently stable through the years.

I am deeply grateful to the eighteen couples in our select group who worked hard and long to give me the material upon which this book is based. It is their hope and mine that from their living example of how marriages can succeed and be rewarding, others will receive inspiration, courage, and information that will help them find a similar fulfillment.

JAMES R. HINE

Contents

PART I

Love Is a Many-Splendored or Otherwise Thing

CHAPTER ONE

Never Marry a Stranger

First, some thoughts about what to do before you say, "I love you."

There is a story about a young man who, on the spur of an inspirational moment, proposed to a young woman he had been dating for a short time. "Will you marry me?" he asked. "Yes, I will!" she replied enthusiastically. The young man lapsed into a strange silence. Puzzled, the proposed-to young woman prompted, "What's the matter? Why don't you say something more?" The young man replied, "I am just thinking I may have said too much already." He may have done just that. Many have, and have lived to regret it.

Joanne had dated Bill for more than a year. She was eighteen; he was several years older. He proposed marriage, and she accepted. As the wedding date drew near, she began to have doubts, but everyone, including her fiancé and her mother, reassured her. "It's just a matter of pre-wedding jitters," they told her. "Besides," she added, "the wedding invitations had been sent, the presents received, the bridal showers in progress, the wedding and reception planned. How do you walk out of a big production like that?" Two weeks after the wedding, Joanne wanted out. "He was a stranger, a total stranger," she confessed. "I didn't know him at all—what he was like, that he had been married before, that he was tied to his mother's apron strings." "How is it possible," I asked, "to have dated Bill for a year and to have found him to be a total stranger?" "It isn't hard at all," she explained, "the whole relationship can be superficial—dances, parties, movies, always putting up a front to impress the other. We never talked in depth or went through any crisis experiences together. We were infatuated and sex kept the relationship stimulating. But we never got to know each other well. If I ever marry again, I am going to take lots of time. And we are going to be honest and know each other as we really are, so that after marriage we won't feel like we are living with strangers." Joanne volunteered to tell her story to a university class in preparing for marriage. Later she made a tape so that her story could be told over and over in years to come. "I want to keep others from making the mistake I made," she explained.

What do you do after you say, "I love you," and find out you said it too soon, with a limited knowledge of the other person, or to someone unsuitable as a marriage partner for you? I hope you will have the wisdom and the courage to admit your mistake and withdraw. In a class I teach on preparing for marriage, we devote a session to the subject of how to break an engagement or a relationship that won't work. It is that important. Betty came at the end of the semester and exclaimed, "I've got good news for you. I've just broken my engagement." Was that really "good news"? It was for Betty. "I know it would never have worked. I see it now. I know what it takes to make a good marriage, and we didn't have it. So, it's over and I'm relieved."

Get your divorce *before* you get married, is one way of putting it. Realizing too late that marriage is a mistake puts one in an unhappy position. Perhaps the problems in such a marriage can be worked out with patience or with the aid of a marriage counselor, perhaps they cannot. In Joanne's case there seemed to be no hope. There were too many obstacles to overcome. Divorce is never easy, and the aftermath is difficult to negotiate. If there are children, they will probably suffer from the breakup of the family unit.

Dave and Judy were a couple with a lot of common sense. They were not engaged, but had been dating a year and were more than fond of each other. Their request was this: "We want to take a good look at ourselves and our relationship before we make a permanent commitment to each other. Will you help us do that?" I was happy to have a couple come to me *before* a wedding date was set. It is not easy to give counseling to an engaged couple a few weeks, or even months (although that is better) before the wedding takes place. All clergymen know the truth of this. Being as nonobjective as most couples are at that time makes it difficult for them to think clearly, or for the counselor to be an effective educator.

What did we do? Premarital counseling differs according to the needs of the individual couple, so I will present the plan in a general way. It would be helpful if some or all of the following goals could be realized.

1. *To come to a better understanding of oneself.* Does it seem strange that preparing for marriage should begin with preparing oneself? Not at all. For marriage is a partnership of two people, each embodying a great variety of personality traits, habits, manners, skills, ideas, experiences, values, and beliefs. Do people recognize these traits and know what they

mean? Not to the extent that they should. But you cannot relate to another person effectively unless you have an adequate understanding of yourself. If you are a mystery which you yourself cannot understand, and if you cannot explain why you think and behave as you do, how can you relate to someone else meaningfully? In the class in preparation for marriage which I teach, each student writes an eleven-chapter autobiography beginning with events in early childhood and moving up to the present, describing how he or she related to parents, friends, pets; early infatuations; learning about sex, love, marriage concepts, religious beliefs, and a philosophy of life. In addition, the student makes a self-appraisal of personality traits, an evaluation of family background, and a listing of priorities in regard to qualities desired in a marriage partner. Many students have said that this experience in self-understanding is the most valuable part of the course.

Self-understanding can lead to self-acceptance, which means neither self-satisfaction nor complacency with what one is. Self-acceptance, in the best sense of that term, can mean a willingness to begin where one is without blaming the past or harboring feelings of self-deprecation. It can mean assuming full responsibility for what one is today and then moving on, determined to be a more loving and a more human person. This resolve raises the level of one's self-esteem, which is necessary for relating to another person. For one cannot love his neighbor unless he loves (respects) himself.

2. *To obtain a sufficient knowledge of the other person.* The title of this chapter is "Never Marry a Stranger." Joanne lived with her husband only two weeks before she discovered that he was a "stranger." She had little knowledge of the real Bill. Dave and Judy were determined not to go into marriage without knowing each other. I tried to give them every opportunity to learn to know each other.

First, they were given a manual especially prepared for couples contemplating marriage.[1] This manual suggested to them areas of exploration and discussion: background, ideas about marriage and home life, compatibility of personalities, ideas, interests, beliefs, value systems, sexuality, role concepts, and religion. They were encouraged to work on the assignments and discuss the results openly and honestly, without avoiding controversial or sensitive issues. The counselor would see them periodically and discuss with them matters that they wished to explore further with him.

They were given an opportunity to take a sex knowledge inventory[2] and a marriage prediction test,[3] and to work on a communication instrument.[4]

Did they know each other more fully at the end of this process, which covered a period of several months? They felt they had confronted each other as truthfully and realistically as possible, and, therefore, were much more able to make a sound decision about their future.

Many young people today (particularly college students) are asking the question: "Wouldn't it be wise to live together as a couple before deciding to marry? In this arrangement wouldn't we come to know each other better?" Cohabitation is increasing on the American college campus. In a study made by Peterman, Ridley, and Anderson at Pennsylvania State University, 1099 students responded to the question: "Are you now, or have you 'lived with' someone of the opposite sex?"[5] A total of 360, or 32.8 per cent responded in the affirmative (33.4 per cent of the men; 32.3 per cent of the women). One half of the cohabitants (180 of 360) said that they had engaged in more than one such arrangement. Males reported shorter cohabiting experiences, 50 per cent reporting that their longest arrangement lasted less than a month, while 31 per cent of the cohabiting females had liaisons lasting less than a month. For the most part, they described their longest cohabiting experiences as "love" or "intimate" relationships. We do not know how many considered them as "trial" marriages.

In a survey of my marriage education classes during four years, 929 women and 257 men responded to the statement: "I would like to have the experience of living with a person before deciding to marry, if this were socially acceptable," as follows:

TABLE 1-1

		% Yes	% No
1972	Men	95	5
	Women	54	46
1973	Men	89	11
	Women	64	36
1974	Men	84	16
	Women	71	29
1975	Men	89	11
	Women	67	33

Our study indicates that a large percentage of men and an increasing percentage of women are interested in this arrangement.

What will all this mean for the future of marriage and the family? Will cohabitation as it is currently being practiced lead to better decisions by couples before entering marriage and thus lessen the possibility of divorce? Will the "trial" marriage become socially acceptable and eventually legalized, as Margaret Mead and others suggest it should? What will contribute to sounder and more lasting relationships between husbands and wives?

We do not have sufficient evidence at this time to answer these questions adequately. From my own clinical experience dealing with couples who are or have been cohabiting, I would have to say that many problems attend this kind of an arrangement, where often there are no ground rules, no permanent commitments, a limited sense of responsibility, and, too frequently, a difference of opinion as to what the relationship really means. Some couples have reported that it helped them decide that a marriage for them would work. Some said it saved them from what might have been a disastrous marriage. For many it was inconclusive.

Sociologists Lyness, Lipetz, and Davis concluded that "to a very striking degree, living-together couples did not reciprocate the kinds of feelings (of need, respect, happiness, involvement, or commitment to marriage) that one would expect to be the basis of a good heterosexual relationship."[6]

The eighteen couples in our study, who represent the attitude of parents and of an older generation, were not in favor of cohabiting as a means for a couple to get to know each other better. They felt their method worked quite well for them and without the hazards of cohabitation.

We do know that a more thorough knowledge of each other is essential for the couple who wishes to make a good marriage choice. We are still searching for ways of accomplishing this more effectively.

3. *To evaluate the relationship of the couple.* A successful marriage consists of two people who are able to relate together in a loving, harmonious manner. Will and Patty were students of mine who later became very close friends of our family. We became very fond of them and admired them for the fine people they were. When they announced their intention to marry, we were extremely happy. It seemed to us that such a marriage would be among the best. They married and moved to another city, and we received letters from them periodically, always full of optimism and hope. Then one day there came word that Will and Patty had separated. Shocked, we asked, "How could this happen to such a fine couple?"

Most of us have had similar experiences with friends or relatives. There is no simple explanation, but it can be said that two excellent prospects for marriage might be highly incompatible together. It is not easy to predict whether or not a couple will be compatible.

Temperamental compatibility is the most important, perhaps. People are like chemicals; some blend well when put together; others explode. Agreement on roles, values, beliefs, and goals helps immeasurably. The eighteen couples in our select group all scored high in the area of compatibility, as we shall see later.

When Dave and Judy were tested on compatibility of interests, values, and role concepts, they learned about areas of mutual agreement, and had lengthy discussions about matters on which they disagreed. The very fact that they were willing to talk in depth with each other was evidence that they were moving into a higher degree of compatibility. The counselor was impressed with the honesty and understanding with which they related to each other.

What about sexual compatibility? We discussed that, too, and suggested some reading material. But it is my opinion that good sexual relations are a part of a good total relationship. A gynecologist, Dr. Herbert Pollock, a close friend for many years, puts it this way, "If they get along well in the kitchen, they will probably get along well in the bedroom."

I have often used a formula to try to describe what a successful marriage relationship is.

$$M g_1 + F g_1 = \text{Successful Marriage}$$

The elements can be described as follows:

M = male

F = female

g = good prospect with characteristics such as: friendliness, warmth, optimism, emotional maturity, responsibility, ability to cope and communicate, etc.

p = poor prospect with characteristics such as selfishness, irritability, coldness, emotional immaturity, pessimism, inability to communicate, disorganization, etc.

1 = set of characteristics compatible with all other 1's

2 = set of characteristics compatible with all other 2's

Additional numbers indicate other sets of characteristics; the farther they are from 1, the less compatible they are with 1 characteristics. Thus: $M g_1 + F g_2$ would be more apt to be compatible than $M g_1 + F g_7$. $M p_1 + F p_7$ would signify a disastrous marriage, combining two poor prospects with very different and incompatible sets of characteristics.

4. *To help develop skills needed in the relationship.* Marriage is a vo-

cation that calls for greater knowledge and a wider range of skills than do most vocations. Heavy demands are made upon people as husbands, wives, and parents. In my opinion, it is more difficult and more complex to be a parent or a partner today than it was in former years. People are subjected to more stresses and strains in our modern, urban, industrial society than they were in the earlier rural and small-town setting. Many couples who succeeded in marriage in the early 1900s might have failed today. What comes after you say, "I love you," involves harder decisions, tougher problems, the ability to cope with change and transition, to meet greater expectations, and to rear children in a society of confused morals and meanings.

In the equalitarian home, which is the ideal of many contemporary married people, the art of communication and the skill of negotiation are necessary. In discussing this in a clarification session with our select group, it was made clear that no couple felt it had mastered this art or fully achieved this skill. All couples acknowledged that these skills were paramount, but said they had to work constantly to arrive at understanding and to formulate compromises satisfactory to the relationship.

Perhaps the development of these skills is what we should emphasize most with Dave and Judy. If we can help them learn more about how to handle conflict, how to communicate effectively, and how to arrive at decisions that will contribute to the best interest of both of them, we will have given them help where help is most needed in a marriage.

5. *To help the couple know more about available resources.* We were interested in the fact that our successfully married couples stressed the importance of knowing how to meet crises. Meeting a crisis demands resourcefulness. They had read books on how to live, how to handle money, and how to nurture children. They had attended classes, workshops, church groups, and study groups where family problems were discussed. They were interested in health, recreation, religion, community service, and generally in a fruitful, productive life. In times of trouble they knew where to go for help.

We shall discuss this more later. In our marriage education classes, we inform our students about the resources available in the community, including clergy, physicians, marriage counselors, home economists, lawyers, investment counselors, and insurance advisers. We also try to acquaint them with the best pamphlets and books in all these areas. Learning about resources available to a couple is an important part of getting ready for a life together and becoming more realistic about marriage and family life.

REFERENCES

1. James R. Hine, *Grounds for Marriage.* Danville, Ill.: Interstate Printers and Publishers, 1971.

2. Gelolo McHugh, *Sex Knowledge Inventory.* Saluda, N.C.: Family Life Publications, 1967.

3. Ernest Burgess, *Marriage Prediction Schedule.* Saluda, N.C.: Family Life Publications.

4. James R. Hine, *Marriage Counseling Kit.* Danville, Ill.: Interstate Printers and Publishers, 1970.

5. Dan J. Peterman, Carl A. Ridley, and Scott M. Anderson, "A Comparison of Cohabiting and Noncohabiting College Students," *Journal of Marriage and the Family,* Vol. 36, No. 2 (May 1974), pp. 344–54.

6. Judith L. Lyness, Milton E. Lipetz, and Keith E. Davis, "Living Together: An Alternative to Marriage," *Journal of Marriage and the Family,* Vol. 34, No. 3 (May 1972), p. 310.

CHAPTER TWO

What Do You Mean When You Say, "I Love You"?

I often begin a class discussion on love by having students decide whether they tend to agree with, disagree with, or are not sure about the following statements. As you read them, make a mental note as to how you feel about each: A=Agree; D=Disagree; N=Not sure.

1. Love is something that happens to you; you can't cause it to come or stay away.   A   D   N
2. Love cannot be analyzed scientifically because it is more emotional than rational.   A   D   N
3. Love is a mysterious thing which doesn't always make sense.   A   D   N
4. When one is in love it prevents one from thinking clearly and objectively   A   D   N
5. One can only come to love another through a slow growth process over a considerable period of time.   A   D   N
6. If you really love a person you are apt to be jealous of that person's relation to anyone else.   A   D   N
7. If you feel you love a person, this is reason enough for marriage.   A   D   N
8. Love at first sight is possible.   A   D   N
9. When you are in love, you will have no doubts about it.   A   D   N
10. There is just one person in the world you can love sufficiently for a happy marriage.   A   D   N
11. One can love two people of the opposite sex at the same time.   A   D   N
12. True love can surmount all difficulties in a marriage.   A   D   N

13. Love means different things to different people.   A·   D   N
14. You can love a person and not like the person.   A·   D   N
15. Genuine married love can be destroyed through carelessness and neglect.   A·   D   N

Without exception, after classes take this test, the students are ready for a spirited discussion. Rarely do we ever get unanimous agreement on any of the statements, although I can't remember anyone ever agreeing with No. 10, "There is just one person in the world you can love sufficiently for a happy marriage." Apparently, the ancient myth that there is that one "Mr. Right" or "Miss Perfect" waiting for you has been dispelled.

At one time or another, most of us have said to someone, "I love you." Some people use the words "I love you" very sparingly, while others say it to almost everyone they meet. Apparently, it means different things to different people. I sometimes think it is the most ambiguous word in our language, and its use ranges all the way from saying, "I love banana cream pie" to referring to "the love of God."

People are at the mercy of the various definitions of love set forth in comic books, movies, television, newspaper accounts of well-known couples loving in and out of wedlock, endless songs about love on records and radio, and ad men selling products that will make one desirable in the love market.

In the movie "Sweet Charity," the naive young woman tells the sophisticated actor that she can never forget the inspiring words he spoke in a picture, "Without love, life has no purpose." He replies cynically, "What a person won't do for money!" One can say the same thing about what has been done for money with a very meaningful word—"love." It has been used to sell almost everything from cosmetics to motor cars; from toothpaste to cruises in the Mediterranean; from magazines to motion pictures. "What a person won't do for money!"

One doesn't need to be a marriage counselor very long to discover the confusion in the minds of many people about what love means. Depending on the occasion and who says the word, it may mean, "I want you," or "I want you to want me," or "I would like to exploit you sexually," or "I need you," or "I desire you for my security," or "I want to help you," or "I accept you for what you are," or "I have decided you are the one I want to live with for the rest of my life." Does the word imply desire, passion, admiration, exploitation, need for protection, loneliness, or what?

In our culture most couples say they marry for love. In a national poll taken a number of years ago asking the question, "What quality do you want more than any other in the person you marry?" the prevailing answer from both males and females was, "Someone to love me." Apparently, we all agree that love is the greatest thing in the world. But what in the world does love mean? Because it means different things to different people, we should be aware of what causes these differences, and what they mean.

If you want to get a reaction from a group of mature people, ask them how many thought they were in love with someone during their middle teen years. Most will admit they thought they were. Then ask how many wished they had married the person with whom they thought they were in love at that time. Your question will be met with much laughter. Their ideas about what love is have changed drastically.

Why is the casualty rate so high in teenage marriages? All studies show that there is a relation between the age at which a couple marries and their marital success. Couples who marry in their mid or upper twenties have less failure than those who marry in their teens or early twenties.[1] It appears that as people get older, they often become more capable of making good judgments and more skillful in managing interpersonal relationships. Their concepts of love mature into more sensible forms. Contrast the difference between the "puppy love" you felt for a childhood sweetheart or the crush you had on a movie star, and the love you developed later on for the person you married. Young love is often a giddy, bubbly, short-lived, extravagant emotional experience. Mature love is one that develops gradually and lasts through the years, if it is nurtured.

What are some of the attributes of an immature concept of love?

1. *High response to eye appeal.* A person can be physically attracted by the appearance of another person. While individuals differ in terms of what may attract them, all of us are conditioned to desire certain characteristics in the opposite sex. The mass media do this conditioning very effectively, portraying the "ideal" man or woman in advertising, the motion picture screen, magazines and newspapers, the TV tube, the campus beauty queen, or the Miss America pageant. From early childhood we are programmed to desire certain physical characteristics. When we see that image in the form of a living being, we are stricken with the idea that this is *The One.* "Our eyes met across the crowded room and we knew we were meant for each other." But, of course, we didn't know. We were only responding to what was appealing to our sense of sight, previously conditioned.

This has led me to believe that many people in contemporary life suffer from what might be called the "cosmetic complex."[2] The word *cosmetic* comes from the Greek word *Kosmetikos,* meaning a skill in decorating the exterior. When people become preoccupied with external appearances at the expense of internal qualities of personality and character, they may be said to have a "cosmetic complex." One of our largest industries has developed to serve this obsession with making the body lovelier and preserving the bloom of youth. With the proper wardrobe, paint, powder, spray, vitamin-enriched ointments, fragrant, airy bubbles, smooth, creamy, luxurious oils, ultra brightening toothpaste, we strive to make our outside attractive, scented, sensuous, and sexually stimulating to the gaze, the smell, and the touch of those around us.

I have no quarrel with anyone who wants to look his or her best. I enjoy seeing people who look clean, neat, appealing, and vital. But let us not be misled by identifying a visual image with what a person really is. The person may be all vogue on the outside and all vague on the inside. Eye appeal has motivated many to believe they were in love. And marriages have resulted, in some cases, much to the regret of those who found the real person wasn't the one they really wanted.

2. *Surface enchantment.* This attribute implies focusing on superficial qualities and seeing them as more important than they really are.

Laura was enchanted with Kenny's athletic ability. He was a football player of considerable talent, and Laura associated his heroics on the field of play with determination, courage, and masculinity. After she married Kenny, she found him to be lazy, irresponsible, and highly dependent. Her admiration for him was centered on a quality that later proved to be unrelated to the things she really wanted in a husband.

It is possible, especially for the inexperienced, to be misled by some characteristic that dominates and stimulates a relationship to make it seem to be something it isn't. A friend of mine fell in love repeatedly with women who were the "clinging-vine" type. Their dependency made them very desirable to him. His friends saw them as shallow, weak, and lacking in strength of character, but he thought of them as extremely feminine and ego-satisfying.

I have listened to college students exude over their dates in such terms as: "He's lots of laughs." "She really knows how to make love." "His folks have a lot of money." "Her family is high up in the social order." "Someday he'll be a big success." "I've always wanted to marry a doctor." "I just love to hear her talk." It is hoped that these are but initial reactions, and that there will be a deeper probing into what the person is really like before the relationship gets too serious, a probing that will prevent a marriage evolving from surface enchantment alone.

3. *Fantasy projection.* We see here a person who has built an image of an ideal marriage partner. When some convenient man or woman comes along, this image is projected onto him or her, and an illusion is created, one to whom the person tries to relate and then love.

Every marriage counselor is familiar with the client who complains about the spouse: "He isn't the man I married"; "She isn't the woman I married." That cannot be true literally. Their partners were not switched. What each means is that he or she did not turn out to be the person "I thought I married." The ideal and the real could not be equated.

A series of lingerie advertisements that was carried in our popular magazines several years ago showed a man looking up at a beautifully attired woman on a pedestal. Like the ad, we tend to construct our loved ones into something we want them to be, and place them neatly on pedestals where we may adore them in our fantasy world. The loved one may feel complimented by this idealization for awhile and try to reinforce it, but sooner or later, reality must be faced.

Often both parties wear masks, assuming characteristics thought to be desirable by the other. In the first chapter, we heard Joanne say that for a year she and Bill assumed false fronts so as not to disappoint each other's expectations. This masquerade creates a relationship between two fantasy figures, not the real people themselves.

Women sometimes project a "father image" upon the men they hope to marry, or men may project a "mother image" on the women they would like to have as wives. The hope is that the spouse will take the place of a parent. When a prospective spouse makes it clear that he or she has neither a desire nor an intention of playing a parental role, the relationship may deteriorate.

4. *Narcissistic love.* In Greek mythology Narcissus is supposed to have fallen in love with his own reflection while gazing into the waters of a spring. Perhaps the basic human problem in relating to another is centered in what might be called the "egocentric predicament." Even while wanting to love another person, one faces the temptation to be preoccupied with his own self-interest. Is it possible then, that one may believe he is loving another, when in reality he is loving himself reflected in the other? While it is reasonable to expect some measure of self-fulfillment in loving another person, genuine love should be more concerned about affirming the other, thus helping that person become fulfilled.

The high school girl who finds it thrilling to be seen walking through the halls with the star athlete is thinking not so much of him as of how people will envy her because she is with him. One can believe that a love for another exists when it is little more than a desire for someone to enhance one's own image. So in saying, "I love you," one means, "I love what you can do for me," which is more like exploitation than love. While sexual attraction is an important ingredient in a love relationship, desiring another for the primary purpose of self-gratification is hardly adequate. Egocentric love is, to say the least, self-defeating.

5. *Love as dependency.* A certain kind of love reveals itself in the form of a dependency on another person. Out of a sense of inadequacy one may turn to another to compensate for one's own feeling of deficiency. Although everyone needs help and support from other people, if carried to an extreme, dependency can result in a relationship resembling an addiction. Stanton Peele and Archie Brodsky have elaborated on this theme in a book which they have titled, *Love and Addiction.* They put it this way:

> Love is an ideal vehicle for addiction because it can so exclusively claim a person's consciousness. If, to serve as an addiction, something must be both reassuring and consuming, then a sexual or love relationship is perfectly suited for the task. . . .

> When a person goes to another with the aim of filling a void in himself, the relationship quickly becomes the center of his or her life. It offers him a solace that contrasts sharply with what he finds everywhere else, so he returns to it more and more, until he needs it to get through each day of his otherwise stressful and unpleasant existence. When a constant exposure to something is necessary in order to make life bearable, an addiction has been brought about, however romantic the trappings. The ever-present danger of withdrawal creates an ever-present craving.[3]

I have observed lovers who followed this pattern and in so doing seemed to lose interest in other people and the world around them. Peele and Brodsky believe that this state of intense absorption is similar to drug addiction in that the "love" becomes something in which they are totally involved for their sustenance and gratification. The lovers cut themselves off from other resources as the dependency on each other becomes paramount. When a breakup occurs, it can be as traumatic as that of heroin withdrawal. This kind of love is apt to be generated in people with low self-esteem and strong feelings of insecurity and inadequacy. It is the antithesis of a love that encourages personal growth and competency and in which each has a concern for the well-being of the other.

All five types of love just described could be classified as forms of infatuation. The word infatuation comes from "fatuous," meaning foolish, unreal, or illusory. Here love tends to be more emotional than rational; more illusory than realistic; more self-centered than unselfish; more naive than experienced; more fatuous than wise. These forms of infatuation are immature and undeveloped in that, in many cases, they are preliminary stages through which many people move to arrive later at more mature levels in their relationships. The process toward a more mature love might be something like this:

1. Man and woman meet. (The thrill of discovery)

2. Man likes what he sees. Woman likes what she sees. (Visual attractiveness)

3. They enjoy communicating. (Superficial interest in each other develops)

4. Each makes a special effort to please the other and meet the other's expectations. This process is mutually reinforcing, so the relationship gets stronger, and they see each other more frequently. (Surface enchantment; they still do not know each other)

5. As they do things together, they discover each other's interests. If these interests are compatible and sufficient in number, the relationship is intensified.

6. As time goes on, the couple becomes more relaxed and disarmed, each showing more of what he or she is really like to the other. Personality characteristics become more obvious. If temperamental compatibility is recognized, they become more fond of each other and more comfortable in the relationship. The ideal is coming closer to the real.

7. An increasing sense of intimacy is realized. A physical, mental, and emotional closeness develops as they relate in expressing affection and talking about ideas, values, beliefs, hopes, dreams, and goals. They find they have much in common, and can share their most intimate inner thoughts.

8. They learn to deal with problems, disagreements, and conflicts. As their lives become more closely entwined, they discover they don't agree on all matters. Quarreling and misunderstandings may arise, or other problems that call for negotiation, compromise, and problem-solving. If they find that they can solve problems reasonably well, they feel even more confidence in the relationship.

9. The bond between them is reinforced by a growing conviction that their needs are being met and they really must love each other. They consider making the relationship permanent.

10. The engagement. A commitment is made for a permanent relationship. They can be relatively sure of each other now. This becomes a time of final testing, and a period of preparation for life together. There is an excellent opportunity to enrich love feelings, and build trust and confidence, at this time.

Of course, love relationships don't always develop according to this pattern. The order can vary with the couple, but surely a mature love, solid enough to support a marriage, must have an evolution of growth and change something like this. Ira Reiss proposes a theory, which he supports through research, that all major cultural types of love develop through a "wheel process" moving through stages of rapport, self-revelation, mutual dependency, and personal need fulfillment. To understand this process, one must investigate the cultural and social factors that underlie it as it applies to various types of young people. The romantic variety of love goes through this same process very rapidly, perhaps in the course of one evening. The sexually-centered type of love limits itself to "one way around the wheel—one way of revealing oneself." The rational type of love is more cautious and takes more time to incorporate "a larger number of rapport, revelation, dependency, and fulfillment factors than of other love types."[4]

The relationship at Points 1, 2, 3, and 4 of our development pattern is, of course, tenuous. Perhaps this is the infatuation phase. Can it be anything more, in the short time that has elapsed so far? At Point 3, some kind of evaluation is being made. How much do we like each other? How are we getting along? How does this relationship compare with others I may be involved in at this same time? Do I want to continue or should I break it off? This evaluation continues periodically through all the remaining steps. Even during the highest level, 10, some relationships are severed. Such was the case of the student (in Chapter 1) who came after class with the "good news" of her broken engagement. "I know now it would never work."

At what point in the process between first meeting and engagement, does one have a right to say, "I love you"? Again we must say it will vary with different people. Perhaps it will be said in some way at Point 7 for most. If the word "love" is to retain any meaning at all, it should not be used too soon.

If we were to analyze carefully what has happened in the development of love through these various stages, what would our conclusions be? Is love something we can break into component parts? I am quite sure we would come up with different answers from different people. Some would stress a set of characteristics that others might consider secondary. Perhaps two people might love each other very adequately without some aspects of love that others might consider essential. With these qualifications in mind, let us suggest that the following attributes might be, and often are, a part of mature love.

1. *Love involves a fondness, respect, and admiration for someone.* Doris and Henry, a couple in our research group, have been married

forty-seven years. When I asked Doris to explain why she had had such a happy, enduring relationship with Henry, she replied, "I liked him at the start, and have continued liking him ever since." Apparently she felt that liking him had much to do with loving him. But, as Zick Rubin points out in his book, *Liking and Loving,* ". . . while liking and loving are surely close relatives, they are by no means identical. The bridge between research on liking and the extensive writings on love remains to be built."[5] Later he compares loving and liking in terms of assisting a couple's progress toward a closer relationship. Research

indicates that liking, too, predicts progress toward a more intense relationship among the romantic students. Liking is not quite so effective a predictor as love is, but it is a reasonably good predictor nevertheless. To some extent this result was predetermined by the fact that love and liking are correlated with one another. It nevertheless appears to be the case that among "simultaneously hardheaded and idealistic" young Americans evaluations of intelligence, maturity, and good judgment and perceptions of similarity play almost as large a role in propelling couples toward more permanent relationships as do the wings of love.[6]

Marriage counselors are familiar with situations in which people declare their love for each other, but admit they do not like each other. Such couples might have a better relationship if they didn't have to live together. But marriage requires propinquity, and to be near each other day after day in so intimate a relationship requires a mutual fondness if the two people involved are going to live in harmony. Love, apart from liking, doesn't get the job done.

Perhaps we could sum up this aspect of love involving liking, admiring, respecting, by calling it affection. This is a warm word that is not easy to define, but it seems appropriate to use to summarize what we mean here.

2. *Love is developing an attachment to a person found to be sexually-socially desirable.* This trait seems to be a happy combination of eros and philia. *Eros* is the driving force that propels us toward union with our beloved. It aids us in bridging the gap that separates us from the experience of completeness and fulfillment. According to Rollo May:

In regard to our preoccupation with the orgasm in American discussions of sex, it can be agreed that the aim of the sex act in its zoological and physiological sense is indeed the orgasm. But the aim of eros is not: eros seeks union with the other person in delight and passion, and the procreating of new dimensions of experience which broaden and deepen the being of both persons. . . . It is this urge for union with the partner that is the occasion for human tenderness. For eros—not sex as such—is the source of tenderness. Eros is the longing to establish union, full relationship. . . . The two persons, longing, as all individuals do, to overcome the separateness and isolation to which we all are heir as individuals, can participate in a relationship that, for the moment, is not made up of two isolated, individual experiences, but a genuine union. A sharing takes place which is a new Gestalt, a new being, a new field of magnetic force.[7]

The second part of this combination is *philia,* a Greek word relating to the family line. We find the meaning of ourselves, not alone, but in union with another member or members of the family. There is a bond, almost indestructible, in kinship. Could we not say that *eros* has fused us into this bond?

Some have given the word *philia* a liberal translation to mean a close friendship. Is it unreasonable to suggest that lovers should be good friends? Some are not. They may passionately embrace each other physically, but they do not embrace each other mentally or spiritually. Our successfully married couples unanimously endorsed the importance of companionship. They enjoyed one another socially, shared common interests, activities, and goals. They liked to be together, and they liked to be together with other people.

In a love that partakes of *eros* and *philia,* people overcome their isolation in union with another. Life is never quite the same again.

> Two lovers
> come together
> at the confluence
> of merging hopes and dreams,
> and loneliness is lost.

3. *Love is a concern for another—a desire to affirm, to help, to serve.* Let us turn to the Greek again for help in understanding the many-sided nature of love. The word *agape* is impossible to translate, for there is no word in the English language that carries its meaning. Paul, in First Corinthians, writes, "Love bears all things, believes all things, hopes all things, endures all things."[8] Here he uses the highest word for love he knows, *agape. Agape* is a self-giving, compassionate love. It has within it that emphatic sense that helps one know how another feels, and gives one the desire to share the burden. It is an active love that moves to assist and help.

In this sense it is the opposite of hate; where hate desires to destroy, this love desires to affirm and give life to the loved one. It accepts, without condoning, the faults and weaknesses of the other. It seeks to understand where understanding is difficult. It is ready to forgive, to reconcile.

Is this kind of love too far beyond the capacity of a human being to be put into practice? Perhaps we have seen it in the love of a mother for a child, or a saint's willingness to give his life for others without thought of self. But can we expect it to operate in a marriage? Perhaps this love is seen too seldom in marriage relationships, but we have observed it in the lives of the successful married couples in our study group—not all the time, but often enough to convince us that it is a very vital, renewing type of experience for married couples to have.

4. *Love is a search for completeness and fullfillment through another person.* We have discussed under No. 2 the kind of love that overcomes loneliness and isolation through union. Here one is motivated from a sense of deficiency or incompleteness. In a profound sense, no male or female can claim complete independence from the other. No one is physiologically equipped to be self-sufficient. Male and female need each other to reproduce the human race, and to satisfy their sexual needs. In sexual intercourse, male and female are joined in a functioning entity. So, there seems to be a built-in safety factor to keep a human being from declaring himself or herself independent of all others and thus destroying the pairing of the human race.

> Then the Lord God said, "It is not good that the man should be alone; I will make him a helper fit for him. . . . Therefore a man leaves his father and mother and cleaves to his wife, and they become one flesh."[9]

Is there not also a need for a mental and emotional completeness that can come only from a heterosexual union? However you may want to define it, there is something we can observe as masculinity and femininity, and each has its own distinct qualities. The blending of these qualities makes each feel a wholeness.

While we like to think we can help our children grow up to be independent, this independency, at best, is insufficient to meet life's demands. Everyone has some feeling of inadequacy. At times, the strongest feel anxious and insecure. One of the exciting experiences of being in love for each of us is the recognition that someone believes in me, thinks I'm worthwhile and wants to help me, comfort me, support me in times of need. This is a healthy dependency, in contrast to the addictive type referred to earlier.

Everyone has a set of needs that he cannot fulfill by himself. When someone enters the scene and begins to fulfill these needs, a feeling of well-being is generated. After working for many years with couples in the pre-marital stage, I have come to believe that once a person recognizes that his needs are being met by another, a dramatic change comes into the relationship. For the relationship to thrive, this recognition must be mutual—two people meeting each other's needs. Here we have a functioning partnership giving each partner a sense of fulfillment and security. We see here a coming together of what we discussed under No. 3, and what we are talking about now—each saying to the other, "I need you," and at the same time, "I want to help you." Harry Stack Sullivan put it very well when he said, "When the satisfaction or the security of another person becomes as significant to one as is one's own satisfaction or security, then the state of love exists."[10]

5. *Love is a decision and a commitment.* A psychiatrist friend of mine announced to me one day that he had gained a new insight into the nature of love. "I have come to believe," he said, "that love is a decision." What kind of a decision is it? A partial answer might be that it is a decision made in the light of the facts of the case, after a careful evaluation of the relationship, to love another person, and to help this love grow and develop through the years to come.

Rollo May in discussing stages in therapy says:

> The process of therapy with individual patients involves bringing together the three dimensions of wish, will and decision. As the patient moves from one dimension to the next in his integration, the previous dimension is incorporated and remains present in the one that follows. Intentionality is present on all three dimensions.... Decision, in our sense, creates out of the two previous dimensions, a pattern of acting and living which is empowered and enriched by wishes, asserted by will, and is responsive to and responsible for the significant other-persons who are important to one's self in the realizing of the long-term goals.[11]

In this sense, decision leads into a commitment, and love becomes a commitment to, and a covenant with, this significant other. Love, then, is something much more than the way we feel today and the way we feel tomorrow. It is a journey with another person which we have both decided to make and complete in a certain way. Love, like marriage itself, is more than the ingredients that go into it. It is an ongoing process sustained by determination and creative effort. We shall want to discuss this further when we talk about successful marriages.

In a day when the importance of sexual adjustment to love and marriage is so highly emphasized, let us look back on a conclusion reached by Alfred Kinsey and his associates after their exhaustive study of sexual behavior:

> There are few married persons who have not, at least on occasion, recognized a serious need for additional information to meet some of the sexual problems which arise in marriages. On the solution of these problems the stability of a marriage may sometime depend, although we have previously said, and reassert in the present volume, that we do not believe that sexual factors are the elements which most often determine the fate of a marriage.

We have also said that there seems to be no single factor which is more important for the maintenance of a marriage than the determination, the will that that marriage shall be maintained. Where there is that determination, differences between the spouses may be overlooked or forgotten and minor disturbances may be viewed in a perspective which emphasizes the importance of maintaining the marital union.[12]

Certainly a love that has within it this kind of dedication and determination will take a couple a long way toward marital success.

What do you mean when you say, "I love you"? You are speaking out of an experience of a number of years, conditioned by your social, cultural, and religious environment. What you think of when you say "love," has been learned in the past, and developed in your various experiences in loving and being loved. What you mean depends on your personal definition of love, the way you have reacted to the reinforcement and rewards you have received from the person you believe you love, and the kind of personal investment you intend to make in the relationship. This means taking what you say in the words "I love you," very seriously, with all the rationality and determination you can muster.

How do I love thee. Let me count the ways.[13]

REFERENCES

1. Judson and Mary Landis, *Building a Successful Marriage.* Englewood Cliffs, N.J.: Prentice-Hall, 1963, p. 128.

2. James R. Hine, *Come Prepared to Stay Forever.* Danville, Ill.: Interstate Printers and Publishers, 1966, p. 69.

3. Stanton Peele with Archie Brodsky, *Love and Addiction.* New York: New American Library, 1976, p. 70. (Originally published by Taplinger Publishing Company, New York, 1975.)

4. Ira L. Reiss, "Toward a Sociology of the Heterosexual Love Relationship," *Marriage and Family Living,* Vol. 22, No. 1 (February 1960).

5. Zick Rubin, *Liking and Loving.* New York: Holt, Rinehart and Winston, 1973, p. 211.

6. *Ibid.,* p. 335.

7. Rollo May, *Love and Will.* New York: Dell Publishing Co., 1973, pp. 74, 75.

8. *First Corinthians* 13:7.

9. *Genesis* 2:18, 24.

10. Harry Stack Sullivan, *Conceptions of Modern Psychiatry.* New York: W. W. Norton and Co., 1946, pp. 42–43.

11. Rollo May, *Love and Will,* pp. 262, 267.

12. Kinsey, Pomeroy, Martin, Gebhard, *Sexual Behavior in the Human Female.* Philadelphia: W. B. Saunders Co., 1953, p. 11.

13. Elizabeth Barrett Browning, *Sonnets from the Portuguese,* 1850.

PART II

Love Is Well and Living in Some Marriages

CHAPTER THREE

What They Did After They Said, "I Love You"

Some years ago, Dr. O. Hobart Mowrer, well-known clinical psychologist, said to several of us would-be counselors, something like this, "If you want to learn how to negotiate a difficult situation, talk with people who have already been through it successfully." This is what I had in mind when I began my study of successful marriages in the summer of 1972. I thought that if I could talk with and study in depth couples who are successful in the marital enterprise, perhaps I could find out what they did to bring about this happy situation. Eighteen couples have been generous in giving time and effort by writing the history of their marriages, coming together for discussions, taking tests, making tape recordings, and giving in-depth interviews.

One of the first things we did after we had received a great amount of material from our couples, including papers many of them had written on why their marriages had succeeded, was to list as many of their reasons for success as we could find. From this list we selected the items that appeared most frequently, and developed a testing instrument containing thirty-nine characteristics. We sent this instrument to our eighteen successfully married couples as well as to fifty-six additional couples, some of whom were having serious marital problems and were in counseling. We asked each person to fill out this instrument without consulting his or her spouse.

In addition, we asked all spouses to rate their marriages on a scale from 0 to 100, from completely failing to excellent. Each one was to do this without consulting the other, so we could compare ratings of spouses in a given marriage to see how close or far apart they were. Below are the instruments for evaluating characteristics in a marriage and the Marriage Success Scale.

MARRIAGE EVALUATION INVENTORY

Use the graduated scale to rate how these characteristics function in your marriage. Please do not consult with your spouse in the process of making your evaluation.

Key: a = an outstanding characteristic of our marriage
      b = fairly successful in this area
      c = a contributing factor to a lesser degree
      d = not one of our strong characteristics
      e = not a characteristic of our marriage

Circle letter that applies

	a	b	c	d	e
1. We both have always had a will to succeed.	a	b	c	d	e
2. We share goals which we want to achieve.	a	b	c	d	e
3. Our children contributed much to our marital happiness.	a	b	c	d	e
4. We delayed having children until we had adjusted to each other.	a	b	c	d	e
5. Each respects the privacy and independence of the other.	a	b	c	d	e
6. We give each other support and reinforcement.	a	b	c	d	e
7. Each tries to please the other.	a	b	c	d	e
8. We recognize and meet each other's needs.	a	b	c	d	e
9. We have characteristics which are different, but which complement each other.	a	b	c	d	e
10. We communicate effectively.	a	b	c	d	e
11. We are able to talk through a problem.	a	b	c	d	e
12. We share decision making.	a	b	c	d	e
13. We have empathy for each other (the ability to understand).	a	b	c	d	e
14. We can meet crises successfully.	a	b	c	d	e
15. We trust each other.	a	b	c	d	e
16. We share common interests and activities.	a	b	c	d	e
17. We can forgive and forget.	a	b	c	d	e
18. We practice good money management.	a	b	c	d	e
19. Our values are very much alike.	a	b	c	d	e

20. Our religious beliefs and practices are
    compatible.   a   b   c   d   e

21. We are excellent companions.   a   b   c   d   e

22. We respect each other.   a   b   c   d   e

23. We like the other as he or she is.   a   b   c   d   e

24. Our sexual life has been satisfying to both.   a   b   c   d   e

25. We know how to deal with conflict.   a   b   c   d   e

26. We have the ability to "give and take."   a   b   c   d   e

27. Our personalities are very compatible.   a   b   c   d   e

28. We agree on the roles and responsibilities
    each assumes as spouse, parent, male,
    female.   a   b   c   d   e

29. Our loyalty and faithfulness have meant a
    great deal to our marriage.   a   b   c   d   e

30. We have always been truthful and open.   a   b   c   d   e

31. We have lived a considerable distance
    from in-laws.   a   b   c   d   e

32. Our in-laws have been a great joy to us.   a   b   c   d   e

33. Our backgrounds are similar.   a   b   c   d   e

34. Each has a good sense of humor.   a   b   c   d   e

35. We know how to have fun together.   a   b   c   d   e

36. We agree on how to rear children.   a   b   c   d   e

37. We both have displayed unselfishness.   a   b   c   d   e

38. Our family does many things together
    (projects, activities, games, etc.)   a   b   c   d   e

39. We show affection to each other.   a   b   c   d   e

Check: Filled out by ____wife. ____husband. Number of years married ____.

Your name_____ (unless you wish to be anonymous.)

Let us now look at some of the results obtained from couples using the Marriage Evaluation Inventory. One hundred forty-eight married people scored themselves on the Inventory. Each item was scored as: a—an outstanding characteristic of our marriage; b—fairly successful in this area; c—a contributing factor to a lesser degree; d—not one of our strong characteristics; e—not a characteristic of our marriage.

MARRIAGE SUCCESS SCALE

As a summary evaluation, check the point that best describes how you believe your marriage is functioning.

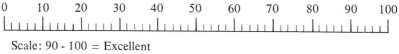

Scale: 90 - 100 = Excellent
       80 - 89 = Above average
       70 - 79 = Average
       60 - 69 = Passing but below average
       50 - 59 = Not functioning well but hopeful for improvement
       40 - 49 = Not functioning well but only slight hope for improvement
       Below 40 = Poor to completely failing

Note: Intermediate points may be checked for a closer evaluation.

First, we will consider all people who scored 85 or above on the Marriage Success Scale. These people are in the upper portion of the above-average group, the very successful group. In what areas were they most competent? Where did they rate themselves as functioning on an "a" level—"an outstanding characteristic in our marriage"? In Table 3-1, the fifteen leading characteristics are listed in the order in which the 102 people ranked them.

TABLE 3-1

		%
1.	Trust each other	85
2.	Respect each other	79
3.	Loyal and faithful	74
4.	Affectionate (mutually)	68
5.	Shared values	68
6.	Will to succeed	65
7.	Shared religious beliefs	65
8.	Support and reinforce each other	64
9.	Shared goals	63
10.	Shared decision making	62
11.	Have fun together	62
12.	Meet crises successfully	59
13.	Excellent companions	58
14.	Truthful and open	56
15.	Agree on roles and responsibilities	55

We concluded that the people who felt they were doing well in their marriages, did so because of competence in certain areas of their married life, particularly trust, respect, loyalty, and faithfulness. Although the percentages may not appear to be so high, when we compare them to the percentages of the group doing poorly in marriage, we shall see quite a difference. So now let us see how all 148 people rated themselves in these fifteen areas. The statistics were compiled according to four different classifications:

I. Our select group of 18 couples all rating 90 or above on the Marriage Success Scale.

II. The 51 couples rating 85 or above (the results noted earlier).

III. The 23 couples rating below 85.

IV. The 14 couples rating below 60. (Most of these couples had serious marital problems.)

TABLE 3-2

Group classification	I %	II %	III %	IV %
1. Trust each other	94	85	37	25
2. Respect each other	83	79	30	21
3. Loyal and faithful	81	74	33	11
4. Affectionate (mutually)	83	68	24	7
5. Shared values	75	68	24	21
6. Will to succeed	72	65	26	25
7. Shared religious beliefs	64	65	48	36
8. Support and reinforce each other	69	64	13	11
9. Shared goals	72	63	15	11
10. Shared decision making	64	62	22	14
11. Have fun together	61	62	11	7
12. Meet crises successfully	58	59	13	4
13. Excellent companions	58	58	4	4
14. Truthful and open	64	56	22	14
15. Agree on roles and responsibilities	64	55	15	11

Groups I and II, both functioning very well in their marriages, are very close in their evaluations, with Group I somewhat higher. When we consider all people scoring below 85, we note that the percentages drop off considerably, and those below 60 show a radical difference from those in the high group. These people scored poorly in all fifteen areas. And note the areas in which less than 10% felt that they excelled: Mutually affectionate—7%; have fun together—7%; meet crises successfully—4%; excellent companions—4%.

Let us take another look at our four groups, this time to see if there are any areas in which our select group of eighteen couples is fully functioning without exception. In other words, if a person rates an "a"—"an outstanding characteristic of our marriage" or "b"—"fairly successful in this area," we will rate that person as 100% satisfactorily functioning in that area. Then we will compare them with the other groups rating themselves in these same areas. Table 3-3 gives us the results of this comparison.

TABLE 3-3

	Group classification	I %	II %	III %	IV %
1.	Respect each other	100	99	76	64
2.	Meet crises successfully	100	97	43	25
3.	Loyal and faithful	100	95	57	29
4.	Support and reinforce each other	100	95	48	29
5.	Truthful and open	100	95	54	43
6.	Shared values	100	92	63	50
7.	Affectionate (mutually)	100	91	50	25
8.	Shared goals	100	91	59	50

I. Select group of 18 couples with marriage evaluation 90 or above.
II. 51 couples with evaluation 85 or above.
III. 23 couples with evaluation below 85.
IV. 14 couples with evaluation below 60.

Here we discover that our select group was 100% satisfactorily functioning in 8 out of the 39 areas. Every spouse in the eighteen marriages rated all 8 of these areas with an "a" or "b." This was true of this group in none of the remaining areas in our list of 39. When we look at Group IV, all rating below 60, we see an appreciable difference in those being able to score an "a" or "b." We see particularly low scores in the ability to meet crises—25%; the showing of affection to each other—25%; loyalty and faithfulness to each other—29%; the giving of support and reinforcement to each other—29%.

The order of seriousness in failure to function in the IV Group is as follows:

TABLE 3-4

	Area in which select Group I functioned 100%	*% below Group I, scored by Group IV with marriage rating below 60%*
1.	Meet crises successfully	75
2.	Affectionate (mutually)	75
3.	Loyal and faithful	71
4.	Support and reinforce each other	71
5.	Truthful and open	57
6.	Shared values	50
7.	Shared goals	50
8.	Respect each other	36

Although we will continue to do research in this matter in the future, we have the beginning of some evidence that, if a couple is to function reasonably well in a marriage, they must function in the eight areas listed above (Tables 3-3 and 3-4).

In Chapter 1 we mentioned that Dave and Judy came asking for help in making a decision about a possible marriage. It would have been helpful to tell them that many marriages are successful because in them couples meet crises successfully, show affection, are loyal and faithful to each other, are alert to the importance of giving each other support and reinforcement, communicate truthfully and openly, share similar values and goals, and admire and respect each other. These are among the most important areas in which a couple must become competent if they expect good things to happen to them after they say to each other, "I love you."

CHAPTER FOUR

How To Succeed in Marriage with a Lot of Trying

It was my opinion from the beginning that we could not say very much about why marriages functioned or failed to function by passing out questionnaires to large numbers of married people, compiling the replies and drawing our conclusions. Oscar Lewis, for many years a professor of anthropology at the University of Illinois, employed a very effective technique in his study of family life.[1] When he wanted to study families, he traveled to the people's homes and spent large amounts of time talking with them and observing their manner of life. I felt that I needed to study some families I had known over a period of ten to fifteen years, and that I would need to talk with other couples from time to time over a period of several years. Taped interviews, written material including histories of the marriage, personality studies, role-concept comparisons, and other tests of important areas of the marriage would augment my personal observations. By now, I feel I have come to know most of the eighteen married couples in our select group quite well, many on a close friendship basis.

It is not easy to summarize the reasons these marriages function so well. The thirty-nine statements of the Marriage Evaluation Inventory in Chapter 3 include most of the reasons given by the couples themselves. Perhaps we can distill these reasons into a form that is easier to comprehend. But first let us take a brief glimpse at some of our couples.

Jack and Josie met in high school in a small town and dated for two years, until Jack left for college. When Josie graduated from high school, at age eighteen, they were married. Jack was twenty. Josie worked to help Jack get his degree, after which they had two daughters two years apart. Once the girls were in school, Josie enrolled in college. Now she has her degree. This marriage, in the first years at least, experienced considerable stress, which, in many marriages, would have led to a breakup.

Josie, like most girls at age eighteen, was not ready for marriage. She worked to assist Jack in getting a college education, and there was little money to pay the bills that kept coming in. Josie explained it this way: "We started with no money. When we had little, we spent little. When we had more, we spent more. Later Jack took a cut in pay because of a job opportunity. It was a difficult time but we knew it would not last. It seems that many wives don't have enough confidence in their husbands to encourage them to make that kind of a decision." When Josie began to feel her life was unfulfilled, Jack and the children urged her to start working on a college degree. This gave her a new feeling of confidence and direction. She is now working on a master's degree and may go on to pursue a career.

I asked them: Why is your marriage successful?

JOSIE: We enjoy it. We're good for each other. He's got a lot of integrity and a great sense of humor.

JACK: We have a lot in common. We spend a lot of time talking over matters. We've had some problems, especially when the children were young. Josie seemed unsatisfied and we were growing apart. So we did something about that.

JOSIE: You have to develop toleration, and accept your partner as he is. Don't expect to change him. You need to grow together in love and intellectually, too.

JACK: You must remember that the two people are going to change through the years. And you have to adjust to that. Allow for individuality and the fact that each will and should have outside interests.

JOSIE: I felt I knew Jack before I married him. I knew there were more likeable than non-likeable things about him. We spent a lot of time together in each other's homes and that helped us get to know each other. At the beginning love was being absorbed in pleasing the other. This led to an identity crisis on my part. I had to learn to be a person in my own right. At first, I cried a lot doing the routine housework, thinking it was very unimportant. Jack and I talked it over, and that is when we set some goals for my future.

I asked: What, more than anything, makes a marriage go?

JOSIE: Jack is what makes it go for me. He's the right guy. I like the person he is: good, honest, dependable.

JACK: We both feel we have rare marriage partners. I've never met another man's wife who I thought could be my wife.

JOSIE: Jack is above the average. He has more to give. He has a lot of energy and gets a great many things done. I'm so proud of him!

JACK: And we enjoy just being together by ourselves. We have many friends and go out a lot, but I love to be home. It's the best place for me. I tend to work late and I know Josie doesn't want it that way but she understands. Within an hour after being home from work, I'm relaxed and happy.

JOSIE: A lot of little thoughtful things we do for each other—that's what keeps a marriage going. And do you know, after 16 years of marriage, Jack still holds my hand.

Jack and Josie have a marriage that ranks near the top of all the marriages in our study. Yet it is one that has come through considerable stress and strain. It did not coast to its present level. Many problems had to be faced and worked out. There were critical periods when the outcome could not be predicted. Some couples would have failed at points where Jack and Josie came through stronger than before. What makes the difference? We can note several factors. Both Jack and Josie have the character and the temperament that make them good for a marriage. Even though they were quite young when they were married, each showed evidence of maturity. They had to assume more than an average amount of responsibility in the operation of their own homes. Both of Josie's parents worked, so she had to be responsible for many of the tasks of keeping their home operating. Jack's father was a farmer in Texas and experienced seven crop failures in ten years. He and his brothers took turns going to school and working on the farm. Both sets of parents, in spite of hardships, must have had a positive and enriching influence on their children.

After listening to their tapes once again, I would say I am impressed with the following characteristics of their marriage. They like each other intensely and are good friends and companions. They share a great many interests. They have similar values and beliefs which give them a sense of unity and direction. On the tape, they talk about their religious faith and church activity. Josie remarked, "We joined a church soon after marriage, and it probably helped our marriage to succeed. It seems to be a unifying factor for our family." They have developed the skill of problem solving. They face problems honestly and openly, and communicate and negotiate until they arrive at the point that seems best for both, and always in a persistent but friendly manner. Both are endowed with a sense of humor, which acts like a shock absorber to get them over rough ground. They are tolerant and accepting and do not try to manipulate each other's lives. They are sensitive to each other's needs and ask daily what can be done to help the other. They maintain a unity and a closeness, yet each allows for the independent growth and fulfillment of the other. Again it must be said, though their marriage is thoroughly enjoyable to both, it is where it is today as the result of a great amount of concerted effort, daily determination, and just plain hard work.

Dan and Betty comprise another of our "success couples" who have put a large amount of creative effort into their marriage. Both admit that the home life they experienced in their formative years was not what they want in their own marriage. Betty's mother and father were divorced, and she felt the effects of a broken home. Dan tells about his teenage years when his father did not hold a job. His family life was full of anxiety. How were bills going to be paid? What would happen to his father? How were the children going to get an education? Both Dan and Betty say that they entered marriage with certain apprehensions resulting from their experiences with their own parents. Betty has uneasy feelings about the amount of time Dan might spend with his work or other activities that could take him from time at home with the family. Dan admits that he is tempted to be success oriented as the result of his father's lack of ambition and failure to give his family economic security. They are still very much concerned about their parents and what will happen to them eventually. They must work on their own marriage without the model that some couples have when they come from happy, stable family backgrounds.

I asked them: What more than anything else has made your marriage work?

BETTY: I think the main thing is the fact that we can really talk to each other. We communicate our needs, our goals and priorities, and by doing that we can learn about each other and what each other needs, and can come to an agreement that leads us to be satisfied and happy with what we are doing.

DAN: I would say we have a strong desire to make the marriage work. We like each other very much and we want it to work. We enjoy doing things together. When we have problems we are willing to talk about them. We may not always agree, but we can talk them out, and come to a mutual understanding one way or another.

I asked: Are you conscious of actually working to make it succeed?

DAN: Yes, I am conscious of this. A marriage does take work. It is not something that just happens, eternal bliss made in heaven. It takes two human beings who understand each other, or want to understand each other and who want to work and help each other.

I asked: Betty, on certain days do you say that you are going to do certain things to make your marriage better or to make yourself a better marriage partner?

BETTY: Now, to a certain extent that is almost true. We will go for a long time discussing a certain problem in our marriage, or area of conflict; and after long discussions, maybe over several days, each of us comes up with ideas of ways we have to change or new ways of looking at things and handling things, new priorities that we want, or I learn of a new need—I'm constantly learning of a new area of need that Dan might have. And I might spend time actually thinking, I'm going to have to actively take care of that—change my way of doing one particular thing or my way of thinking about it.

DAN: For me, if I see a need, or Betty has brought to my attention that we have a need, or something to be done, from that standpoint we work to fulfill that need, or if we can't, we try to find some mutual understanding on the problem. You, consciously, have to realize that you have these problems coming up and you do have to work with them, and I think we do this very well.

On another tape, Dan and Betty had this to say about problem solving.

BETTY: There are some small problems, which when you can't reach an agreement, tend to grow into big problems; while some of our most important decisions have been the easiest for us to make.

DAN: I do think you have to deal with problems when they come. We talk about them just before going to bed, and try to come to some understanding before the day ends.

BETTY: Sometimes, I feel that we are the only ones having problems, but I realize more and more that every marriage has its own problems. I used to think that people who argue are incompatible with each other. This was a worry since I have a volatile nature; but I now see it can be an asset in getting tensions worked out.

Dan and Betty met in college and began to feel serious about each other after two months of dating. Two years later, Dan left for his first year in the Air Force. Dan's absence in military service meant a year of separation before they could be married, which Betty thinks now, was a good idea. "It helps one develop a perspective over the whole relationship," she commented. They realized that there were problems at that time and they are grateful now that they waited, so that with growing maturity and effort, their marriage had a better start. While Dan was in the Air Force, they needed to plan the future and his career. Dan and Betty agreed that he should enter law school as soon as he was free to do so. Law school meant three years of hard study, borrowing money, and a very meager standard of living while raising a daughter. But they made it, and now Dan is doing well as a practicing attorney.

No one looking carefully at their seven years of marriage can say that it was a smooth, easy trip, but Dan and Betty feel the journey has been worthwhile and rewarding. And both have grown stronger and become more capable of meeting challenges as the years have passed.

What can we learn from their experience? First, that courage and determination play a large part in the success of a marriage. Both Dan and Betty have come a long way from the type of home environment they experienced in their youth. They were determined not to repeat the errors of the marriages of their parents. This determination is to their credit, as it is all too easy for people to fall into the life style to which they have been conditioned in their youth. Perhaps the skill which Dan and Betty have developed most completely is that of communication—talking, discussing, listening, arbitrating. This skill has become apparent to their friends, and it reinforces a conviction I have had for a long time: it is not the problems that cause difficulty in marriages; it is the inability to meet the problems constructively. All couples have problems. It depends on whether they think of these problems as enemies trying to defeat them, or challenges to their skills and abilities to overcome them, and thus, a friend in disguise. If the latter is the case, then the marriage will grow stronger with a greater sense of confidence as each challenge is met.

Gregory and Barbara have been married almost ten years. Gregory was twenty-five and Barbara twenty-four when they were married. They have a two-year-old boy. The marriage of Gregory and Barbara was founded on a more rational basis than most. They were older than the average couple getting married, and both were in graduate school. They dated for two years, during which time they evaluated the relationship very carefully, and during the engagement period they enrolled in a pre-marital education seminar together. Barbara feels that all couples, including themselves, begin a marriage with an immature love, and, as she puts it, "If this is all they have, the marriage will probably end in disaster. In fact, I am not sure it is real love at all—maybe infatuation would be a better word. It has to be nurtured by communicating, by sharing, and by becoming companions. There is little resemblance between the love we felt for each other at the time we were married and the love we have now." And Gregory had this to say:

GREGORY: From the very time I met Barbara, I did not view the situation as something that would lead to marriage as much as an opportunity for companionship. We were people with common interests who enjoyed doing things together. And we felt we were getting along very well together. In the later states, we did discuss matters pertaining to marriage; but I believe the marriage developed naturally out of the companionship we enjoyed when we were dating. I'm glad I waited until I was twenty-five because I was more ready in terms of being prepared professionally and desiring to enter married life. We have both commented that if we had met earlier we never would have married each other—that's for sure, and I think the reason is we both had very different interests in our earlier days.

BARBARA: That is certainly true, for when I was an undergraduate, I was very much concerned with being a party girl, which wasn't me at all. I enjoyed pretending. If I had met Gregory in those days I wouldn't have been the least interested, but by meeting later we knew that basically we were very much alike, sharing the same goals and interests.

By the time Gregory was twenty-five, he had formulated certain ideas about the kind of woman he wanted for his wife. "There were certain traits which would be essential, and I think these would include such things as a certain tendency toward intellectual endeavors, and being systematic and orderly about doing things. There were other desirable things, but they would be less important." These are not the highly romantic images of a woman that some men would conjure up, but Gregory found a woman who had them and they helped make the marriage a highly stable one.

Barbara referred to her sister's marriage, which ended in a divorce. She saw it as a clash of two people with the same undesirable personality trait—stubbornness. "Neither one was able to give an inch. Although Gregory and I are both aggressive, we don't clash. We seem to be able to give at the appropriate time." This capacity to "give" is not a quality that is developed overnight. Barbara and Gregory have worked at this and consider it to be an accomplishment of their marriage. Gregory explained that they had also worked hard to develop the capacity to meet each other's needs. He had the tendency to keep matters that bothered him to himself. Barbara could sense this and help him express his feelings.

GREGORY: This does two things: it helps relieve the tension I feel about this problem; secondly, it gives her a feeling of being able to help me. And the same has happened for her in regard to her work and things that may be bothering her. We have been both comforting and fulfilling to each other.

BARBARA: A need that became very clear to me in graduate school, when I developed special interests, was the need to become independent, and to have my own life—to be me as well as Gregory's wife and Steven's mother, and it is a need which Gregory has satisfied. He has always encouraged me to pursue things that I have wanted very much to do, that in no way involved him. He has wanted me to feel independent and able to take care of myself if anything happened to him. It takes an unusual man to do this. There are a lot of men who are threatened by that need in a woman, and he has never been. It isn't a case of his being wishy-washy, or that I run the show. We do all of that jointly.

Barbara pointed out that they saw their roles very much in the same way. Gregory did not feel that he was or wanted to be head of the house. He explained, "We think of ourselves as making decisions together. We both feel an equal responsibility for our child. At the time Barbara's income was greater than mine, I was not threatened by that. Basically, we share the same goals, values and beliefs. If two people build their lives together from this common base, it certainly helps."

When a child came into the life of Gregory and Barbara, it called for a major readjustment. Steven came after they had been married almost eight years, though Barbara stated that they had hoped to have one three years earlier, but "it didn't happen." Barbara describes the experience as almost traumatic, although she doesn't like to use that word.

But it has brought about quite a change. Our free time—our time together has diminished considerably. In fact it has almost entirely disappeared, at the moment anyway. By the time Steven is in bed at night we're so tired we don't have much time to communicate with each other without his presence. Right now I feel as though at times we are very much out of touch—that sense of very good communication that we had before is missing right now. We try to make the best of the time we have together, but it really is scarce. We are happy focusing on Steven, but I do miss the opportunity to focus just on Gregory.

I asked Gregory if all this bothered him. He responded:

One of the things that made it difficult for me resulted from habits we had established early in our marriage; we had meal times to discuss our problems and our mutual interests. We had the habit of taking long walks late in the evening after our work was completed to discuss things. There is a realization on our part that we can't do things exactly as we want to. Now we find our schedules regulated by Steven. In the beginning, I found this very difficult— being constantly interrupted in what I was trying to do. But I find out now how to handle the problem. We are concerned about the danger of neglecting each other, however, and are trying to find new ways of communicating.

Barbara feels that her life has changed even more than Gregory's.

BARBARA: At least eight hours of his working day remain the same. While that eight hours for me, which was sometimes on a job, and again just my time to do with as I wanted,—that time has changed completely for me, as have the other hours of the day. So I feel that the adjustment I have had to make is greater than that of Gregory. [Gregory agreed.]

GREGORY: When I arrive home in the evening, Barbara is tired. I am, too, but in a different way. And what I need to learn to an increasing extent is how to relieve her of some of the responsibility of taking care of Steven, which she assumes all day. I've learned from the weekends when I have had to be there all the time that it can be very wearing. But I feel that our child is a joint responsibility and I need to do my part.

Barbara felt there was something she wanted to say about what parents need to watch out for when children come into the marriage.

BARBARA: Because of the difficulty we have in finding time to communicate with each other, I can easily see how twenty years from now when the children are raised you suddenly realize you don't know each other. This is something I had never thought of before Steven arrived, but now I know.

GREGORY: I think the idea that having a child will bring a marriage together that was not sound before, is just nonsense.

BARBARA: I think it is a beautiful experience. We have found great joy in Steven. But people seem to forget the other side which says you are going to have to change your style of living considerably when there is another person involved, especially when it is a little person who can't adjust his way of life to yours.

Students in class who have listened to the tapes of Barbara and Gregory often comment that this couple seems too rational, too realistic, and that they lack the sentimental approach some parents seem to take toward their children. How could any parents feel that a child is a disruptive force and deprives them of many things they would like to do! But I have observed this marriage since the beginning, and I have great respect for it. I like the rational, common-sense way these people go about doing things. It seems to be good for the relationship, and I believe it will be good for their children.

This marriage illustrates the fact that two mature people are more apt to make good choices of mates, and approach the problems of marriage with less conflict and better decisions. Marriage is for adults and not for children. Adults have a much better chance of achieving a well-functioning marriage. Immature adults who act like children very likely will get into one predicament after another, until the marriage can stand the strain no longer, and breaks.

Barbara and Gregory represent maturity and all that goes with it—responsibility, sound judgment, ability to adjust, to communicate, and negotiate, and a more definite idea of who they are and where they are going.

We have taken a look at three of our couples in some detail. There are fifteen more couples in the group in which we are especially interested. There are Dick and Dorene and their three children, who seem too good to be true. They are perhaps the most perfectly matched couple we have studied. Their backgrounds are almost identical. Both came from midwestern farms. Their parents have become close friends and do many things together. Both families are warm, affectionate, easy-going, unselfish, and church- and community-oriented. In their sixteen years of married life, they have never had a serious quarrel. They like living on a farm and rearing their children on a farm and wouldn't want to be any other place. They have occasional misunderstandings, but they deal with them promptly and openly. And while they agree on values, roles, and religion, each seems to have a distinct individuality. When I asked them if this blissful life wasn't a bit bland and monotonous, they denied it intensely. They really like being married to each other and everything connected with it.

There are Doris and Henry, mentioned earlier, who have been married forty-seven years and feel that they like each other more each succeeding year. Shirley and Harry have interests that are quite different. She likes art and music, while he is involved in science and mechanics. Each has learned to appreciate the other's interests, and has developed the ability to agree to disagree when necessary.

Joan and Martin met in the ninth grade and never really cared for anyone else. Martin is doing some creative things in his professional field and Joan admires him greatly. She believes he is good for the world in general and her in particular. She thinks he is the ideal father of their three children. Martin feels the same way about Joan. "Everyday reinforces my admiration for Joan as a person and as one who does so much for people. We love and respect each other, and those two characteristics cannot be separated in a good marriage."

George and Margaret have been married for sixteen years and have two adopted children. When they married, they recognized they would have to change to make the marriage work. George said he had to learn to compromise and be unselfish. Margaret had found it easy to "fly off the handle at little things," and had to change her way of dealing with stress. Despite difficulties, they were able to achieve common goals. This marriage required a considerable amount of adjustment, especially during the first ten years. At the present time, they feel the marriage is functioning in a smooth and efficient manner, and affection flows freely.

Joe was a farm boy and Carrie was a city girl, but Carrie likes outdoor life, so she has adapted to farm life. They are different but very accepting. Carrie likes to get up late and Joe early, but this does not bother them. Carrie describes it this way: "He is easy-going and I'm anxious. We balance out. He tends to be on time; I tend to be late; so we are not too late. He is very good at giving support and assurance." Joe says, "Carrie is very helpful. She is a good cook, a good mother and a good companion. I don't always give her as much affection as she wants. This is one of the differences we have had throughout the marriage." A close study of their relationship reveals common interests, beliefs, goals, and an excellent ability to communicate.

I knew both Jim and Vicki several years before they were married. They were very much alike in that both were easy-going, friendly, gentle people. They would rather listen than talk. Their family backgrounds were similar in location, type of family activity, values, and religion. Both Jim and Vicki were "only" children, but I never saw any evidence of either being spoiled. I once kidded them about being so much alike that their marriage might be unexciting. They later informed me that this did not prove to be the case.

Vicki pointed out that in the process of dating for two years, they developed a trust that has continued to grow and sustain their marriage. "It shows up in little ways. I can be reasonably sure that Jim will come home on time. I know about how he will spend money, giving considerable thought before making a purchase. I trust his judgment in his part in the discipline of our two children. The decisions he has made about job changes have worked out well. I feel we have a lot going for us in that we both trust each other, particularly our judgment."

Jim and Vicki married when he was twenty-nine and she was twenty-two. Jim feels that their adjustment to marriage was made easier because they were older, more settled and mature. "I'm glad I didn't marry any of the girls I dated earlier. It wouldn't have worked out nearly so well," he stated. They have worked out a system to prevent unnecessary hassling in their relationship—something neither of them likes. "I almost had to be hit over the head before I realized that Vicki was trying to tell me something. This was aggravating to her. Therefore, I made up my mind I was going to start to listen to what she was trying to say to me. Listening was not something I was in the habit of doing. When I put this into practice I was able to respond to her more fully, and as a result I never get nagged." Vicki added, "And the interesting thing is we are able now to communicate in other ways than talking. It could almost be called communication of feelings. And as Jim says, listening is so important."

Jim and Vicki both agree they get a great amount of support from their friends, who share many of their same values and goals. Many of these friends are from the church Jim and Vicki participate in with their children. They have particularly benefited from their church study groups. And they had these interesting things to say about their relationship with their children. Vicki: "When our first child was born, someone suggested to us that we learn to enjoy our children at each step of their development. This takes children out of the category of being problems to their parents and helps us accept them and appreciate them." Jim added this: "Our daughter, age fourteen, and I began having disagreements and she felt in doing so, I was putting her down. So, I explained to her that I wanted to think of her as an adult able to engage in discussing differences. Since then our relationship has been altogether different."

Jim and Vicki say they are conscious now of preparing their children to become independent, so that when the time comes for them to leave, both parents and children will be ready for the transition. Jim recalls that when he left home, the situation for his parents was just short of being traumatic. It took them some time to adjust to living with just the two together.

Here is a stable marriage aided by two people who are mutually easy to get along with, who operate in a low key, and use large doses of common sense in their judgment and decisions. There have been problems, but they were solved in a rational manner as they arose.

Ken and Christy went through a serious period of adjustment and re-ordering of their relationship early in their marriage. They married late, when Ken was thirty-five and Christy in her late twenties. Shortly after their marriage, they had two children eleven months apart; seven years later they had another—all boys. Christy is a very sensitive person, and somewhat of a perfectionist. Although she is quite domestic, she has certain career goals. She was a very successful teacher when she married, but upon the arrival of their first child, she felt she had to resign her teaching position. Ken is a research scientist and very much involved in his work. At one time he devoted himself to a sixty-hour workweek. Christy explains, "The years when the children were small were difficult. It seemed I was home about 100% of the time. I didn't know how to take care of one baby, let alone two. And I wasn't getting the attention I needed from Ken. Of course, he wasn't giving up much, but I had to completely change my roles—teaching, going out with friends, and spending leisure time with Ken." It took Ken some time to realize that he had to do some radical changing to help a situation that was getting increasingly serious. He pitched in and helped with the housework and the children. He later arranged for Christy to get away for a vacation with friends in Canada. This apparently had a marked influence on Christy, who saw Ken's concern for her welfare, and the start of his willingness for her to have a new freedom and independence.

One is impressed with the fact that here is a marriage of two very different people, perhaps the most different of all our eighteen couples. Ken is reserved, conservative, scientifically oriented, and "thick skinned," as he puts it. Christy is outgoing, vivacious, socially active, articulate, and very sensitive. Fortunately, their differing characteristics are complementary. Christy has great respect and admiration for Ken and his accomplishments, while he feels her "beautiful personality" is one of the most important factors contributing to the success of their marriage.

They believe, as do some of the other couples, that their maturity has been an important factor in their capacity to work through their problems. Ken said, "I was sure that my love for Christy was not infatuation." And Christy explained, "We are able to express resentment before it builds up. I have to express my feelings or I'm unhappy. Ken is supportive, mature, responsible, and doesn't get hurt easily. When I'm upset, he is calm, and that helps a lot."

Two excerpts from their tape illustrate two important factors contributing to the functioning of their marriage. The first concerns their value system.

CHRISTY: I think this has been one of the strengths of our marriage. Ken and I have been very close together both in interests and in values. We value the same types of persons. We have the same goals, essentially. We are close together.

The values they hold in common seem to give their lives a sense of direction and make important decisions less complicated. They both feel this factor has given them a sound base on which to operate their marriage and family life.

The second segment reveals a decision Ken made about family life.

KEN: I believe that everyone after reaching his main career goals, which I have met, should turn much toward the family. In the last two years I have done this, and have given much more time and attention than I had in the past. And this has been very satisfying to me. I could go on working this sixty hour workweek and contribute more and more to my technical field, but I have to say to myself while this might be possible and I do have the ideas and ability to go ahead with this, yet I feel I need to modify my role at this time in terms of devoting more time to the family before the children move away. So, for the next six or seven years I will give myself to the family and hold these ideas that I have for my research efforts in abeyance till that time. This is a major decision to make, but I have made it and I think it is a logical one.

I believe this statement to be an important illustration of the way a parent can gain insight into an important family need and make a crucial change in his life style to meet it. In a day when the family is fragmented by the many demands made on each member by contemporary society, and where fathers are absent all too much from homes because of their obsession with getting ahead in the world of work, business, and professional life, it is well to reflect on Ken's decision to break through the vicious circle.

Perhaps these vignettes taken from the lives of people trying and succeeding in the essential, the exciting, the precarious adventure of marriage and family life will help us understand more clearly what it takes to make marriage and family life move toward creative and productive ends benefiting all who participate in them, and renewing society from within.

In the next four chapters we will see if we can put all this together in a systematic model that will give us an overview of the kinds of marriages that function adequately and will have some kind of general application to most marriages today.

REFERENCES

1. Oscar Lewis, *Five Families.* New York: New American Library, 1959.

PART III

The Anatomy of a Healthy Marriage

CHAPTER FIVE

Personal Characteristics

The search will go on endlessly for a definition of the fully functioning, healthy marriage. And this is good, because we need all the assistance we can get in helping people know what it takes to make a marriage work. No definition and no formula will be adequate, for people on all levels of the socio-economic ladder, comprising various ethnic groups, religious denominations, and other cultural, racial, and geographical categories will defy anyone's attempt to make them conform to any one standard of success or happiness. Marriage counselors are continually puzzled by seeing couples who, seeming to have the attributes that make for a good marriage, are failing or divorced; and, on the other hand, being confronted by others who, though violating most of the rules for marital success, would not even consider splitting up.

The safest approach I can take is to say that I am suggesting attributes for a healthy marriage which seem to characterize the successful marriages I am studying, and which I have observed in the past twenty-five years as a marriage counselor and family educator. All of the top-level marriages do not have all of these attributes. Some may have but a few, but those they do have are outstanding. When we have reviewed our conclusions and evaluated them, perhaps we can pick out those which are the essentials, and suggest some that are universally true for all couples everywhere.

First, there are the personal characteristics that distinguish an individual and seem to make him or her a good prospect for marriage. Our couples, who are doing well in their marriages, seem to have these personal characteristics.

1. *Dependability and trustworthiness.* We noted in Chapter 3 that the outstanding characteristic in the marriages of the "select group" was, "We trust each other." In reviewing what couples said about each other

on the tapes, we find the word "trust" being used again and again. Trust, according to a dictionary definition, is, "reliance on the integrity and justice of a person—confidence. . . ." It can be as simple as being relatively sure a spouse is going to show up for a meal on time, to believing that his or her love will endure through all the circumstances of their life together. The word "dependable" is linked with "trust," for on it all trust depends. A dependable person is trusted because experience has proven that he has earned that right. I recall a couple that came in for counseling. The problem was caused by the wife's inability to trust her husband. Had he given her any reason for distrust since they had been married? No, he had not. When we explored their relationship before marriage, we discovered that he had had numerous sexual relationships with other women about which he had bragged to this new girl friend. She could not free herself of the conviction that her husband would continue his "affairs" after marriage. And without trust, her relationship with her husband was miserable. Where there is trust, there is a solid feeling that all is well and the future will be good. It is both a gift one gives to another and a feeling built on past experiences with a person who is dependable and predictable.

2. *Warmth and affection.* Cold people are unresponsive. They shun other people. They do not like to touch or be touched physically or emotionally. They appear to be preoccupied with themselves, uninterested. They have an abnormal desire for privacy. In marriage they deny the unity that marriage intends. Warm people are affectionate. They like others, and show interest and concern. They display feelings of compassion, empathy, and the need for friendship. They communicate signals of acceptance and understanding. They express their feelings through words and acts. They reach out and touch another with their fingers and their souls. They are good for a marriage because it is intended there that body meet body, mind meet mind, and soul meet soul, melted in the heat of two warm hearts.

Where does it begin? For each of us it begins beyond the far stretch of our memory, back to someone who loved us, fondled us, and made us feel secure and accepted. If there is that warmth within us, we felt the transfer from others who loved us and taught us to love, conditioned us to love, and who made us feel good about ourselves. And so we like others as we come to like and accept ourselves.

Lovers often mistake "sexiness" for warmth. A prostitute may know all the moves, positions, and techniques of coitus, but be as cold as ice to her partner. Genuine warmth must have within it respect, concern, and friendship. It is the way a person thinks, feels, lives, and relates. As Allan Fromme has written:

Our ability to love is established not so much by fervent promise as by oft repeated deeds. Perhaps it is more helpful to think not of the ability to love, but the ability to remain loving. This emphasizes its history and presently continuing character. It stresses the reality of the daily pleasure we find in human relationships. This constantly reinforces our ability to love, freeing us more and more from the prison of self. Life runs more smoothly, leaving less to impair the ideal growth of some special love of our choice.[1]

The couples in our select group show a great deal of love and affection for each other and rate them very high in their listing of the outstanding qualities in their marriage.

3. *Generosity and unselfishness.* These traits did not rank high in the lists of accomplishments of our couples, but that does not mean they did not feel the importance of them. Perhaps they were among the more difficult characteristics to achieve. If a human being's greatest problem is the temptation to be preoccupied with his own self-interest, it is as true in marriage as anywhere else. The "egocentric predicament" rears its ugly head between husbands and wives as much as between neighbor and neighbor, or between people of different races and classes. In Chapter 4 we saw in Ken's struggle between his desire to rise in his scientific profession and the needs of his family, the competition between concern for one's self and one's significant others. Fortunately, the others won in this case. Many divorces stem from a selfishness that would not accept the fact that marriage demands persons who can give generously. The philosophy of "what's in it for me?" is self-defeating if one wants a union that can exist only in the larger dimension of "what's in it for us?"

4. *The ability to meet crises.* We noted that in our select group of eighteen couples this characteristic ranked as functioning in all cases. For these people the ability to meet crises was a necessity. I have discussed this with several groups of married couples to get their reaction. The consensus was that married life consists of a series of crises: births, illnesses, accidents, sudden surprises, changes in jobs and residences, helping children adjust to new situations, differences of opinion, quarrels, separations, even death itself. How do people meet these unexpected, trauma-filled events? From our survey of our couples, we find them meeting them surprisingly well. We noticed in so many of these people a quality of calmness and confidence in the face of a crisis. One wife mentions the ability of her husband to remain calm when they faced unusual stress. This characteristic seemed strong enough in most of our

couples to enable them to face events, unpleasant though they be, with the question, "What is the best thing to do about it now?" Then they put their answer to work and pulled through the crisis stronger than before.

5. *Mental and emotional maturity.* Perhaps this quality is directly related to, and responsible for, the one we have just discussed. A mature person is one who is particularly adept at meeting crises and solving problems. He is not thrown off balance by misfortune, the need to change directions, or sudden and unexpected events in his life. Richard H. Klemer defines a mature person as:

one who behaves with calm decisiveness in difficult situations, who plans and solves problems intelligently, who seeks help from appropriate specialists when he needs it, and who is adaptable enough to change himself and so adjust to the realities of the situation that confronts him. All of these behaviour characteristics are crucial in effectively dealing with the difficulties in marriage and in family living that will inevitably arise. It is probable that a family will be successful to the degree and extent to which this kind of maturity exists in both of the marriage partners.[2]

In immature people we notice the inability to be objective and rational. They seem to be unable to think clearly about a problem situation and initiate a plan for solving it. They are more apt to be emotionally upset and act irrationally, oftentimes aggravating the situation. These people often find it impossible to communicate sensibly, and they may say and do things which afterwards they regret.

Becoming mature is a life-long process. The beginnings go back to wise parents, who help children learn what maturity is and how to achieve it. But it is never too late to start; one starts by making a self-appraisal of individual needs, and then formulating a plan of action which must be faithfully carried out.

6. *Honesty and openness.* The partners in our well-functioning marriages expressed both honesty and openness. On the other hand, fewer than half of those in the failing group were truthful and open. These qualities are necessary in order for a person to communicate what he really thinks and feels. To be honest is to "tell it as it is." To be open is to clear the channels for the transmitting and receiving of messages.

Earlier we discussed the importance of trust. Honesty is one of the foundation stones that supports trust. The marriage counselor often hears the haunting question, "How can I ever trust him [or her] again?" After a dishonest act or betrayal, one must work to restore the trust, temporarily lost; the other must work to reinforce the restoration. In response to a question I often ask couples: "Would you modify the truth to avoid unpleasantness in your relationship?", a large proportion of people would reply, "Yes, of course." That answer bothers me to some degree. I would want to have some careful discussion at that point with the couple to clarify that reply and its implications.

Openness is receptivity to the truth when it is stated, and willingness to reply in kind. Transactional analysis defines this as an Adult-to-Adult transaction with no games being played. Albert Camus once said, "We do not need to reveal ourselves to others, but only to those we love. For then we are no longer revealing ourselves in order to seem but in order to give." Camus is saying that some forms of openness are expressed in order to create an impression. But between two loving people there is an openness that is a reciprocal givingness that links their lives together in a profound meaning.

7. *The will to succeed in the marriage.* We spoke earlier of Kinsey's observance of the importance of two people determined to make the marriage work. The importance of this factor cannot be emphasized too much. In Gestalt therapy we are taught that "I can't!" quite often means, "I won't!" Some couples who "can't" get along, really "won't" get along. Marriage counselors often are frustrated in working with a couple who ought to be getting along, but who seem to persist in failing to do so. On the other hand, the couple who comes saying, "Our marriage is not functioning as it should, but we both want to do something about it," presents a situation in which there is hope.

Pat was a young woman who had been married five years to Alan, who was more dedicated to his work than he was to her. Pat wanted Alan to go with her to a marriage counselor when she first saw trouble on the horizon, but he refused to go. Now she felt the marriage was all but over, but she was a woman with determination. First, she told Alan she was leaving him. He protested violently. He would do anything. "If you are willing to work on it, so will I," she told him. When she first came with Alan, she stated that she could see no way they could make the marriage work, but that she would do anything in her power to mend it, if that were possible. For a year these two people did work with determination, and at the end of the year they were ready to try again. Today, ten years later, the marriage is functioning very satisfactorily. They "could" and they did.

The eighteen couples in our group, without exception, began their marriages with the idea that they were going to make the relationship permanent, and that it was going to be a satisfying one to both. They did not view marriage as an endeavor of grim determination, but as an exciting adventure. Of course, mistakes can be made in the choice of a mate, and people do grow apart in the course of the years, but even these handicaps can be overcome in many circumstances, if there is a will to succeed.

The authors of *Born to Win* speak of "winners" and "losers" in life.[3] Winners do not see themselves as powerless in the face of adversity; they respond authentically and positively to the challenges of life. Losers avoid responsibility, feel helpless, give up easily, and blame others for their bad luck. In this sense, "winners" find a way to keep up good relationships in a marriage. They do have the will to succeed.

8. *Durability*. What is this interesting quality known as durability? I am not sure I know. I know that some shoes wear better than others, because there is a quality of substance and workmanship in them that makes them last. One of my students is studying marriages that have lasted fifty years or more. We are all anxious to study the results of her research to find out more about what it takes to keep a marriage going through more than a half century. These people have a combination of many qualities, of course, but they seem to have an extra amount of dedication, loyalty, tolerance, patience, persistence, grit, and all those things that go into mature love to give them "staying power." Should I add, they have physical stamina?

When my son was in college, he was a member of the cross-country team. He and his teammates would run five miles or more in a meet that frequently took them over rugged, up- and down-hill terrain. I marveled at the ability of these runners to go that far and still be as strong as they were at the end of the race. They all had physical endurance. On the other hand, there were the short-distance runners who excelled in the "dashes." They would go at great speed for a short while, and that was it. If they were asked to run a long distance, they would fall by the wayside. So it seems to be in marriage. I received a telephone call one afternoon from a woman whose voice indicated that she was in a state of distress. Her story went something like this: "My husband just told me he is quitting our marriage. We have only been married three years, and I thought things were going along very well, as did most of our friends." "What reasons did he give?" I asked. "That's the trouble," she replied, "He says he still loves me, and there is no great problem, but that he is just tired of being married." This man, it appears, is a sprinter. For a short while he did very well. Then he was through. Doris and Henry, in our successfully married group, have been together forty-seven years and seem to like it more every year. They are among the long-distance runners.

Perhaps some of the couples who have made it fifty years or more have done it on sheer grit. Maybe they are not altogether happy, and some would argue that it might have been better for them and for their children if they had separated long ago. I would want to consider the matter very carefully before making a judgment. I often think about the married life of my own parents. We children knew there were problems in the marriage. We observed the discord that occurred from time to time, and we were conscious of the unhappiness that appeared now and then. Yet my parents were not ones to call it quits, and they worked it out together, although it took a long time. My father died at the age of ninety-six, shortly before they were to celebrate their seventieth wedding anniversary. The last thirty-five years of their married life were years of happiness and contentment with the added joys of frequent reunions with their children and their grandchildren. I, for one, am grateful that they stayed together. How different life would have been for all of us if they had not.

I am not trying to suggest that all marriages should remain intact in spite of everything. In some cases with which I have been associated professionally, a divorce seemed the only way to go. But it is my conviction that a great many couples, perhaps as high as 50 percent of them, give up too soon. They are sprinters who fall by the wayside because they lack the endurance of the long-distance runners.

What is most needed? As we think of the thirty-six people making up the group we have been evaluating, what personal characteristic seems to be predominant? One is reluctant to name one attribute over the rest, or to discard any as less important, but there is one attribute that most of them seem to have that is a key to their ability to function well in a marriage. They are likeable. If you were to meet them, and come to know them, you would enjoy having them for friends. They have the warm, positive dispositional characteristics of people with whom you would like to associate. This is in contrast to people who are cold, negative and sometimes neurotic, about whom you might be tempted to feel, "I want to get away from these people as soon as possible."

Our successfully married persons seem to have the capacity to like and be liked, to love and be loved, to give and to receive, to encourage and be encouraged. In the best sense of the word, these people are mentally and emotionally healthy. To be this way, one generally has a long history of personal development along the avenues of positive thinking and living, leading to a strong feeling of acceptance of oneself and others. Allan Fromme writes about

. . . the child who has had a sunnier climate in which to discover himself, a climate that was more approving than disapproving, more encouraging than critical. He, too, will find reinforcement for his developing image of himself. He may be only average in his school grades, but because he has a sunnier face his teachers tend to smile and encourage him instead of frowning and reproving. . . . He does not need to be perfect and above reproach in order to feel accepted and loved. . . .

In a word, he feels adequate. And with this sense of his own adequacy he can forget himself and enjoy the world, people, things.

Anyone who has a reasonable feeling of adequacy about himself is a pleasant person to be with. He is not given to complaining about his lot and the way the world treats him. He does not assume in advance that people will be unkind or untrustworthy, that they will try to take advantage of him. . . .

It is easy for people to like such a person because he begins by liking people. It is easy for them to be interested in him because he is interested in them. He is a person whom it is easy to love. . . .

When he falls in love, he brings to his love all his other loves, all his other attachments. He is rich in enjoyments and he says to his love, "Here, enjoy this! Share this with me, and this, and this." He brings to the love of his life a wealth of things to share.[4]

It may seem simplistic to say that what is wrong with the world is people, but it does come down to that. We have come into an age of "responsibility" therapists, who keep telling us that we must assume personal responsibility for what happens to us. Blaming others or blaming circumstances is most unproductive. A decent world begins with the people who live in it and are responsible for it. A healthy marriage depends on the people who are a part of it and contribute what they are to it. If that contribution is a warm, loving, accepting personality, it will go a long way in helping marriages move toward a satisfactory and rewarding conclusion.

So much that comes after a person says, "I love you," depends on that person's concept of himself, how he is responsible for the development of his personality in higher levels of understanding and relating to other people, the realization of a dream that he might find fulfillment in his complete potential for loving and being loved. The prayer of St. Francis is appropriate:

> . . . grant that we may not so much seek
> To be consoled, as to console.
> To be understood, as to understand.
> To be loved, as to love; for
> It is in giving, that we receive. . . .

REFERENCES

1. Allan Fromme, *The Ability to Love.* New York: Simon and Schuster (Pocket Books), 1966, pp. 309, 310. (Originally published by Farrar, Straus & Giroux, Inc., New York, 1963, 1965.)

2. Richard H. Klemer, *Marriage and Family Relationships.* New York: Harper and Row, 1970, p. 317.

3. Muriel James and Dorothy Jongeward, *Born to Win: Transactional Analysis with Gestalt Experiments.* Menlo Park, Calif.: Addison-Wesley Publishing Co., 1971.

4. Allan Fromme, *The Ability to Love,* pp. 81, 82.

CHAPTER SIX

Compatibility Factors

Marriage might be compared with an omelet. An omelet is composed of eggs and other ingredients combined in the proper proportion. The quality of what goes into the omelet is important; that is where the omelet begins. But an uninformed or inexperienced cook might spoil the finished product even though the best ingredients were used. All the basic elements must be put together and cooked properly, and they must be served in an appealing and appetizing manner. So it is with a marriage. The ingredients are the characteristics of the people who go into the marriage. We have just discussed how important these characteristics are. If you will pardon the expression, we must have "good eggs." But we cannot stop there; for now we must consider the second important matter—who marries whom. And what about the importance of the compatibility of the combination?

If we look back to the formula in Chapter 1, we see the symbol for the good marriage prospect: $M\ g$ (male) and $F\ g$ (female). Now it is hoped we can get two good prospects together who will be compatible. Characteristics considered to be the most compatible are represented by the same numbers, 1, 2, 3, 4, 5, etc. A set of characteristics "1" in the male is highly compatible with a set of characteristics "1" in the female. Putting male "1" and female "2" together might still be fairly compatible, because they represent characteristics that come close to matching. But if male "1" and female "5" were put together, then there would be difficulty in their attempt to live harmoniously. Later we will attempt to illustrate this point.

First, let us consider the areas in which compatibility is most needed. In our select sample of eighteen couples, there seemed to be five areas, although it is difficult to limit the list to these five. These areas appeared to coincide with my observations through the years of married couples who got along well together.

1. *Husband and wife liked each other.* Mentioned earlier were Doris and Henry, married happily for forty-seven years. I asked Doris what came to her mind as one of the outstanding characteristics in their marriage.

DORIS: I have believed from young womanhood, that the ability to like a person is the most important prime thing. After that can come loving; but if you do not like, you can't possibly love. If you do like and thoroughly like, then you can go on to any situation.

QUESTION: Did you feel you came to like Henry a long time before you came to love him?

DORIS: Yes, I liked him very much.

QUESTION: What did you like about him?

DORIS: I had great respect for him. I liked his mind. We liked to talk about the same things, and we liked to do the same things.

QUESTION: Do you think that today, people about to choose a marriage partner could take that more seriously?

DORIS: Yes, I think young people are attracted so much to each other physically that they forget to find out whether or not they like the person.

Would you agree with her statement, ". . . but if you do not like, you can't possibly love"? I suppose it would depend on an individual's definition, but there are those who feel that liking and loving are separate. There was a line in a "rock" song of several years ago, in which a girl sings about her boy friend, "He's no good, but I love him just the same." And it is not uncommon for a marriage counselor to hear, "I love my husband [or wife], but I have no respect for him [or her]." What is the nature of this love? Sexual attraction, infatuation, compassion, loyalty might account for some of these love feelings. A long-haired son says to his bald-headed father, in a *New Yorker* cartoon, "Gee, Dad, just because I have contempt for your politics, social standards, religious beliefs, and moral code doesn't mean I don't like you. I really like you a lot."[1] Here we might ask, did he mean "like" or "love," and what is the difference? Perhaps it is possible to like someone who is very different from us.

But it seems, for the most part, that we tend to like people who are like us. And when people agree with us, don't we tend to find them "agreeable"? We did discover in the couples classified as highly compatible in our study that there was a tendency for them to come from similar geographical, religious, educational, and socio-economic backgrounds, and from families whose life styles were quite similar. Zick Rubin noted this tendency in much of the research that has been done in the past years.

If similarity dictates our choice of friends, it even more certainly dictates our choice of spouses as well. Hundreds of statistical studies, dating back to Francis Galton's study of hereditary genius in 1870, have found husbands and wives to be significantly similar to one another not only with respect to such biographical and social characteristics as age, race, religion, education, and social status, but also with respect to physical features like height and eye color, and psychological characteristics like intelligence. It is still possible that there are times when opposites attract, as when a dominant person hits it off with a submissive one, or an outgoing person is drawn to a more contemplative sort. But the operation of such an "opposites attract" principle in mate selection has never been conclusively demonstrated, whereas the impact of physical, social and attitudinal similarities has been demonstrated repeatedly.[2]

The married persons we are studying prefer their mates to others. If they had to marry all over again, it would be to the same person. They list "respect" at the very top of outstanding characteristics of their marriages. When they talk about each other, there is a note of admiration in what they say. They are "proud" to be seen together among their friends and relatives, and at public gatherings. They like the way their spouse looks, acts, talks, and thinks. Without a doubt, where husband and wife like each other, there is a solid foundation for a compatible life together.

Is there any way one can test his "liking" for another person? In his current research, Zick Rubin is using a 9-item "liking scale" as a method by which one person can evaluate another in such areas as maturity, intelligence, making judgments, ability to gain admiration, win respect, and be liked by others. He asks that one consider how he would react to statements such as:

I think _____ is unusually well-adjusted.
I would recommend _____ for a responsible job.
_____ is the sort of person whom I myself would like to be.

By this method one can test whether or not he finds another person agreeable to his tastes and able to meet his expectations. Liking another person and feeling comfortable in this favorable atmosphere are very important in a relationship and need to be considered carefully in making a marriage choice. We saw clearly in our studies of our eighteen couples that each could say to his partner with conviction, "I really like you!"

2. *Personalities related harmoniously (temperamental compatibility).*

Personality traits are like chemicals. Mix some together and they will unite to form something new and beautiful and useful. Some simply will not mix, and if you do put them together, they will explode. A couple should find out as early as possible during their courtship days whether their personality traits blend or explode.[3]

A question frequently asked by students in the marriage class is, "Should I marry someone with similar personality characteristics, or would it be better to marry someone whose personality characteristics are different from mine?" Sometimes they add, "Wouldn't it be monotonous to live with someone whose personality is the same as mine?" This kind of question deserves a careful answer. It matters a great deal about what characteristics one has in mind when talking about "similar" or "different." Suppose you have friendliness as a personality characteristic. Would you want to marry a friendly person or an unfriendly one? The answer is obvious, "A friendly one," of course. Suppose you are aggressive and always ready to take the initiative. Should you marry someone who is quiet and somewhat passive? Now, we aren't so sure. Most of us would say, "It all depends." Two such people might be compatible, while two aggressive people might not be. The degree to which complementary personality characteristics aid in marital functioning is dependent on a number of other factors.

All of us have married friends who appear to be getting along very well, but who seem to have different personality patterns, although personal observation may be very misleading when it comes to judging whether the personalities are really different or alike. These people appear to be very acceptable to each other. When they relate and function together, there is an unmistakable harmony. They may be playing different instruments, but they make music together. What then is temperamental compatibility? It exists when the personality configurations of one person combine with the personality configurations of another in a harmonious arrangement.

How aware of this are couples who are in the process of mate selection? Probably not as aware as we might think. It would be safe to say that most couples are not conscious of picking a mate as a result of a careful analysis of the personality interaction operating in their relationship. They are conscious that two personalities are interacting, but they are not sure as to just why and how. This may be the reason why it is difficult to predict whether or not a marriage will succeed on the basis of personality matching, although we do know that some personality matches are good and others are poor.

The proof of the pudding, then, is in the eating. While we know that temperamental compatibility is desirable in a marriage, we have difficulty in saying just what that is. But when we are with another person for a period of time under a variety of circumstances, we can learn if that compatibility exists or not. As someone is supposed to have said, "I know nothing about music, but I know what music I like." I may not be altogether sure what a person is like, but I do know whether or not I like that person.

Another matter that must be mentioned is that personality characteristics change over the course of time, so that no two people are the same after the passing of the years. They may have changed for the better or for the worse. They may have grown more compatible in terms of personality, or they may have grown farther apart.

We have had the opportunity to observe seven of our couples over a 15-to-20-year period. From these observations we will attempt to draw several conclusions:

a. In all cases, both spouses possess a number of positive personality characteristics mentioned in Chapter 5. These positive characteristics appear to interrelate harmoniously.

b. In many cases the personality configurations in the spouses in a given marriage seem to be somewhat different, but nevertheless compatible. Here complementarity seems to operate. A dominant male may be more comfortable with a submissive female, and vice versa. A talkative wife may enjoy a husband who would rather listen than talk. It may even be true that a person possessing a less favorable trait could increase his chances of marital success by choosing a partner who could compensate with a more favorable trait in the same area.

c. Persons with similar personality weaknesses who marry are likely to have severe trouble, particularly if there is evidence of a number of such weaknesses. One dominant weakness may be enough to upset the marriage. You may remember that Barbara felt that her sister's divorce was the result of two very stubborn people who could not adapt or compromise.

The following personality inventory was used with some of the couples in our study group.[4] We asked each husband and wife to consider the list to see if each possessed a reasonable number of the qualities, and whether or not the characteristics of one partner blended or conflicted with the characteristics of the other. Three forms were given to each couple so that each could rate himself or herself, each could rate the other, and third parties could rate each. The couple would then take the results for discussion and evaluation.

PERSONALITY INVENTORY

Husband is rated with "H."   Wife is rated with "W."

| *Characteristic* | *Rating* |

Characteristic	Lacks	Possesses to Some Degree	Possesses to Considerable Degree	Excels
Dependability				
Adaptability				
Maturity				
Unselfishness				
Sense of humor				
Thoughtful of others				
Geniality				
Warm-heartedness				
Enjoys people				
Well organized				
Emotionally stable				
Relaxed				
Domestic				
Energetic				
Neat				
Communicative				
Shows affection				
Takes initiative				
Cheerful				
Frugal				
Practical				
Articulate				
Good listener				
Truthful				
Tolerant				
Optimistic				
Courageous				
Not easily discouraged				

3. *Shared interests and activities.* A number of years ago I was giving some pre-marital tests to a couple who were planning to be married within a few weeks. One of the tests was constructed so couples could see the number of interests, hobbies, and leisure-time activities they had in common. The results, for this particular couple, showed that neither participated in many of the forty-five listed activities at all, and that they had only five in common, none of them very significant. Out of curiosity, I asked them what they planned to do on their honeymoon. The groom-to-be answered, "We're going fishing." That happened to be one of the few things he liked to do, although the bride did not list it as one of her favorite pastimes. I met them a few weeks after they returned from their honeymoon, and asked how they enjoyed it. "We had a good time," the husband replied, "I fished and she sat in the boat." One could wonder what the future held in store for them as an exciting adventure in pursuit of things they both enjoyed doing.

During the past twenty-five years, I have given a common-interest test to a number of couples who have come for marriage counseling. I have been impressed with the fact that couples who were doing very poorly in their marriages scored low on this common-interest test. On the other hand, we find that the eighteen select couples in our high adjustment group scored fairly well. Sixteen out of the eighteen couples took the following test.

INTERESTS, HOBBIES AND LEISURE-TIME ACTIVITIES

Husband and wife should rate themselves in their respective columns and compare, using summary at the end of the inventory of interests, hobbies ,and leisure-time activities for evaluation.

Key: Circle the number that describes your feeling: 1 = Find very important. 2 = Enjoy. 3 = Might enjoy but haven't tried. 4 = Do not care for. 5 = Dislike intensely. 6 = Would like to interest our children in this.

Wife							*Husband*				

						Quiet Games						
1	2	3	4	5	6	Table games	1	2	3	4	5	6
1	2	3	4	5	6	Chess or checkers	1	2	3	4	5	6
1	2	3	4	5	6	Bridge or card playing	1	2	3	4	5	6
1	2	3	4	5	6	Billiards or pool	1	2	3	4	5	6
1	2	3	4	5	6	Other _____	1	2	3	4	5	6

Participation in Athletic Activities

1 2 3 4 5 6	Tennis	1 2 3 4 5 6
1 2 3 4 5 6	Swimming	1 2 3 4 5 6
1 2 3 4 5 6	Bowling	1 2 3 4 5 6
1 2 3 4 5 6	Golf	1 2 3 4 5 6
1 2 3 4 5 6	Table tennis	1 2 3 4 5 6
1 2 3 4 5 6	Badminton	1 2 3 4 5 6
1 2 3 4 5 6	Trap shooting	1 2 3 4 5 6
1 2 3 4 5 6	Other _____	1 2 3 4 5 6

Outdoor Activities

1 2 3 4 5 6	Hiking	1 2 3 4 5 6
1 2 3 4 5 6	Mountain climbing	1 2 3 4 5 6
1 2 3 4 5 6	Picnics	1 2 3 4 5 6
1 2 3 4 5 6	Fishing	1 2 3 4 5 6
1 2 3 4 5 6	Hunting	1 2 3 4 5 6
1 2 3 4 5 6	Horseback riding	1 2 3 4 5 6
1 2 3 4 5 6	Boating	1 2 3 4 5 6
1 2 3 4 5 6	Skiing	1 2 3 4 5 6
1 2 3 4 5 6	Flying an airplane	1 2 3 4 5 6
1 2 3 4 5 6	Other _____	1 2 3 4 5 6

Mental Activities

1 2 3 4 5 6	Reading books	1 2 3 4 5 6
1 2 3 4 5 6	Reading magazines	1 2 3 4 5 6
1 2 3 4 5 6	Discussion groups	1 2 3 4 5 6
1 2 3 4 5 6	Writing poetry or prose	1 2 3 4 5 6
1 2 3 4 5 6	Puzzles	1 2 3 4 5 6
1 2 3 4 5 6	Other _____	1 2 3 4 5 6

Service Interests

1 2 3 4 5 6	Attending church	1 2 3 4 5 6
1 2 3 4 5 6	Working in the church	1 2 3 4 5 6

1	2	3	4	5	6	Teaching in church school	1	2	3	4	5	6
1	2	3	4	5	6	Voluntary community service	1	2	3	4	5	6
1	2	3	4	5	6	P.T.A.	1	2	3	4	5	6
1	2	3	4	5	6	Other _____	1	2	3	4	5	6

Entertainment

1	2	3	4	5	6	Movies	1	2	3	4	5	6
1	2	3	4	5	6	Television	1	2	3	4	5	6
1	2	3	4	5	6	Musicals	1	2	3	4	5	6
1	2	3	4	5	6	Concerts	1	2	3	4	5	6
1	2	3	4	5	6	Ballet	1	2	3	4	5	6
1	2	3	4	5	6	Amusement parks	1	2	3	4	5	6
1	2	3	4	5	6	Dancing	1	2	3	4	5	6
1	2	3	4	5	6	Parties	1	2	3	4	5	6
1	2	3	4	5	6	Plays or opera	1	2	3	4	5	6
1	2	3	4	5	6	Night clubs	1	2	3	4	5	6
1	2	3	4	5	6	Other _____	1	2	3	4	5	6

Spectator Sports

1	2	3	4	5	6	Basketball	1	2	3	4	5	6
1	2	3	4	5	6	Baseball	1	2	3	4	5	6
1	2	3	4	5	6	Football	1	2	3	4	5	6
1	2	3	4	5	6	Rodeo	1	2	3	4	5	6
1	2	3	4	5	6	Other _____	1	2	3	4	5	6

Creative Work

1	2	3	4	5	6	Woodworking	1	2	3	4	5	6
1	2	3	4	5	6	Leatherwork	1	2	3	4	5	6
1	2	3	4	5	6	Sewing or weaving	1	2	3	4	5	6
1	2	3	4	5	6	Pottery	1	2	3	4	5	6
1	2	3	4	5	6	Photography	1	2	3	4	5	6
1	2	3	4	5	6	Playing a musical instrument	1	2	3	4	5	6
1	2	3	4	5	6	Acting	1	2	3	4	5	6
1	2	3	4	5	6	Stamp or coin collecting	1	2	3	4	5	6

1	2	3	4	5	6	Gardening	1	2	3	4	5	6
1	2	3	4	5	6	Writing letters	1	2	3	4	5	6
1	2	3	4	5	6	Other _____	1	2	3	4	5	6

Cultural and Aesthetic Interests

1	2	3	4	5	6	Art shows	1	2	3	4	5	6
1	2	3	4	5	6	Museums	1	2	3	4	5	6
1	2	3	4	5	6	Antiques	1	2	3	4	5	6
1	2	3	4	5	6	Painting pictures	1	2	3	4	5	6
1	2	3	4	5	6	Sculpturing	1	2	3	4	5	6
1	2	3	4	5	6	Personal meditation	1	2	3	4	5	6
1	2	3	4	5	6	Listening to recordings	1	2	3	4	5	6
1	2	3	4	5	6	Other _____	1	2	3	4	5	6

Going and Seeing

1	2	3	4	5	6	Traveling	1	2	3	4	5	6
1	2	3	4	5	6	Visiting relatives	1	2	3	4	5	6
1	2	3	4	5	6	Window shopping	1	2	3	4	5	6
1	2	3	4	5	6	Exploring	1	2	3	4	5	6
1	2	3	4	5	6	Nature hikes	1	2	3	4	5	6
1	2	3	4	5	6	Other _____	1	2	3	4	5	6

In this list there are sixty-six areas to rate. The average number of areas of agreement scored by the sixteen couples was 31. The highest was 42 and the lowest 18; however, only one couple scored below 25. This means that the couples who were doing well in their marriages had an average of 31 interests, hobbies, and leisure-time activities that they could enjoy together. If you would like to compare your score with that of the select group, count one point for each area in which you and your spouse rank either 1 or 2. Then add up the total.

In all fairness, we must say that our select group did not rank "We share common interests and activities" near the top of the thirty-nine characteristics they were asked to rate. If you will refer again to Table 3-3, you will see that the select group rated 100% fully functioning in eight areas. For "We share common interests and activities," the percentage was 72% fully functioning. This means that there were many characteristics they considered more important to their marriage, and that common interests and activities can be a contributing factor to a lesser degree in a marriage that is functioning quite well. Only one person in the group ranked it as not one of the important factors in the marriage, however.

Shared interests and activities contribute to companionship in a marriage. There is a bit of truth to the saying that "couples that play together, stay together." There is a strong therapeutic factor in enjoying oneself in matters that are of interest, or just plain fun. And when two people share an interest in these areas, the joy is doubled, and a bond between them is strengthened. When children come, they learn to participate with their parents, which is excellent for their personal development, and it gives the family a sense of solidarity. A couple should not neglect doing things together as life grows more hectic as the demands of making a living and rearing a family multiply. When the children leave, parents who have kept doing things together need not feel like strangers with little in common to make their relationship fresh and vital.

A couple, in their seventies, that I knew well, could be seen leaving early in the morning together, making their way to some wooded or lake area near the town in which they lived, to engage in their favorite pastime: birdwatching. This they dearly loved to do, and for them it was a combination of a science and an art. They kept yearly record books of all birds observed, and they were always looking for a new one. This may seem relatively unimportant, but for them it was a constant source of pleasure, and a way of keeping close together as the years rolled by. How much more compatible they were because of the common interest they shared.

4. *Role-concepts agreeable to both.* When Marie married Joe, she thought that they would spend many wonderful evenings together talking and enjoying the satisfaction of participating in common interests. Bowling was Joe's favorite sport and before he was married, he belonged to several bowling teams, and went bowling several times a week. After marriage, Joe continued to bowl just about as much as he did before. At first, Marie was puzzled, then she felt deeply disappointed. Her question to the marriage counselor was, "Isn't a husband supposed to spend his evenings with his wife?" Joe, on the other hand, couldn't see why marriage had to change his life by forcing him to give up something that was so enjoyable to him. What Marie expected a husband to be, and what Joe expected to be, were very different.

Tom was a very frugal man who kept track of every penny he spent. He wasn't happy unless he was putting a certain portion of his pay check in the savings bank each month. If there was a major expenditure to be made, he thought it should be planned for months in advance. Dawn, the woman he married, came from a home where the income had been low and financial security uncertain. Tom was sure that he and Dawn would see eye to eye on financial matters. Much to his surprise, Dawn spent money without keeping track of where it went, looked with disdain on formulating a budget, made large expenditures without planning, and according to Tom, was always asking for more money. "I can't understand her," Tom complained to the marriage counselor, "I expected her to be very careful with money. And I thought we could sit down together occasionally and plan our finances. Aren't wives supposed to do this?" Dawn explained that she had had to pinch pennies all her life and was tired of that way of living. Besides, she said, why should one make oneself miserable over worrying about finances. Tom made a good salary, and they didn't have anything to worry about.

As time went on, Tom became increasingly frustrated at Dawn's method of handling finances. And Dawn began to look at Tom as a miser, a disgruntled haggler, and a nag. No reconciliation of these conflicting views of the way to handle family finances seemed possible. Dawn felt that a husband should not demand an accounting for the money a wife spends, and that life would be freer and happier if money weren't considered so important. Tom insisted that it wasn't the amount of money that Dawn was spending, but the careless manner in which she spent it. Role expectations were not being met at a point on which two people were very sensitive and very stubborn. Eventually, Dawn and Tom were divorced, and there was a great hassle over the financial settlement.

Marriage role concepts consist of what one believes the rights, duties, and responsibilities of a wife, husband, father, mother, male, and female are. When Dawn married, she saw herself as a wife, a female, and a mother in one way; Tom saw her in another way. Tom saw himself as a husband, a male, and a father in a particular way; Dawn expected him to be something quite different. Disappointed expectations can damage a marriage severely if they are not revised or satisfied in time.

It is possible that the role expectations a young person brings to marriage today are so great that they can't possibly be met. These expectations are formulated by television, motion pictures, newspapers, and magazines. Even books and articles on marriage extol the merits of the ideal husband and wife. The ideal husband brings home a more-than-adequate income, keeps himself handsome and athletic, spends his spare time with his wife and children, can repair the plumbing and appliances, is active in community affairs, and is a perfect host when friends or relatives are entertained. The ideal wife is a pleasant companion, an efficient housekeeper and money manager, an excellent cook, a child psychologist and educator, beautiful in face and figure, talented in interior design and decorating, an exciting sex partner, a companion to her husband in his various business and recreational interests, and a woman loved and respected by the whole community.

Such role expectations cannot possibly be met by either the husband or the wife. Most people are not able to function as perfectly and as completely as husbands and wives are supposed to function, according to the ideal picture. One of the objectives in our marriage education courses and in pre-marital counseling is to give people a more realistic idea about what marriage is, and if their expectations are too high, to lower these expectations to a level at which they have a chance of being met. In one of my classes, Barbara expressed the matter very well:

Something, which I have noticed recently, has been bothering me—I have been finding that many people's marriage problems, and/or fears relating to love relationships, appear to stem from one basic problem: they go into the relationship with unrealistic expectations of "love" and marriage. I have talked, lately, with several men about their marriages, and the most common gripe was, "Well, I've become disillusioned—she's not so exciting and marriage is dull and demanding!" Some women I know, too, have expressed the idea that their "white knights" weren't so shining anymore (for similar reasons). I feel this is, in part, a function of the general view held by most people of what marriage is—few realize that marriage is *not* "glamorous" and that it is *not* one long, continuous date! There are jobs to do: laundry, dishes, groceries, toilet training, etc., and the reality of meshing the two lives together. . . . My point is that I regret seeing so many men and women who "get caught" *after* the fact of marrying with reality staring them in the face when they could be helped to perceive it beforehand.

It is good for two people who plan to marry to know what each other's role expectations are, and to discuss these expectations as thoroughly as possible, particularly where there are disagreements. In a time when there is a rapid change in what is considered appropriate for men and women to do and be, it is especially important. Perhaps in no other area of married life has there been a greater change than in role concepts. Men do things that only women used to do, and vice versa. Women are now appropriately taking their places in the business, professional, and political world. Old stereotyped roles of what husbands, wives, males, and females are expected to be have been cast aside.

Marriage today is beginning to be thought of as something that should contribute to the fulfillment of those who participate in it, and not something that limits itself to making confining and restricting demands that shrivel their personalities and chances for development. It is not an end in itself, but a means for the realization of the best interests of all the members of a family.

To help couples understand the role expectations they may have for themselves and each other, we use the following Role Concepts Inventory.[5]

ROLE CONCEPTS INVENTORY

Compare your ideas about what it means to be a husband or a wife.

Key: 1 = Definitely agree. 2 = Agree with reservations. 3 = Not sure. 4 = Disagree in part. 5 = Definitely disagree.

Wife		*Husband*
1 2 3 4 5	1. The husband is the head of the family.	1 2 3 4 5
1 2 3 4 5	2. The wife should not get a job.	1 2 3 4 5
1 2 3 4 5	3. The husband should help with the dishes.	1 2 3 4 5
1 2 3 4 5	4. The wife has the greater responsibility for the children.	1 2 3 4 5
1 2 3 4 5	5. Money that the husband earns is his money.	1 2 3 4 5
1 2 3 4 5	6. Money that the wife earns is her money.	1 2 3 4 5
1 2 3 4 5	7. The wife should spend most of her time in the home.	1 2 3 4 5
1 2 3 4 5	8. The husband should have at least one night a week out with "the boys".	1 2 3 4 5
1 2 3 4 5	9. The wife should always have the meals on time.	1 2 3 4 5
1 2 3 4 5	10. The husband's primary responsibility is to his job while the wife's primary responsibility is to the home and children.	1 2 3 4 5
1 2 3 4 5	11. Money can best be handled through a joint checking account.	1 2 3 4 5
1 2 3 4 5	12. Marriage should be thought of as a partnership.	1 2 3 4 5
1 2 3 4 5	13. Major decisions should be made by the husband.	1 2 3 4 5
1 2 3 4 5	14. The husband should babysit one night a week so the wife can get away and do what she wants.	1 2 3 4 5

1 2 3 4 5   15. The husband and wife should go to church   1 2 3 4 5
             together.

1 2 3 4 5   16. The wife occasionally should initiate lovemak-   1 2 3 4 5
             ing with her husband.

1 2 3 4 5   17. The family should eat out once a week.   1 2 3 4 5

1 2 3 4 5   18. The husband and wife should plan the budget   1 2 3 4 5
             and manage money matters together.

1 2 3 4 5   19. Neither should purchase an item over fifty dol-   1 2 3 4 5
             lars without consulting the other.

1 2 3 4 5   20. The father should be the one to discipline the   1 2 3 4 5
             children.

1 2 3 4 5   21. A wife who has unusual talent should be per-   1 2 3 4 5
             mitted to have a career.

1 2 3 4 5   22. The wife should always have the house neat   1 2 3 4 5
             and clean.

1 2 3 4 5   23. The income should be strictly budgeted.   1 2 3 4 5

1 2 3 4 5   24. The best word to describe a parent's relation-   1 2 3 4 5
             ship with a child is "pal."

1 2 3 4 5   25. The husband should take his wife out for din-   1 2 3 4 5
             ner or diversion twice a month.

1 2 3 4 5   26. The wife should have status equal to her hus-   1 2 3 4 5
             band in family life.

1 2 3 4 5   27. The husband should be expected to do the   1 2 3 4 5
             yard work.

1 2 3 4 5   28. The mother, more than the father, should be   1 2 3 4 5
             the teacher of the children.

1 2 3 4 5   29. The wife frequently should initiate love-mak-   1 2 3 4 5
             ing with her husband.

1 2 3 4 5   30. It is a woman's privilege to be unpredictable.   1 2 3 4 5

1 2 3 4 5   31. Children should be allowed to help plan family   1 2 3 4 5
             activities.

1 2 3 4 5   32. Children do better with stern parents who are   1 2 3 4 5
             strict disciplinarians.

1 2 3 4 5   33. The wife should obey her husband.   1 2 3 4 5

1 2 3 4 5   34. The husband and wife should decide together   1 2 3 4 5
             for which areas each should be responsible.

1 2 3 4 5   35. Neither husband nor wife should bring de-   1 2 3 4 5
             pendent parents into the home to live.

1 2 3 4 5   36. Arguments are detrimental to marriage rela- 1 2 3 4 5
                   tionships.

1 2 3 4 5   37. It is often better to conceal the truth to avoid 1 2 3 4 5
                   unpleasant situations.

Fifteen of our successfully married couples were tested on this inventory. There are thirty-seven statements about which a person can express an opinion. We can also measure disagreements a couple may have. Our couples were quite compatible, according to the scores they received. The average number of disagreements was 7. The highest was 12 and the lowest was 2. This lowest score was that of Doris and Henry, who have been married the longest—forty-seven years. Some of the disagreements were not injurious to the relationship in that they indicated a willingness on the part of one to do more than was expected, such as a husband's willingness to babysit when the wife didn't expect him to do so.

Richard Klemer made an interesting observation about roles when he said, "It sometimes appears that the concept of unmet role expectations might be stretched to cover any malfunction in human relationships, especially in marriage."[6] It might be said that when role expectations are met in a marriage, the couple involved has a good basis on which to build a compatible relationship.

5. *Shared values, goals, beliefs, and religious practices.* There is little doubt about the importance of this source of compatibility in the successful marriages that we have studied. A value system determines what a person thinks is valuable and important in life. It helps one establish a priority of concerns. It helps one live under the banner of "first things come first." A goal is a point somewhere ahead in one's life which he hopes to attain in the course of time, an obstacle to be overcome, an achievement to be accomplished. A belief is a conviction of the truth or reality of life that gives one a basis for thinking and acting. It may be the result of what the believer thinks is positive evidence, it may be accepted on the authority of others in whom one has confidence, or it may be absorbed from one's family or community. Religion is a system in which the quest for reality or the ideal life is made by the individual, generally in community with other adherents of the same religion. Values, goals, and beliefs play an important role in the structure and practice of religion.

In Table 3, in Chapter 3, we noticed that in our selected group of eighteen successful marriages, "shared values" and "shared goals" were fully functioning characteristics of all of these marriages. The fifty-one couples whose marriages were rated 85 or above, ranked in the order of outstanding characteristics in their marriages, shared values as fifth, shared goals as ninth, and shared religious beliefs as seventh. Fifteen of the eighteen couples participated in a religious beliefs inventory that sought to measure the agreements and disagreements the couple had. The Religious Beliefs Inventory[7] contained sixty-five statements of belief to which each spouse was asked to respond. The following are selected from the larger list the couples used.

RELIGIOUS BELIEFS INVENTORY (ABBREVIATED)

Key: A = Agree.   D = Disagree.

1. I think of God as the Creator of everything, the mind and power behind the universe.   A   D

2. God is no more than the sum total of man's ideas and ideals.   A   D

3. I believe in life after death.   A   D

4. I believe God dictated the Bible to his writers and that they recorded it without error from beginning to end.   A   D

5. The Word of God is not the text of the Bible, but God speaking through the Bible to man as he interprets it.   A   D

6. The Biblical miracles do not conflict with the findings of modern science.   A   D

7. Salvation is being saved from going to hell after death.   A   D

8. One fulfills an important part of his purpose in life by giving a considerable amount of effort to the work of the church.   A   D

9. The message of the New Testament is that God loves all people and desires that all should find reconciliation with one another through his love.   A   D

10. God's will for the world is that brotherhood among all races and nations shall be more fully realized.   A   D

11. The Bible and religious faith help people to achieve a higher level of moral values.   A   D

12. All religions of the world are equally valuable and helpful.   A   D

13. Two people whose religious faiths are quite different should realize this might be a point of great difficulty if they should marry.   A   D

14. Parents are responsible for a carefully worked out program of religious education for their children.   A   D

15. Parents should avoid teaching their children religion and wait for the children to decide on their own when they are old enough.   A   D

The Religious Beliefs Inventory from which the statements above were taken works best with people whose religious tradition stems from the main-line denominations of Western culture. Our couples, for the most part, fit into that category. We did not attempt to rank them as orthodox, conservative, liberal, far right, or far left. We simply measured agreements and disagreements. If the reader wishes to use the statements above to test his agreements and disagreements with a spouse, he must remember it is only a partial list, and, therefore, an incomplete measurement.

The average number of agreements for the fifteen couples was 53.5 out of 65, or 82%, making the disagreements 11.5, or 18%. One couple had but 3 disagreements and another 4. Only two couples scored more than 15 disagreements, one 17 and the other 25.

At some later time we hope to give the couples we are studying the Allport-Vernon-Lindzey Study of Values test[8] in order to evaluate their compatibility in the various realms of values. We were able to gain some insight into their values through listening to their tapes, talking with them personally, and reading their written material. Dick and Dorene (discussed in Chapter 4) wrote about these matters. Dick: "We share common goals—both short and long term. We have compatible religious beliefs and needs. There is a total agreement on 'values' and on things which are important to each other." Dorene wrote: "We have common interests, goals and activities, and common religious practices and beliefs. We enjoy singing in the choir together each week. . . . We enjoy our family."

In Al and Carey's writing, Al wrote: "We have mutual life goals." And Carey wrote: "We share a continuing interest in what the other values. Some of these values we share and a few we do not but in all of them we take time to be interested." When we reviewed the work of Barbara and Gregory, we discovered Barbara saying: "We share many goals and interests. We share our religion and many values. We come from similar backgrounds." And from Gregory: "If a successful marriage is defined as one in which the goals of individual members of the family are met as well as the collective goals, then the fact that we have similar opinions and attitudes makes the process easier. These goals might be defined as the development of my career, my role as father, Barb's development as mother and in pursuit of her personal interests, and our common objectives in raising a family."

Our longest-married couple had this to say. Doris wrote, "We have similar goals in financial matters, family relations, and raising children; similar likes and dislikes in friends and recreation, and ability to have fun together." And Henry writes: "We had the desire to establish and maintain a Christian home and to instill these beliefs in our children. Doing for others whenever possible through volunteer work—veterans' hospital, work for the blind, and other handicapped people. We like to work together on projects, and have in the past worked on church boards and committees."

All these couples shared one very important value in that they considered marriage and family life as something to be nurtured and cherished for the rest of their lives. Because it was a top priority value for them, they took it seriously and resolved to succeed in it. Where couples believe differently, have divergent values and goals, and disagree in the area of religious ideas and activities, there is a constant widening of the gap between them; after a period of time, they find themselves in separate worlds, separated by a great chasm.

What comes after you say, "I love you"? The answer depends to a large degree on the number of factors that are working for a compatible relationship where two people move together in a harmonious partnership toward common objectives, finding life together rewarding and fulfilling.

REFERENCES

1. Whitney Darrow, Jr., *The New Yorker Magazine,* 1970.

2. Zick Rubin, *Liking and Loving: An Invitation to Social Psychology.* New York: Holt, Rinehart and Winston, 1973, pp. 137, 138.

3. James R. Hine, *Grounds for Marriage.* Danville, Ill.: Interstate Printers and Publishers, 1971, p. 29.

4. James R. Hine, *Your Marriage: Analysis and Renewal.* Danville, Ill.: Interstate Printers and Publishers, 1976, p. 11.

5. James R. Hine, *Grounds for Marriage,* pp. 24, 25.

6. Richard H. Klemer, *Marriage and Family Relationships.* New York: Harper and Row, 1970, p. 41.

7. James R. Hine, *Religious Beliefs Inventory Kit.* Danville, Ill.: Interstate Printers and Publishers, 1970.

8. G. W. Allport, P. E. Vernon, G. Lindzey, *Study of Values.* Boston, Mass.: Houghton Mifflin Co., third ed., 1960.

CHAPTER SEVEN

Marriage Skills
and Accomplishments

Marriage is a vocation, perhaps the most important and demanding of all. If we think of it as a vocation rather than a nebulous state in which, if everything happens to turn out right, we live "happily ever after," then we can approach it in a more rational manner and expect better results. Vocations require planning, preparation, and the development of skills. You cannot succeed in a job if you have no particular goals and no intention of learning each day how to do your work more effectively. When you apply for a job in an organization, personnel officers want to know what preparation you have had, what your experience in the field is, and what kind of a worker you show promise of becoming. They are looking for people who will grow and develop in their work. They may suggest continuing education and in-service training.

But in the vocation of marriage, we do not seem to be so particular. At the license bureau you are asked if you are old enough, if you have your health certificate, and if you have five dollars. The clergyman or the justice of the peace may not ask any questions either, other than to be sure you have a license. It is about as easy to get a marriage license as it is to get a fishing license. But most people who obtain a fishing license have developed some skills in the art of fishing.

Do we not need to begin to think of marriage as a vocation in the sense that there must be preparation for it, some evidence that we are ready to accept the responsibility before we marry, and a willingness to continue to learn and work to preserve the marriage after it takes place? This leads us to consider what the skills might be. After careful consideration once again of the successful marriages we have been studying in our research, I have concluded that there must be skills in at least four areas. Others may appear later, but we will consider these first.

1. *Skills involving communication and negotiation.* We are beginning

to realize the importance of these skills because of the popular demand for human relations courses, encounter groups, training programs, and workshops that will help people be better communicators.

What is communication? In its simple form it is the giving and receiving of signals. The signal may carry with it a feeling, an idea, a request, information; it may express concern, interest, respect, admiration, or love for another. It may be an invitation to friendship, a desire to argue or a need to reach a common understanding, solve a problem, or make a decision. From the time we are born, we begin to learn how to communicate. A baby's cry is its first attempt to tell the world something. From then on, the child learns to express hunger, discomfort, displeasure, joy, contentment. Signals available are sounds, facial expressions, and body movements. Later come words.

In marriage preparation seminars and in marriage enrichment programs, we study the various ways of communicating, so that couples will learn more about developing this essential skill. Becoming conscious of the variety of ways in which we can and do communicate, consciously and unconsciously, helps us to improve the ways we relate to one another. We might classify methods of communicating into two categories: audible and non-audible.

a. *Audible.* We do something the other person can hear. The most common practice would be to speak words. This is verbal communication. George du Maurier is credited with this description of his reaction to verbal communication. "You fill your lungs with wind and shake a little slit in your throat, and make mouths, and that shakes the air; and the air shakes a pair of little drums in my head. . . . and my brain seizes your meaning in the rough." When you "make mouths" and "shake the air" in a particular way, you use a word that is a symbol agreed upon by people of a particular culture to carry a specific meaning. This is a unique feature of human beings and makes culture, and its continuation, possible. Thus it makes it possible for one human being to say to another, "I love you." And other human beings will have some kind of a notion about what is meant. Note that I said, "some kind of a notion," because though a word carries a definition, it is just that and not the reality itself. This is nowhere more true than when the word "love" is used. Most people use words rather poorly, and only rarely does one find a person who handles his language well. Perhaps this is the reason why verbal communication is not adequate in itself. So there is an audible means without the use of words.

One of the earliest means used by the infant is crying and laughing, signifying an unhappy or happy state. There are other forms of non-verbal vocalizations such as sighing, moaning, humming, using vocal identifiers such as *mmm, ahhh, uh-uh, ooo,* etc. One may make other kinds of noises to indicate his meaning: sighing, gasping, clicking of tongue, snorting, sucking in air, exhaling air, whistling, clapping hands, slapping one's side, stamping one's feet, pounding a table, snapping fingers, even grinding teeth. Some couples have told me that they have their own particular brand of noises, very clearly understood by them, but not by outsiders. For instance, when one wife inhaled loudly, it meant she was somewhat disgusted. Then there are the vocal qualifiers: speaking loudly or softly, in a high-pitched or low-pitched voice, shouting, mumbling, using monotone, whispering, and various other manifestations of personality and feeling that affect our communication.

b. *Non-audible.* Even more interesting in the area of communication are the non-audible forms of transmitting meaning. Of course, there is always writing. I recommend that a courtship contain some period in which the couple writes to each other. There are things one can learn from what one writes that cannot be learned otherwise. Some people who are not adept at expressing themselves in person-to-person situations, communicate very well through the written word.

Then there is the symbolic gift. A young man explained it this way, "I took this new girl friend to a party, and then became preoccupied with visiting some old friends, and neglected her pretty badly. When I took her home she was very cool, and I thought maybe she wouldn't want to see me again, although I did like her very much. It seemed that words wouldn't come to me to explain what I did, to tell her I was sorry. After a few days passed I sent her a dozen roses, and then called her. She seemed quite friendly, and I arranged to see her again." The gift had conveyed the message that he couldn't transmit in words, at least not at first. Once in awhile a husband will see something in a gift shop he believes his wife would enjoy, and he buys it for her, hoping it will say something about a deep feeling he has for her. How many times wives cook that "special" meal for their husbands as a way of saying, "I love you." While words are important for expressing love, they are reinforced by "gifts" that are symbolic of deeper expressions of love.

Your appearance, your manner of dress, and perhaps your fragrance speak for you in a special way. It has often been said that women dress to please men, but I am sure that men do the same thing for women. You may dress to express a particular mood to another person. This is true of hair style, skin color, whether a man is bearded or not, whether a person wears sandals, goes barefoot, dresses formally, uses beads, bracelets, or jewelry. And, of course, there are all the forms of make-up, perfumes, mouth washes, shaving lotions, and perfumed soaps that are on the market today. One cosmetic company advertises: "Let Wind Song do the talking for you." As we discussed earlier, these modes of communication do not always reveal the real person, and sometimes they are deceptive; nevertheless, when one steps into a room, he or she begins to communicate immediately by appearance alone. In other words, presence alone says something about what you are, what you think, and how you feel about others.

Then there is the matter of distance, position, and space. We tested this factor in our marriage class a number of times and decided that when we talk to a casual friend we stand about three feet apart. I noticed in the Middle East that people stood closer than that to me, and sometimes seemed to be breathing in my face; I was uncomfortable, but was told that they like to absorb your presence by being close, and this is a way of saying they want to be friendly. All lovers know that being close is a way of saying something about the relationship. And as lovers quarrel, they tend to sit farther apart. People in our culture require more space than people of other cultures. Someone has described the average American as wanting a "space bubble" about three feet in diameter to keep him at a certain distance from other people. Is this saying we are not as friendly as we might be?

Touching says a great many things. Some people would never think of touching anyone in the course of a conversation, even though that person is a close friend. Others constantly touch their friends when talking with them. Sometimes touching can be a frantic effort to let a person know how one feels. On one occasion, Linus was telling Charlie Brown about the little girl up the street, about whom he had some friendly feeling, "I couldn't think of what to say, so I hit her." She may not have gotten the right message, but his intentions were good.

I have noticed a correlation between the amount of touching a couple does and the quality of their relationship. This is noticeable in social gatherings where in the course of conversations a husband and wife may exchange a gentle touch to indicate a consciousness of the other's presence even when surrounded by a crowd of people. Recently I noticed an elderly couple walking through a park holding hands. Yet I have had wives, in particular, during marriage counseling say that their husbands never touched them except as a prelude to getting them into bed. Touching, particularly at odd moments of the day, is necessary to nourish a relationship in intimacy and affection.

Ashley Montagu believes this means of communication is learned very early in life. When a child is born, it leaves behind the warm, close, secure environment of the mother's womb, and suddenly finds itself in a cold world of space and distance. Unless first the mother, and later the father and other members of the family, compensate for this loss by providing closeness, cuddling, fondling, caressing, the child may lose a sense of being wanted and loved, and never develop the capacity to be close to others. Montagu writes:

Touch and Communication. It has been remarked that in the final analysis every tragedy is a failure in communication. And what the child receiving inadequate cutaneous stimulation suffers from is the failure of integrative development as a human being, a failure in the communication of the fact that he is being loved. By being stroked, and caressed, and carried, and cuddled, and cooed to, by being loved, he learns to stroke and caress and cuddle, and coo to and love others. In this sense love is sexual in the healthiest sense of that word. It implies involvement, concern, responsibility, tenderness, and awareness of the needs and vulnerabilities of the other. All this is communicated to the infant through his skin in the early months of his life, and gradually reinforced by feeding, sound, and visual cues as the infant develops. The primacy of the infant's first perceptions of reality through the skin can no longer be doubted. The messages he received through that organ must be security-giving, assuring, and pleasurable if the infant is to survive.[1]

Montagu discusses, in detail, the effect on the child in cultures where it is carried on the back of its mother and remains close to her body throughout its early life. In the Netsilik Eskimo culture of the Canadian Arctic, the infant spends almost all of its time in contact with its mother's body. This infant seldom cries and later develops "pleasant or altruistic responses to interpersonal relationships. . . ." This characteristic of the Netsilik is greatly influenced by his early childhood experience in relation to his mother's body.[2]

So we learn to touch to express what we feel toward others. We shake hands, pat, slap, tickle, hug, caress, stroke, kiss, and use countless other ways to communicate through touching. If one comes from a family which has not been one to demonstrate affection through touching, or even from a family that has been cold or indifferent, is it possible to acquire the ability to communicate through touching? I have seen it done. It may be more difficult, and it may not come up to the level of someone who does come from a warm, affectionate, demonstrating family; but learning and developing are possible. First, one must develop an interest and concern for people in general. Then this can be followed by practicing communicating by various means of touching, developing a habit that, in time, will feel natural. Certainly the successful marriages I have studied have, in one way or another, developed and practiced this art.

Then there is communicating through body language or *kinesics*. The theory here is that we say a great deal, many times unconsciously, through the movements of parts of the body. Perhaps you have seen a television camera zoom in on the hands of a person being interviewed. You may have seen what appeared to be a calm face, but now you see fingers being twisted nervously. We sit with legs crossed, or feet apart flat on the floor; arms hanging at sides or folded in front; we gesture or sit quietly; we point, nod, or shake the head, shrug, wink, smile, frown, scowl, move eyebrows this way or that. As we talk, our eyes may widen or narrow, we may lean forward or back, drop the head or the hand, switch position of our legs. We look at the person with whom we are talking. We may look him in the eye, then suddenly shift our gaze to the floor (which is sometimes known as "dimming our lights"). Without being aware of what we are doing, we are saying something in these movements of our body. Ray L. Birdwhistell, one who has done as much as any in this field, believes that kinesic behavior is learned and can be analyzed. The study of such behavior is fascinating, and we shall learn much from it. What can we learn that might help us in communicating? We can learn what other people are trying to say to us by being conscious of their body language. This will make us more sensitive to their thoughts and feelings. We can learn to express ourselves more effectively by developing some effective techniques in body language communication.

A wife who came in for marriage counseling said: "I would like to know what you think about a peculiar thing my husband does. When he talks with me, he never looks me in the eye. He looks at the ceiling, or the floor, or he talks with his back turned." What was he saying? Was he beginning to think of her as less of a person and more of an object? Was he trying to hide something from her? Or was he just a poor communicator? She didn't know, but she did know it bothered her considerably. If people were to say, "I love you," to each other, would they not be expected to have some prolonged eye contact? I would think so.

I have recommended one exercise in particular for students in my classes. Perhaps I was motivated by the fact that a teacher sees many faces before him day after day that are dull, flaccid, expressionless. One even observes friends who, in conversations, seem to use their eyes and facial muscles in a limited manner. This exercise is for such people. It has to be practiced in front of a mirror. Now, you are first to practice expressing certain emotions with your face alone: anger, surprise, disappointment, expectation, sadness, joy, love, hate, happiness, fear, trust, and others, as you think of them. This exercise alone will help a person develop the habit of using the face in communication. Now that the first exercise has been practiced, the second is saying something verbally and accompanying it with an appropriate expression of the face: Will you go to dinner with me? I would like to tell you that I'm sorry! I have some bad news! I have some good news! I love you! And so on. Perhaps these simple exercises in body communication can make a person aware of how important it really is to say something more than just words, and with the help of this awareness, to become a better communicator.

The last communication skill to be mentioned here is that of being a good listener. We spend a lot of time each day listening to someone or something. Researchers in the field of listening tell us we are, for the most part, rather poor listeners. Perhaps because we have to listen so much, we have developed methods of not listening even when being talked to. Thus we develop bad listening habits that we carry into marriage and family life. Often we do not listen to our spouses or our children. There are many kinds of listeners, but let us divide them into four types. There is the "not present" listener. A cartoon pictures a man meeting a friend on the street who asks him, "How are things going these days?" The man replies that things are going pretty well, but that his wife has had an operation and is in the hospital. When he gets through his story, his friend replies: "Uh-huh. Incidentally, how's your wife?" During the re-cital of the hospital story, he was not present. Perhaps he was thinking only about what he was going to say when the story ended. Instead of listening, he was waiting his turn to talk. Perhaps he was thinking about what he had to do later.

Then there is the listener who is "tuned out." He may not like what is being said, so he tunes the communication off. He is not receptive to what is going on at all. A third type of listener acts as a "filter." He allows to filter in only what he wants to hear. Something may filter in to complain about, or something to be critical about. Perhaps something that seems to threaten him may filter in, or something to agree with and believe. Many people listen to speeches this way, filtering out bits and pieces to agree or disagree with, but rarely getting the whole message.

Last, there is the "really present" listener. This person says with body, face, and eyes: "I am interested in what you are saying to me." Although what is being said isn't always important, it might be; and it will be helpful to the relationship to treat it seriously. There are times when we are tuned in with every fiber of our being. A loved one is gravely ill, and we ask the doctor, "Is he going to live, or is he going to die?" We are lost on a mountain trail, and we meet a forest ranger, "Can you tell me how I can get to where I want to go?" In such cases, we are, as it is often said, "all ears." I have found that to be a good listener when I *want* to be, I have to discipline myself to be an attentive listener most of the time. It is a skill that I can develop consciously when I put my mind to it. And when a spouse speaks, or when a child speaks, it is well to listen carefully to what is being said, for in so doing one can create the empathy that is so needed in family relationships.

If I were asked to estimate the values of different ways of communicating, I would make an educated guess and say that the total impact of this important process can be broken down to something like 25% verbal; 30% vocalizations, vocal qualifiers and identifiers, and meaningful sounds; and 45% body language, including facial expression. If this breakdown be anywhere near the truth of the matter, then it behooves us all to learn how to communicate effectively in all possible ways.

Equally as important as communicating is the skill of negotiating, for communicating alone is not enough. Negotiating is the process by which we communicate about something on which we differ, and find it necessary to reach a compromise, or a point that seems to serve the best interests of both parties. Because negotiating is such an important factor in a marriage, we will deal with it at greater length in a later chapter.

2. *Adaptability and adjustment skills in marriage.* A neighbor of ours lost his wife shortly after his retirement. A very good friend of theirs lost her husband about the same time. The two started to date, and after several years decided to marry. Each owned a beautiful home filled with furniture that had been carefully selected over the lifetime of their first marriages. When they married, they had some difficult decisions to make: Which home would they keep and which would they sell? What furniture of each would they keep to use in the house in which they chose to live, and what furniture would they sell or give to their children? In addition to these decisions, they had to apply themselves to the important matter of joining their two separate life styles into a harmonious pattern. This situation symbolizes what every couple brings to a marriage: years of accumulated habits, manners, ideas, beliefs, personality traits, and personal belongings. How do they put all of this together and make it work? The skills used to do this are those of adaptability and adjustment. A wife once said to me: "A human being is a very complicated thing and difficult to understand. Now think of putting two together and expecting them to get along!" To be sure, they are not going to be able to do this unless they have considerable skill in adapting and adjusting. Robert Bell writes:

Given the various ways in which modern middle-class marriage roles may be filled, the ultimate measurement of successful marriage is the degree of adjustment achieved by the individuals in their roles and in interaction with one another. In the following discussion, adjustment and success are both used in essentially the same way to refer to the degree of satisfaction with marriage. . . . Given the complexity of the roles and role relationships, as well as the personalities of different individuals, no marriage is absolutely adjusted or maladjusted. Even in marriages assessed as highly adjusted, some areas of conflict for or between the partners will exist. A marriage in which absolute personal and social acceptance and satisfaction always prevail is hard to imagine. . . . Whether or not a marriage is successful is determined by the interaction between the two partners over the time span of their marriage.[3]

Several years ago I made a study of 170 couples who had been married more than five years. I wanted to find out what areas of their marriages required up to five years for a satisfactory adjustment. The survey showed the following results.

TABLE 7-1
A STUDY OF ADJUSTMENT PATTERNS OF 170 COUPLES
(340 PERSONS)

Problems which took up to five years for satisfactory adjustment, in order of frequency	*Number of individuals having adjustment problems*
1. Adjustment to each other's personality	192
2. Sexual relations	190
3. Ability to talk through problems	135
4. Handling finances	123
5. Agreement on child rearing	102
6. Getting along with in-laws	100
7. Social activities and recreation	73
8. Religion, church	72
9. Selecting mutual friends	48

What this tells us is that in most marriages there is quite a bit of adjusting to do, no matter how well the marriage turns out in later years. Many of the couples in the study indicated that, at the time of the survey, they still had areas in which an adjustment had not been accomplished. It must be taken into consideration, also, that people change in the course of the years, and changes may call for additional adjustments.

Adjustment includes changes in a number of special areas, including the following:

a. *Adjustment to each other's personality.* Although a courtship period of a year or more should help people get to know one another fairly well, living together in a new setting requires personality modification on the part of both, and adaptation to, and acceptance of, each other. If temperaments are fairly compatible to begin with, this adaptation can be accomplished over a period of time without undue strain. If they are not, the adjustment will require much more time and attention.

b. *Sexual relations.* Some couples are surprised when they are told that a satisfactory sexual adjustment may take five years. This is true because a good sexual relationship depends on a good total relationship, and a good total relationship is not accomplished overnight.

c. *Ability to talk through problems.* This ability is a matter of communication, negotiation, and the handling of conflict. This we will want to discuss in more detail later.

d. *Handling finances.* Money can be a big problem, especially if there isn't enough of it, and there usually isn't, at the beginning anyway. There are two matters more important than the amount of money a couple has, though, and the first is the value system of the couple. Have they agreed to, and adjusted to, a system of values that will serve both of their needs as adequately as possible? Each comes from a family that considered the meeting of certain economic needs as necessary for their well-being. Have they discussed these needs to the point they can adapt to what is best for them? The second matter is financial planning. Robert Kelley writes:

Money is an important factor in marriage; some workable pattern of organizing expenditures is a must for every family. Any young couple about to begin managing a family income must be realistic about their financial situation. If the husband insists on continuing the use of his money in the same way he did before marriage, or if his wife imagines that she can maintain the same standard of living she was accustomed to in her parents' home, where her living expenses were paid for her and her whole income was available for her personal expenses, they are in for a rude shock. They must recognize that it takes intelligence, a certain amount of time, and a good deal of common sense to build a working financial partnership in the family.[4]

The couples in our current study, who have done well in the area of money management, have done so by means of effective communication and negotiation; arriving at a plan of budgeting, saving, and spending; and formulating short- and long-term financial goals. A division of labor is generally agreed upon in regard to who keeps records, whether there is a joint or separate checking account, and who pays which bills. Sometimes one of the spouses may enjoy, and be particularly efficient at, handling finances. After an agreement is reached, this person may take charge of most of the financial responsibilities of the family. This person may or may not be the one who is considered the "breadwinner."

e. *Agreement on child rearing.* Fortunate is the couple who has had the opportunity to take a child development course together or separately sometime before the first child arrives. Often couples find themselves disagreeing about child rearing, having come from families with different ideas about infant care, toilet training, discipline, and other matters. In this case it would be important for them to enroll in a class on child development, or at least get some of the better books, and read and discuss them together. But there are some attitudes that are still more important than the knowledge they may have acquired. The research team of Chess, Thomas, and Birch points this out:

> There are some universal requirements for good parenthood. Good parents plan room in their lives for a child. . . . Good parents clearly, simply, and directly communicate their feelings, attitudes, standards, and demands. What they communicate to the child is personally and socially healthy, appropriate to the situation, to the child's level of development, and to his temperament. . . . Within these universals there is room for the widest expression of individuality. . . .
>
> To say that children need love is to belabor the obvious. An unloved and unwanted child is a tragic and innocent victim of his parents and society. But the bland prescription of love and more love as an emotional panacea for all parent-child issues is quite another matter. . . .
>
> There is no mystery about good parenthood. If parents cultivate with their children the qualities they use to make their other close and deep relationships work, there will probably be no need to worry about whether the child is sufficiently loved.
>
> Sometimes parents seem so weighed down with instructions and commandments that the joys of parenthood are quite obscured. This is indeed sad. Children are one of the most reliable and richest sources of pleasure in life.
>
> Parents who enjoy their children in their own individual ways can be sure the children are also benefiting. If there is one thing above all that children will thrive on, it is their parents' pleasure in them.[5]

Adjusting and adapting to children would then consist, for the most part, in learning the basic techniques of child development, and maintaining an attitude that you are going to love and enjoy your children every step along the way.

f. *Getting along with in-laws.* Adjusting to in-laws can be an acute problem for couples whose in-laws are constantly interfering with the marriage or have failed to accept it. In this case, putting considerable distance between the couple and in-laws seems to be the only solution. However, 66 percent of the 340 married people in our study said they made the adjustment with in-laws early in the marriage. All but 12 spouses said they had made the adjustment by the time the marriage had gone through the fifth year. Also, studies by Blood and Wolfe[6] and others, show that problems with in-laws tend to decrease fairly rapidly and almost disappear in the later stages of the family life cycle.

g. *Social activities and recreation.* Our study of well-adjusted couples shows that couples with similar interests at the time of marriage have an advantage over couples whose major interests are dissimilar; but that couples who are willing can develop many interests and activities in common as they move together creatively in their marriage.

h. *Religion and church involvement.* Our studies show that the adjustment is much simpler if married couples belong to the same religious denomination and participate to the same extent in that religious community. Just carrying the same religious label is not sufficient. Or if both are non-religious or anti-religious, this makes for an easier adjustment than when one is devoutly religious and the other is not. Most of the couples in our select group of eighteen couples were related together in some religious group, and felt strongly that this contributed positively to their marriage, both for sociological and religious reasons. If there are major religious differences before the marriage, it is highly advisable that the couple arrive at some mutually satisfactory decision about how they are going to reconcile these differences and what they are going to do in the future about religious instruction for their children. If the marriage takes place without this agreement, it is most difficult to solve the problem in the new context.

i. *Selecting mutual friends.* In our study and in those conducted by Judson Landis,[7] this area proved to be the one in which the adjustments were most readily made. Where they are not made, the situation can be an uncomfortable one. Renee came into the marriage counseling office complaining about the fact that her husband's friends were unacceptable to her. "He has the strangest taste in friends," she explained. "They are not like us at all, and I find nothing we have in common with them. But he insists that I be friendly with them, partly for business reasons." Renee's husband refused to join with her in selecting new friends that would be mutually acceptable. As a result, their social life is unsatisfactory, and Renee is considering a separation. If her husband had been willing to do what must be done in such cases, namely, make new friends together, all might have worked out in the course of time. Unacceptable friends on the part of one spouse tend to phase out as new ones are cultivated by the couple.

The Landis study considered all the areas we have been discussing with the exception of "adjusting to each other's personality," and "ability to talk through problems." Some of their conclusions are:

The study of the 409 couples showed that a close relationship existed between agreement or early adjustment to differences and happiness in the marriages. Over one-half of the couples rated the marriages as very happy if agreement had existed from the beginning or if they had been able to get together on differences immediately, whereas only one-fifth rated their marriages as very happy if they had been unable to adjust at the beginning.

Some couples rated their marriages as very happy, even if there was one area in which they had never been able to agree. But if there was failure to get together fairly well in two areas, 77 per cent were average or unhappy, and all those who reported unsatisfactory adjustment in three or more areas rated their marriages average or unhappy.[8]

Adaptability and adjustability are two of the great arts of a healthy marriage. They call for personality types and acquired skills that are indispensable. If rigidity, stubbornness, uncompromising attitudes, or unwillingness to accommodate and change prevail, the clouds of impending disaster will continue to gather on the horizon. One of our successfully married couples said they thought "flexibility" expressed best the way they worked together. Another said, "Learn the ways of each other, adjust by trying to fit them together, and when you can't, use toleration." This is good advice.

3. *The skill and accomplishment of meeting each other's needs.* Everyone has his own individual set of needs. Mine may be very different from yours. Some persons may have healthy needs, while others may have neurotic needs. Also, there are those who maintain that there are basic needs shared by all human beings. W. C. Schutz, after intensive research into the field of interpersonal relations, concluded that all people have three basic interpersonal needs in common:

inclusion (which) has to do with the degree of commitment, belongingness, and participation an individual requires in human interaction; *control* (which) has to do with the degree of influence and power an individual requires; and *affection* (which) has to do with the degree of closeness, intimacy, an individual desires.[9]

These needs are expressed in our relationship to others, and at the same time, there is a desire for the others to fulfill these needs in their relationship to us.

As early as 1954, Abraham Maslow was beginning to construct his *hierarchy of needs* in his book, *Motivation and Personality,* which he enlarged later. His theory is that all people have basic needs, the most obvious of which is the need for survival: air, water, food, shelter, sleep, sex. Then there was their need for safety and security. This was followed by what Maslow called *being values* or growth needs, which led toward self-actualization: love, belongingness, self-esteem and esteem by others, meaningfulness, playfulness, justice, completion, individuality, aliveness, beauty, goodness, truth, and other *metaneeds*. Many of these needs could not be met by an individual living alone and separated from his fellow human beings. They could be met only in an interaction with another human being. Behind the anxiety that we all suffer, the loneliness that we cannot altogether escape, is the need motivating us to reach out for another, and beyond this, to some ultimate concern that will fill the lonely void and give us a sense of union and fulfillment.

I have always thought that marriage was an attempt to meet a person's basic need for union, for security, and for meaning. How this need is met by marriage depends on the nature of the marriage and how the needs of both husband and wife are met in the relationship. We used an inventory to try to see how people who seemed to be having satisfactory marriages had their needs met, and in turn, met the needs of the people they married. The following is an adaptation of this inventory.

INDIVIDUAL NEED ANALYSIS AND COMPATIBILITY FACTORS[10]

In column 1, indicate how you feel about this need by choosing one of the four statements in Key I, and recording the symbol.

In column 2, indicate to what extent these needs are being met in the relationship by your partner, by selecting the appropriate statement in Key II, and recording the symbol.

Key I	*Key II*
Key for Column I to be used to indicate the need.	Key for Column II to be used to indicate how you feel the need is being met by your partner.
IN = Intensely felt IM = Important for my well-being FL = Feel this is a need at times but to a lesser degree NO = Not a felt need	VS = Very satisfactorily met MO = Moderately so PM = Partially met UM = Unsatisfactorily met NR = No response needed here, or doesn't apply to my relationship with my partner.

The Need	1	2
1. I need to be reassured frequently and told that I am appreciated and wanted.	____	____
2. I am very dependent and need constantly to have someone to "lean on."	____	____
3. I like to be noticed, admired, and to feel I have made an impression on others.	____	____
4. I want to be free, uninhibited, uncommitted to conventions, traditions, and independent of what others think I ought to be.	____	____
5. I need to have opportunities to organize, direct and influence programs and people.	____	____

The Need	1	2

6. I feel most secure when I am with someone who is strong in conviction and firm in decision making.   _____   _____

7. I am apt to take the more safe and conservative step to avoid problems, danger, or failure.   _____   _____

8. I feel most at ease when I have my affairs in order, my surroundings neat, and my work organized.   _____   _____

9. I like to be free of responsibility most of the time. I tend to shun involvement.   _____   _____

10. I need a great amount of privacy in my life, away from people and events.   _____   _____

11. I have a desire for a considerable amount of gaiety and fun through going places and doing pleasurable things.   _____   _____

12. I put considerable emphasis on economic security.   _____   _____

13. I need better than average clothes, home, car, furniture, and money to do extra things.   _____   _____

14. I get most of my satisfactions from non-material sources: friends, music, art, beauty of nature, good literature, etc.   _____   _____

15. I have a strong religious feeling implying a need for God, worship, giving thanks, thinking high thoughts, exercising faith.   _____   _____

16. I have a strong sexual drive and need frequent satisfying sexual experiences.   _____   _____

17. A great deal of the time I like to be quiet, avoid crowds, noise, the busy world, in order to reflect and maintain emotional stability.   _____   _____

18. I am uneasy unless I am saving money.   _____   _____

19. I am more comfortable when I conform to the ideas, manners and styles of the people around me.   _____   _____

20. I tend to want to be a part of group activity, organizations or clubs that provide opportunities for social experiences or doing things together.   _____   _____

21. I like good food, have a healthy appetite, and relish opportunities to eat with friends or family at home or in restaurants.   _____   _____

	The Need	1	2
22.	I enjoy competition and will work to improve my ability to do a better job, or play a better game.	___	___
23.	I receive a great deal of satisfaction in winning over others with whom I am competing.	___	___
24.	I enjoy being the life of the party and have the capacity to generate activity in groups.	___	___
25.	Talking is more important to me than listening when I am with other people.	___	___
26.	One of my tendencies is to feel compassion for others, particularly those in trouble.	___	___
27.	I will go out of my way to help, understand, console, and comfort people in need.	___	___
28.	I find a sense of fulfillment in devoting time and energy to a cause, feeling that I am a part of a movement for the betterment and well being of mankind.	___	___
29.	I am curious and want to know the answers to questions.	___	___
30.	I enjoy exploring new areas; I need explanations of ideas presented even by authority figures. I like to feel I have worked out things by myself.	___	___
31.	I enjoy arguing, matching wits with another, defending my convictions.	___	___
32.	I like to win a "contest" if I can.	___	___
33.	When I am criticized, proven wrong, corrected or disciplined, I feel good about it. It keeps me humble and in my place.	___	___
34.	I need physical activity and like active games, hikes, picnics, etc.	___	___
35.	I consider myself to be the outdoor, athletic type.	___	___
36.	I need someone to help me get through frequent feelings of depression.	___	___
37.	I am sensitive to criticism and need a partner who takes this into consideration.	___	___
38.	I enjoy being touched by friends or relatives who desire to show affection.	___	___
39.	I find satisfaction in demonstrating my affection to people I like (kissing, hugging, etc.)	___	___

The Need	1	2
40. Intellectual discussions and pursuits are very necessary to me.	———	———
41. When I have a problem, I want to get it out in the open and talk about it.	———	———

Perhaps using this instrument can bring about a better understanding of your own and your partner's needs, and, as a result, you will both strive to find ways of meeting these needs and thus a greater fulfillment individually and together.

4. *Competency in marriage roles and goal accomplishment.* We began this chapter by stating that marriage is a vocation, perhaps the most important and demanding of all. The demands are made upon husband and wife to perform their roles adequately and to accomplish the goals they believe to be necessary for family achievement. We note in the successful marriages studied that there is a general agreement on role concepts (rights, duties, and responsibilities). Also, there is an understanding about short- and long-term objectives to be accomplished; and both husband and wife do their jobs rather well. What kinds of roles are needed in the family, and who performs which?

The traditional terms used to indicate the difference between roles of husband and wife are "breadwinner" and "homemaker." Talcott Parsons refers to the "husband-father" role as that of the task specialist, and the "wife-mother" role as that of the social-emotional specialist. In Korea the husband is known as the "outside master," while the wife is known as the "inside master." These designations have not always been appropriate in our culture, for in pioneer days, when America was largely rural, the woman was "task oriented" to a high degree, and spent a great amount of time outside the house.

One will find differing role concepts held in contemporary America, but by and large, the tendency is to make husband and wife roles fluid and flexible. And in spite of all the labor-saving devices conjured up by our industrial designers, the "task" roles to be performed in the average home are numerous. Consider the following.

income producer
child-bearer
child specialist
gardener
cook
cleaning person

athletic coach
parent
companion
repair person
engineer
business manager

interior decorator	bookkeeper
seamstress	therapist-comforter
dietitian	nurse
shopper-buyer	mechanic
educator	reconcilor
musical director	secretary
tour guide	social director
chauffeur	arts and crafts specialist

This list could go on and on. Now look down the list again and decide which seems to be the husband's role and which seems to be that of the wife. It is not easy, is it? And almost all of these roles are interchangeable. Only one role seems to remain constant, and that is the wife's as child-bearer; this we will be able to depend on for some time to come.

How does one become competent in the role that seems appropriate for him or her? Most of us who have been married for a long time feel that in marriage we continue to learn and develop skills in the roles for which we come to be responsible. My wife and some of her neighbors are learning to do macrame. Some other women are taking courses in auto mechanics, and a number of men and women are enrolled in the local community college learning new skills.

What about goal accomplishment? First, a family needs to set goals. Where do they want to be a year from now, five and ten years from now? What kinds of goals are important to them? George Levinger made a study of family goals ranked by sixty couples and found that the couples ranked them in this order of importance:

1. *Affection*. Having family members satisfied with the amount of love they give to each.
2. *Companionship*. Having family members enjoy doing things together and feel comfortable with each other.
3. *Happy children*. Personal development. Giving each family member the opportunity to develop as an individual.
4. *Religion*. Living according to religious principles and teaching.
5. *Economic security*. Keeping up or improving the family standard of living.
6. *Attractive home*. Having a place which is comfortable and attractive to live in.
7. *Wise financial planning*. Making sound decisions in budgeting for present and future purchases, and making intelligent use of money.
8. *A place in the community*. Giving family members a respected place in the community.[11]

When husbands and wives ranked these goals separately, there was a surprising closeness in their ranking. Affection, companionship, and happy children ranked in the first three for couples, husbands and wives. While different rankings would be obtained from different socio-economic groups, the tendency is toward the companionship marriage with a democratic structure and a participating membership for each person.

Earlier in this book, we attempted to establish that the marriage that continues to function well and does not lose its luster for the husband and wife within it, is the one in which the couple have determination, a will to succeed, and a desire to work to improve it as the years go by. In this kind of a marriage, the skills can be developed that will help the family reach the goals that will give it a sense of fulfillment.

REFERENCES

1. Ashley Montagu, *Touching.* New York: Columbia University Press, 1971, pp. 194, 195.

2. *Ibid.,* pp. 261, 262.

3. Robert R. Bell, *Marriage and Family Interaction.* Homewood, Ill.: The Dorsey Press, 1967, pp. 296, 297.

4. Robert K. Kelley, *Courtship, Marriage and the Family.* New York: Harcourt Brace Jovanovich, 1974, p. 441.

5. Stella Chess, Alexander Thomas, Herbert G. Birch, *Your Child Is a Person.* New York: Viking Press, 1965, pp. 198–203.

6. Robert O. Blood, Jr., Donald M. Wolfe, *Husbands and Wives: The Dynamics of Married Living.* Glencoe, Ill.: The Free Press, 1960.

7. Judson T. Landis and Mary G. Landis, *Building a Successful Marriage.* Englewood Cliffs, N.J.: Prentice-Hall, 1963, pp. 288–90.

8. *Ibid.,* p. 289.

9. W. G. Bennis, E. H. Schein, F. I. Steele, D. E. Berlew, *Interpersonal Dynamics.* Homewood, Ill.: The Dorsey Press, 1968, p. 19.

10. James R. Hine, *Will We Meet Each Other's Needs?* Danville, Ill.: Interstate Printers and Publishers, 1978.

11. George Levinger, *Sociometry,* Vol. 27 (1964), 433–48.

CHAPTER EIGHT

Situational Factors

Briefly, we will consider here the effect of situational factors on a marriage. The setting, the environment, the climate, the background, current circumstances relating to income, health, children, friends, relatives, and many other situational factors have a pronounced effect on the functioning of a marriage.

A review of the written and taped material in which our eighteen couples gave reasons for their marital success yielded very little information about the effect of situational factors on these marriages. One of the husbands said: "We have been fortunate. We have experienced no catastrophic physical, mental or financial problems." His wife had this to say: "From the arrival of the first pay check after marriage we both have agreed that it is important to spend less than we earn. As these savings funds have grown, they have relieved us of financial worries and have made it possible for us to support some of the relief programs of our church and other like-minded organizations. We have realized from early adulthood that neither of us has robust health so have deliberately limited the number of commitments we make to social and community affairs. We can see that there would be conflict if one had much more abundant energy than the other."

Another wife writes: "I feel our move to another state, away from our in-laws, was a real strength builder; we had to learn to depend on each other more and adjust to some hardships all by ourselves." As ninth in her ranking of important factors, another wife lists "We have had an adequate salary." Another wife remarks: "The fact that we decided not to have children right after we were married proved to be an asset." A husband writes: "I have been relatively successful in a dynamic, interesting, growing vocation, which has given us financial security and a sense of achievement." Another husband and wife mention good health and a job that pays well, and postponement of children for several years.

In the Levinger study mentioned in Chapter 7, sixty couples ranked in their list of family goals, happy children as third, economic security as fifth, attractive home as sixth, wise financial planning as seventh, and a place in the community as eighth. But affection and companionship took precedence over all of these. Most of the outstanding characteristics of the successfully married couples in our study fell into the categories of respect and admiration for each other's personality and character traits, and the quality of the interpersonal relationship they enjoyed. A number of couples mention that they appreciate the fact that they both come from similar backgrounds, and they give this factor a lot of credit for their marital success. That, I suppose, would be a situational factor. It has been a well-known fact for many years that people from similar backgrounds, provided they be healthy ones, tend to make an adjustment to each other much more easily than couples from different backgrounds.

If the couples in our study had not had financial security, good health, attractive homes and surroundings, would there have been a difference in their evaluations of their marriages? Perhaps it is because most of their basic needs were met that they concentrated on the higher needs mentioned in the Maslow hierarchy of values. In the study of the research in the 1960's on marital happiness and stability, Mary Hicks and Marilyn Platt report:

People who report very happy marriages are more likely to concentrate on relationship sources of happiness, while those reporting less happiness in marriage tend to concentrate on the situational aspects of marriage (home, children, social life) as sources of their marital happiness. Conversely, in the association with sources of unhappiness, we see that those happier in marriage—when they give any reasons for unhappiness—tend to focus on situational sources, while the less happy stress difficulties in the relationship (or the spouse). Thus, feelings of happiness in marriage bear a clear relationship with the extent to which a person is satisfied or frustrated in the relationship aspects of the marriage.[1]

We might conclude from this that our happy and successfully married couples, if asked about problems in their marriage, might refer to situational factors, because what is most important—their interpersonal relationships—were functioning quite well.

Though they be of secondary importance, situational factors need to be looked at among all the other attributes affecting a healthy marriage.

1. *Background circumstances.* Since many of our couples mentioned the importance of background and similar backgrounds, let us look at

that first. Many years ago, Lewis Terman made a study of background circumstances most predictive of marital happiness. He discovered ten characteristics:

a. Superior happiness of parents
b. Childhood happiness
c. Lack of conflict with mother
d. Home discipline that was firm, not harsh
e. Strong attachment to mother
f. Strong attachment to father
g. Lack of conflict with father
h. Parental frankness about matters of sex
i. Infrequency and mildness of childhood punishment
j. Premarital attitude toward sex that is free from disgust or aversion[2]

If two people marry who come from backgrounds with these characteristics, then they have had a good start on a healthy marriage. Most of us carry a basic life style developed in our childhood families. This life style we carry into marriage. If the person we marry has a similar life style, we are much more apt to be compatible. In our select group of couples, Dick and Dorene came from farm families incorporating many of the qualities Terman mentioned in his study. They are among the best functioning of all our couples. And though the parents of this couple did not know one another before Dick and Dorene started dating seriously, after the marriage they became close friends and even traveled together on vacation trips.

In *A Marriage Prediction Schedule* by Ernest W. Burgess,[3] an instrument to help people know the probability of their success in marriage, the first part is devoted entirely to a study of the backgrounds of the couple involved. When two people want to know about their chances for success in marriage together, a consideration of their backgrounds and how they might fit together is highly advisable.

2. *Education.* Most studies show that the more education one has, the better are his chances for success in marriage. It would seem that education tends to broaden one's knowledge and interest in life, thus increasing his potential for a more satisfying life. J. Richard Udry concludes:

The relationships between education and marital success are well documented, and the results are consistent: the more education one has, the lower his probability for divorce and the higher his probability of good marital adjustment. . . . Furthermore, on practically any measure of success one cares to choose, the better educated have the more satisfactory marriages. This holds for both sexes as well. The better educated women are, the more satisfactory their marriages.[4]

It also seems that the more similar husband and wife are in educational advancement, the more satisfied they are with the marriage. Where the wife has more education than the husband, there is more likely to be dissatisfaction. There are some indications that the more educated, though happier in marriage, have higher expectations of what marriage ought to be; they also are more prone to be sensitive to problems and analyzing situations. In my marriage counseling practice, I find the more highly educated indulging in long periods of analyzing and scrutinizing even small details in their married life. Thus, education also produces hazards and tends to complicate life at times.

3. *Economic status.* What can we say about this factor? Certainly, no couple can be comfortable living on an income below subsistence level. The anxiety and insecurity resulting from unemployment and poverty are unmistakable. Every couple needs enough money to take care of the basic needs of life. Beyond this, in middle- and upper-income levels, the difference in happiness related to the level of income is more difficult to determine. I suppose I have had just as many serious marital problems to deal with among the affluent as among those who make just enough to pay their bills and have enough left over for a few luxuries. What matters most is the expectation each spouse brings to the marriage, and whether these expectations can be met financially. Add to this a consideration of the ability to communicate and negotiate financial matters, and we will know more about how economic status will affect a marriage.

4. *Location.* Some people need to be in specific areas of the country for health or job reasons. Jody is unhappy because her husband accepted a job advancement in a neighboring state. Everything about their new location was unsatisfactory to Jody. But she is beginning to adjust and see some advantages to living there. If she continues to adjust, it will be to her credit, and all will be well. If she fails to adjust, it may be that she is displaying signs of rigidity and inflexibility, which will militate against marital happiness regardless of location. Young people, for the most part, seem quite capable of moving about and finding contentment in whatever location seems best for them vocationally at the moment. When they are older, they may be able to be more choosy. We will say that location seems to be of minor importance.

However, an acceptable neighborhood is more important because that is where friends are made, and children find their closest companions. Ted and Julie have just moved from one part of town to another and are much happier. In their new neighborhood, they are able to make the kind of friends they need, the schools are better for their children, and the atmosphere is more conducive to their style of life.

Most couples these days must live in large urban areas. Our couples who live on farms feel this is unfortunate. In our interview with Dick and Dorene, I asked, "Farming is becoming rare these days. Are you glad you are farming and live on a farm?" Dorene answered, "Yes, very much so. It gives children a place to feel important and needed. I enjoy gardening, growing vegetables and fruit. The children help by picking, pitting and canning. They enjoy it and it makes for family solidarity. Just the other day our son came in from helping his dad milk the cows and said, 'Gee, Dad needs me, doesn't he?' " Dick added: "We think it's healthy here on the farm, and children share more in our life here than they would if we lived in the city. This need is vital, and the lack of it may be what is causing breakdown in family life these days."

If rural living is more desirable, it simply is not available to most of the population, for more than 90 percent must live in large towns and cities, in the nuclear family, often far from the nearest relative. Is urban life more impersonal, more dehumanizing? Many say it is. Others argue that cities have many advantages to offer to enrich the lives of the people who live in them, and more services that are needed by the modern family. Most mature people will continue to adjust to the kind of environment in which they find it necessary to live, whatever it may be.

5. *Health.* Is good health a prerequisite for happiness in life? Some people have the quality of character to find satisfaction in life in spite of bad health. The capacity of human beings to negotiate the many problems life puts before them in spite of failing health is an inspiration to us all. But, for the most part, health is a great asset in helping us live life to the fullest. One couple came to me for marriage counseling, and the husband, though still a young man, was failing rapidly. He could no longer participate in the recreational activities his wife and children enjoyed; he did not always feel like going to the many places they wanted to visit. His feelings of inadequacy increased. Although his wife and children were sympathetic, it didn't help, and he withdrew physically and emotionally from them and from life. The marriage eventually ended in a divorce, partly because of the husband's poor health and the depressive state that resulted from it. On the other hand, I know of another couple in failing health whose marriage seemed to grow stronger because of their feeling of empathy and dependence.

Because of the stresses and strains of the business life of contemporary husbands, heart attacks are not uncommon, even for young men. Perhaps a change in value systems and life style might enhance the health of these young men and give them many years of happiness they might not have otherwise.

6. *Children.* Parents who know how to relate to children and help them grow, enjoy their children. All of the couples we have studied told

us that children added to the happiness of their marriage, but it must be noted that these people liked children and knew something about child nurture. For people who do not like children, and many parents do not, children are a nuisance and a source of frustration. So we cannot say that children are an asset to all marriages. In some marriages they can be divisive and disruptive, which may be the fault of the parents, of course.

7. *Vocation.* There is an important relationship between a husband's satisfaction with his job and how he reacts in his family situation. Men who are satisfied in their work and find a sense of fulfillment in it, are more content in marriage and family life than those who are not. Women apparently take a great deal of pride in a husband who is doing well in his vocation, and they have an added feeling of security as well. Many wives find satisfaction and fulfillment in a job or a career, and this seems to add to their happiness. Hicks and Platt, referred to earlier, conclude that recent studies show that "husbands of working wives indicate a significantly greater amount of poor marital adjustment suggesting that the working wife may be perceived as a threat to the husband's culturally defined dominance and that the male believes the children will suffer from the wife's absence."[5] However, this attitude is changing and husbands show an increasingly favorable attitude toward the wife's working, whether it be for income or in a career.

8. *Length of marriage.* Does the length of time a couple spends together in a marriage increase the happiness level? All couples in our study reported that it did. One responded, "Each year as it comes brings us new experiences, greater challenges, and more love for each other." Studies vary in what they show about whether marriages tend to improve or disintegrate. Pineo's studies indicated a gradual decline over the years in such areas as companionship, demonstration of affection, love feelings, etc.[6] Of course, the direction in a marriage depends on the people who motivate it, care for it, and enhance it through creative effort day by day. Neglect and indifference to such matters take their deadly toll.

9. *Contemporary society.* Many studies indicate that the stability of marriage and family life is upset by conditions that characterize our contemporary society. Currently, our attention is being focused on the sad plight of the battered child. We also need to consider the problems of the battered parents, who find themselves at the mercy of a society that imposes painful stresses, excessive demands, and urgent priorities that cause frustration, distraction, and brokenness in their lives. These forces batter and scatter parents and children. The fragmented family is not a healthy context for the nurturing of happy parents or children.

Many parents recognize the importance of family unity and the time it takes to cultivate good family relationships in which parents and children can participate in one another's worlds. Yet these same parents may feel they are fighting a losing battle in the face of the demands of life around them. The actual time that husbands and wives spend together, and that parents spend with children, has been decreasing year by year over the past twenty-five years. Job demands, organizational obligations, time spent commuting, events on the social calendar, television watching, all of these have contributed to the fragmentation and dehumanization of the American family.

This problem is dramatically illustrated in an interview with Urie Bronfenbrenner by a correspondent for *Psychology Today* magazine. This specialist in child development states:

> Increasing numbers of children are coming home to empty houses. If there's any reliable predictor of trouble, it probably begins with children coming home to an empty house, whether the problem is reading difficulties, truancy, dropping out, drug addiction, or childhood depression. . . .
>
> It's not because parents are irresponsible or children are intractable—although children having received inadequate care are more difficult these days. What's destroying the family isn't the family itself but the indifference of the rest of society. The family takes a low priority.[7]

We cannot go back to the family life of earlier times, but society in general, and parents in particular, need to reconsider the fact that the family is the heart and center of our civilization. In view of the fact that the future depends on family unity and stability, all of us together must design new attitudes, establish higher priorities, and build more adequate structures for the improvement and enrichment of marriages and family living.

We cannot deny the effect of trying circumstances on marriage and family life. We must do the best we can to create favorable situations in which people can grow, develop, and find fulfillment. Yet, for all of us, the situations we meet must be looked upon as a challenge, and not as something that will defeat us. I am continually amazed and inspired by people who have the power to overcome challenging or even tragic circumstances and move on to a satisfactory and rewarding life. A good illustration of this came to me by way of a letter a woman wrote me after she viewed a television program in which I discussed successful marriages.

Dear Dr. Hine:

> I heard you on Morning Line program and decided to write to you about my marriage and let you decide if it is a success or not. I've worked hard to try and make it a success and I feel that I have.
>
> I was married at the age of 16 and my husband was 20. We will celebrate

our 33rd wedding anniversary on June 22nd. We come from a small town of 750 population and everyone seemed to think that our marriage would not last, but I decided to prove them wrong.

Our first son was born 11 months and three days later so we did not have to marry like most people thought. Our second son was born 4 years later, shortly after that I had major surgery and then was unable to have any more children, which I didn't mind at all although I would have liked to have had a little girl. My husband was in the delivery room when our first son was born and in far off India during the war when our second son was born.

When our youngest son was eight years old he was hit by a car and we were told by our Doctor that he would not live through the night but another Doctor was called in and he said, "Where there's life there's hope." He was unconscious for three weeks and had to learn to walk and talk all over.

I had just recovered from a nervous break down at the age of 28 years, just before the accident happened, so it set me back a little. Things were pretty rough for us and we moved to Arizona in August 1958 as my Doctor suggested as I was suffering with arthritis.

My husband got a job with the city and brought home $139.00 every two weeks but we were on a budget and did pretty good. He was making $3.00 a day when our first son was born.

We have two fine sons—ages 32 and 28. Our youngest son has paid his own way since he was 16 years old working in a grocery store. Our oldest son went to the U of A for one year and entered the service and saved his money. Our youngest son wanted to enlist also but has a nerve hearing loss from the accident. Our two sons went to Sequoia National Park in California to work and married girls they met at work there. They were both 24½ years old when they married. One son works for the telephone company and has a nice wife and a boy six years old and a three year old girl. The other son works in a bakery and has a nice wife also and a two year old girl. Both of them are buying their own homes.

My husband was 48 years old before he had his first new car. We moved into our first new home 18 months ago and are very happy. My husband now brings home a good pay check.

I have no outside interests but my husband golfs once in a while and I go to the bowling alley to watch him bowl one night a week during the winter months.

I'm happy just being able to keep our home nice and clean; keep our yard nice and neat; and talking to friends on the phone. I now watch more T.V. as I know what people meant when they told me I was so nervous that I ought to sit down and relax and take it easy. I do, all but about five hours a week for washing, ironing and cleaning.

We have taken a vacation every year for a number of years; we've all seen the five great lakes and the two oceans and also have been in Canada.

My dad died when I was 12 years old and my mother was left with four children at the age of 38 and went to work for $40.00 a month to support four children. I guess that's when I really learned the value of money and to budget my husband's pay check. My husband is 53 and I'm 49 and these past 18 months has been the happiest time of my life, since I'm free of most of my pain and all the hard work I used to do. My husband has been with the city for eight years and he's looking forward to retirement so we can buy a trailer and travel.

I've always felt that it's not what you have, it's what you do with what you have, that really counts. I feel that all our sorrows, pain and struggling have brought us closer together.

Yours truly,

A HAPPY WIFE, MOTHER, AND GRANDMOTHER

The saints and the psychologists conspire to try to teach us that it is not so much what life brings us that shapes our destiny, but how we shape the circumstances and events of our lives into a destiny. The Biblical heroes and prophets speak of courage, overcoming, faith and victory. Alfred Adler reminds us that it is not what one has inherited that is important, but what one does with his inheritance.[8] It is for us to decide to be responsible, to work, love, and move through the dark of night into the light of day. As the Happy Wife, Mother and Grandmother said in her letter, "I've always felt that it's not what you have, it's what you do with what you have, that really counts."

REFERENCES

1. Mary W. Hicks and Marilyn Platt, "Marital Happiness and Stability: A Review of the Research in the Sixties," *Journal of Marriage and the Family* (November, 1970).

2. Lewis M. Terman, *Psychological Factors in Marital Happiness.* New York: McGraw-Hill Book Company, 1938, pp. 110, 111.

3. Ernest W. Burgess, *A Marriage Prediction Schedule.* Published with permission by Family Life Publications, Saluda, North Carolina.

4. J. Richard Udry, *The Social Context of Marriage.* Philadelphia: J. B. Lippincott Company, 1971, p. 290.

5. Mary W. Hicks and Marilyn Platt, "Marital Happiness and Stability."

6. Peter C. Pineo, "Disenchantment in the Later Years of Marriage," *Marriage and Family Living,* Vol. 23 (1961), pp. 3–11.

7. Urie Bronfenbrenner, "Nobody Home: The Erosion of the American Family," *Psychology Today,* May 1977, p. 41.

8. Alfred Adler, *The Science of Living.* Garden City, N.Y.: Doubleday and Company, 1969, p. 5.

PART IV

The Other Side: The Anatomy of Divorce

CHAPTER NINE

The Marital Breakdown: Symptoms and Causes

So far, we have been looking at marriages that are healthy and successful. In these marriages the people have said, "I love you," married, and stayed together in what appear to be well-functioning relationships. But this is not always the case. There are many who say, "I love you," and get married for what they think will be a permanent relationship, but then come to a parting of the ways. For them love seems to have disappeared, and a meaningful relationship no longer exists. I am sure that anyone who works with couples who stay married and couples who get divorces, is always bothered by the question, "Why do some marriages attain stability and permanency, while others deteriorate and come apart?" We will try to apply what knowledge and experience we have had in this field to give some response to this haunting question.

How serious is the phenomenon of divorce in our society? Some deplore it as a sign of the breakdown and decay of our civilization. Others accept it as a natural outcome of a society so wracked by stress and strain that two people can hardly be expected to stay together for a lifetime.

There are those who will argue that all people who get divorces, as well as their children, are affected adversely, and some are scarred for life. Others will point out that divorce, for many, has ushered in a new life, free from the damaging effects of a bad marriage on spouses and their children. In most of the cases with which I have worked, there has been a note of sadness and tragedy, even though the divorce itself seemed inevitable. I believe that many of these divorces would not have occurred if the couple had acted earlier to solve some of the problems that had irritated their marriages for many years. By waiting so long, deep resentments, negative attitudes, and bad habits had become so deeply ingrained that it seemed impossible to eradicate them.

The couples we have been studying have been married on the average for about twenty years. They believe that staying together is a decided asset and that it brings many rewards. They are not restless. They would marry the same person if they had to do it over again. They have few regrets about what has happened so far in their marriages; divorce seems to be the farthest thing from their minds. Our society cannot help but benefit from marriages and families like these. How much happier and more stable it would be if most marriages were like those we have studied. Yet this does not seem to be the case. Most people would think of our sample as exceptions to the rule, but we must not paint too dark a picture before we examine the facts. All marriages are not breaking up, though in reading some of the articles in magazines and newspapers, one might conclude that we are moving toward a point where everyone *will* be divorced. Recently, in a responsibly written book, it was commented that it will simply be a matter of time until we will all be living in a society of the remarried. One also hears friends saying, "Almost everyone I know is getting a divorce." And it isn't uncommon to read statistics that give the impression that 50 percent or more of marriages are ending in divorce.

With this in mind, let us first look at what is happening to marriages in terms of the likelihood of their ending in divorce. It is difficult to determine the divorce rate in the United States. Many have been careless in their handling of statistics and the conclusions drawn from them. For instance, some would attempt to determine the present divorce rate by comparing the number of divorces with the number of marriages occurring in a particular year. Suppose we do this for three different locations during the year 1968, as seen in Table 9-1.

TABLE 9-1

Location	Marriages	Divorces and annulments
Los Angeles County, California	61,067	28,820
Cook County, Illinois	52,068	15,505
Dade County, Florida	12,328	6,094
Maricopa County, Arizona	8,959	6,619

Source: U.S. Department of Health, Education, and Welfare, *Vital Statistics of the United States,* 1968, Vol. III, Marriage and Divorce.

If we were to use these statistics to compute the divorce rate, Los Angeles County would have 47%, Cook County, 29%, Dade County, 49%, and Maricopa County, 73%. But this measurement would not be accurate, because people getting divorces in 1968 were married in previous years, from one to perhaps thirty years before. And the nature of the marriages taking place in one year may be very different from that of those taking place in other years. So we must look to other figures to help us get a more accurate picture of what is happening.

TABLE 9-2
MARRIAGES AND DIVORCES (AND ANNULMENTS) IN THE
UNITED STATES (SELECTED YEARS, 1920-68)

Year	Marriages	Divorces	Divorces per 1,000 married women age 15 and over
1920	1,274,476	170,000	8
1935	1,327,000	218,000	7.8
1946	2,291,045	610,000	17.9
1955	1,531,000	377,000	9.3
1967	1,927,000	523,000	11.2
1968	2,069,000	584,000	12.4

Source: U.S. Department of Health, Education, and Welfare, *Vital Statistics of the United States,* 1968, Vol. III, pp. 2–5.

When we look at the divorces per 1,000 married women who are age 15 and over, we see a different picture. There is a greater stability than we have been led to believe. Although there is an increase in the divorce rate, it is not so radical as it has often been made out to be. A great number of divorces occurred in 1946 after World War II, evidence of the marital breakups that occur after every war. The figures for 1973 showed that 18.2 divorces took place for every thousand women. This rate represents a slight increase over the 1946 figure.

In 1972 John Scanzoni titled a chapter in one of his books, "The Myth of Marital Disintegration," and wrote:

If we focus chiefly on the "refined" divorce rate, what generalizations can we make about current divorce trends and patterns of marital stability? On the one hand, the rate of 11.2 . . . for 1967 means that for every 1,000 married women, approximately 11 experienced divorce. (The figure is, of course, almost identical for every thousand husbands.) This is little more than 1 percent. Clearly, if better than 98 percent of the married women (and men) do not seek divorces in any given year, there seems little indication of mass dissatisfaction with marriage, or wholesale rejections of it as a viable institution. The publicity given to Hollywood divorces and the misuse by some of certain kinds of divorce statistics combine to distort the actual stability of the great majority of American marriages.[1]

Later John and Letha Scanzoni wrote:

Census data do not necessarily indicate widespread disenchantment with marriage but rather that persons appear to expect more from that institution and are less willing to settle for relationships that do not live up to their expectations. At the same time, we must keep in mind that the statistics show that most people are not getting divorced.[2]

Also, it is interesting to note that, of the 315,957 people who got married in 1968, 43,625 men (about 14%) and 106,869 women (33%) were under the age of twenty. Marriages taking place under the age of twenty are very hazardous, and divorce statistics are profoundly affected by the fact that so many do marry at an early age. If more couples would wait until they are over twenty to marry, the stability of the institution of marriage would be greatly enhanced by that action alone.

What is happening to the institution of marriage during the decade of the seventies? We do know that divorce is increasing year by year, at a rate that outstrips the rate of population increase. What are the causes of divorce in general, and how do we account for the increase each year?

If people who are in the process of getting a divorce, or people who already have obtained a divorce, were asked, "Why are you getting a divorce, or what was the cause of your divorce?" many of them would not be clear in their answers. I have often thought that one object of a marriage counselor's work with a couple with marital difficulties should be to help them understand what the basic problems are. So many do not seem to know. They know that they are unhappy, that the marriage isn't functioning, or that there is a great amount of conflict, but they are not sure why. It is something like asking a person who is ill, what is wrong with him, and having him reply, "My problem is that I don't feel well," or "I have a pain in my stomach." He is describing symptoms but not causes. Many women say that their husbands are not giving them enough money to live on, or that they do not like the way their husbands handle money. They may say that he drinks too much, or he is cruel, or has affairs with other women; frequently a number of reasons are cited. Men may complain that their wives are not good sexual partners, that they nag, that they are poor housekeepers, or they may recite a variety of circumstances that tend to make them unsatisfied and unhappy. None of these may be the real cause of their trouble. They are likely to be the "pains," the symptoms of a deeper trouble.

It is also difficult, perhaps impossible, to find out the real causes of divorces by examining the grounds on which they are sought. Most of the legal reasons used are in such categories as: cruelty, desertion, adultery, neglect to provide, or a combination thereof. None of these tells the story, partly because people tend to use the grounds that are most accessible to them, regardless of whether they are valid or not.

Marriage counselors often have difficulty getting a couple to make a thorough analysis of what is wrong with their marriage. This is particularly true if one party or both are very unhappy with the situation and want to get to the divorce as soon as possible. Marilyn was very much like that. She came to the marriage counselor because her husband begged her to do so before applying for a divorce. He wanted to save the marriage and was willing to work with Marilyn and the marriage counselor to do so. But she kept saying that it was too late, and that if her husband had wanted to save the marriage, why hadn't he done something about it long ago. The sessions we had were not productive, because Marilyn was restless and anxious to get on with the business of the separation and divorce. She never indicated a willingness to take a good look at the relationship in order to understand it or ask what might be done for it. So nothing much could be done except try to reconcile the husband to the fact that his wife did not want to save the marriage, or even take a thorough look at it in order to understand what the basic problems were. Marilyn hurried off to get her divorce. Soon afterwards we discovered that there was another man in the picture, and, as is often the case, her interest in him blocked the way to any cooperative attempt to discover what the problems were.

In our study of why marriages were successful, we did a comparison study of 14 couples whose marriages were failing. Some of these couples were considering divorce; several were already committed to a divorce. Although this is a small sample to study, we did gain some insights into why these marriages were failing. One of the evaluations recorded in Chapter 3 attempts to show in what areas successful marriages excelled. In order to obtain a rating of excellent in a particular characteristic, a spouse needed to give it an "a" rating. The couples whose marriages had serious marital problems or were failing rated themselves as follows in those areas:

TABLE 9-3

Characteristic	% spouses rating characteristic as excellent in marriage
Excellent companions	4
Meet crises successfully	4
Having fun together	7
Mutually affectionate	7
Agree on roles and responsibilities	11
Share goals	11
Support and reinforce each other	11
Loyal and faithful	11
Truthful and open	14
Share decision-making	14

Here 28 people indicate that in a failing marriage there are special deficiencies in the ability to excel in certain characteristics. They scored very low in a quality that I would rate as one that becomes increasingly important as the years unfold—companionship. Equally poor was the capacity to excel in meeting crises. We have noted that every marriage faces crises that must be negotiated if the marriage is to make progress to higher levels of achievement. Certainly the marriage counselor observes the lack of good times in the lives of these people; they do not have fun together. There is little gaiety and joy in their lives. Sometimes showing affection ceases almost entirely, and the fire goes out of the relationship, leaving only ashes.

We also took the characteristics that all the successful marriages rated as fully functioning characteristics (that is, rated as "a" or "b") and measured them in the failing marriages to see how far below the fully functioning level the latter marriages fell.

TABLE 9-4

Fully functioning sample (100%)	*% of functioning of failing sample*
Meeting crises successfully	25 (75 below)
Show affection	25 (75 below)
Loyal and faithful	29 (71 below)
Give reinforcement and support	29 (71 below)
Truthful and open	43 (57 below)
Shared values and goals	50 (50 below)
Respect each other	64 (36 below)

Tentatively we concluded that the characteristics listed in Table 9-4 were necessary in a marriage if it was to function adequately. Our failing marriages indicate that they are functioning very poorly in these requirements for a successful marriage.

In Chapters 5 through 8 we suggested attributes for a healthy marriage and categorized them in four major areas:

1. *Personal characteristics.* Individuals who are warm, kind, generous, affectionate, truthful, mature, courageous, etc., make better marriage partners than those who are deficient in these attributes.

2. *Compatibility factors.* The people who, when paired, prove to be compatible in such matters as role concepts, values, beliefs, temperament, interests, etc., tend to function well in marriage.

3. *Skills and accomplishments.* Where certain skills and accomplishments are present, the marriage is enhanced.

4. *Favorable situations.* Where certain favorable situations exist, a healthy context is provided in which the marriage can grow and develop.

If we turn each of these around and look at the reverse side, we see factors that will cause unhealthy marriages to develop, and with them, the possibility of divorce. A divorce might very well develop where any one or more of the following conditions exist in a marriage:

1. *A marriage in which one or both partners have characteristics that might be symptomatic of personality or character disorders.* One type of personality disorder is that of the neurotic. Anyone possessing neurotic qualities is difficult to live with. We have mentioned on several occasions that marriage is accompanied by a series of crises that occur from time to time throughout the marriage. Our mature spouses seem to meet these crises with a degree of calmness and rationality. They evaluate them and then see what can be done to relieve them. The test of a mature person is in his ability to meet frustration, difficulty, and failure itself. In such circumstances, he experiences anxiety, but learns how to deal with it. Percival Symonds puts it this way:

Anxiety has been differentiated into that which is normal and that which is pathological or neurotic. Since anxiety is inevitable for every individual, this distinction depends upon how the anxiety is met rather than on the presence or absence of it. The first distinction is that normal anxiety is responded to by a protective adjustment. The healthy individual finds some way of meeting the anticipated threat, either by preparing to eliminate it or to protect himself against it. In neurotic anxiety, however, the adjustive phase is less evident, and the response is inappropriate, exaggerated, and ineffective.[3]

I suppose it is possible for some couples to go through a courtship period without meeting much frustration and therefore without suffering much anxiety. Often each will do all in his or her power to keep out frustration. Therefore, they are never tested before marriage in a way that might reveal how they deal with anxiety. But one need not be married long before he discovers many types of frustration that lead to anxiety. Then the test begins. Mary couldn't believe that Harry would get angry because she did not have his meal prepared on time. Here they had been married only two weeks, when dinner was late for the first time, and he became very upset. What kind of man was he to make so much of something that to her was relatively unimportant? When Harry was faced with frustration, he responded in a way she felt was inappropriate. If he had been tired, or feeling ill, it probably would have been quickly forgotten. But as Harry continued to become upset and angry over matters that displeased him, his neurotic tendencies became apparent. Mary then began to see that she had a husband with whom it was going to be difficult to live.

Picture trying to live with someone whose responses to frustrations are "inappropriate, exaggerated, and ineffective." These people are immature, irritable, jealous, dominating, pessimistic, moody, easily discouraged, unfriendly, insecure, stubborn, rigid, easily upset, tense, and nervous. They over-react, and what they do often results in straining relationships and leaving problems unsolved or exacerbated. If my memory serves me correctly, many of the people who have come into my office through the years with very serious interpersonal relationship problems have displayed some of these neurotic characteristics.

Character disorders are not easily defined or differentiated from personality disorders. But certain kinds of complaints that spouses make about each other seem to come under this classification. My husband drinks too much. My wife won't tell the truth. He gambles away our income. She cheats on me when I am out of town. He is irresponsible and lazy. She sleeps till noon every day. Maybe some of these are what seem to the spouse as "bad habits." It may be a matter of different standards practiced by different families. A husband says, "In my family we were brought up to drink wine and beer. But my wife thinks it is terrible to drink." In some cases, a person's behavior might come under the classification of a "deviation" or being "far out." A wife comes in aghast at discovering that her husband is a homosexual. Should she divorce him? Another husband wants to "swing" with other couples. But his wife thinks it is immoral and outside of anything she could ever think of doing. If one spouse suspects the other spouse of having a character disorder, then trust and confidence break down, and trouble deepens.

2. *A marriage in which there is a general state of incompatibility.* Two individually good marriage prospects may not necessarily be good together. We haven't yet quite figured out why Jan and Tommy got a divorce. They were both good friends of ours, and we liked each of them as persons. They were stellar people by almost any criterion by which you might wish to judge them; intelligent, friendly, amiable, talented, and mature. They displayed no neurotic tendencies that my wife or I could ever detect throughout the twelve years we had known them. And yet one day they announced that they were separating and would probably get a divorce in due time. This announcement came as a shock. We will probably never know what happened. We do know that although they were close at the start of their marriage, they moved apart as time passed. Jan became more interested in friends, the children, and doing things with those who were close to her. Tommy became deeply engrossed in the business world, taking trips to make new contacts and contracts. Gradually, as they committed themselves to two different worlds, they found themselves doing less and less together. Perhaps their value systems were incompatible at the start but it had seemed less obvious to them then. Finally, Jan recognized the difference. She complained, but nothing happened to bring them closer together.

Sylvia was moody, easily depressed, insecure, and in need of constant reassurance. Yet she loved her husband, her children, and her friends. She was talented, intelligent, affectionate, and compassionate. In a way, she was an idealist, dreaming dreams of what life should be. Will, her husband, was practical, rational, stable, lacking in sentimentality, slightly amused by Sylvia's idealism. In their courtship period they seemed to complement each other—what one lacked, the other had. Would not their complementary characteristics make a complete marriage? They might have. Their marriage counselor had hopes for an adequate adjustment to the differences that seemed to be troubling them. "We wanted it to work, and we really thought it would. But as time went on, the differences became magnified, and we couldn't tolerate them any longer. It was too much of an emotional drain. When we separated we were both very sad. We never thought it would end this way." In words like these, Sylvia tried to describe the incompatibility that became increasingly severe after ten years of married life. Was their marriage a mistake at the beginning? Or did they fail to recognize their differences in time to make a concerted effort toward accommodation? These questions remain unanswered.

Marie and Rocky were two young people everybody seemed to like. Although they differed in some ways, both were friendly and nice to be with. Marie thought Rocky would settle down after he was married to her. She didn't approve of many things that Rocky did before they were married. He was the typical playboy, the one who drank too much at parties and became loud and boisterous. Marie was a quiet, thoughtful, business-like woman, very sure of herself, and with no doubt that she could handle Rocky, once she got him into the comfortable environment of home life. She expected to domesticate this wild animal. Much to her surprise, Rocky did not respond to her mothering instincts and her desire to nurture him into a sober, settled, home-loving husband. He continued his role as the fun-seeking boy, with a flair for wine, women, and song. His old friends encouraged him to stick with them in all the after-work drinking sessions, with occasional all-night flings. Marie had a responsible job for which she was paid handsomely, and she shouldered the responsibility for most of the bills that kept coming in. But there came a time when she admitted that their life-styles were incompatible. They are still good friends, but neither can tolerate the other's idea of what the role of a married person should be. Here were two good people who were not "good" for each other.

Ogden Nash once jokingly wrote that incompatibility existed in a marriage when the husband ceased to bring in an adequate *income* and the wife lost her *patibility*. It depends, in part, on the expectations each brings to the marriage. What are the wife's expectations regarding her husband's role, and his achievements in business and the community? What does she expect his values, beliefs, and goals to be? What kind of a person does she believe he needs to be in order to function temperamentally with her? What does the husband expect of the wife in terms of what she needs to do and to be, to make him feel comfortable and happy with her? The answers to these questions will determine whether they make it together or not. If disappointment is a continuing response on the part of either or both, the marriage will not last.

3. *A marriage in which there is a lack of ability or there is an unwillingness to develop the necessary skills and accomplish the expected goals to make the marriage function.* Two people bring the raw materials to a marriage, and they must work together with skill, determination, and a sense of direction to produce a growing relationship from these materials. Sometimes one does not need the best of materials to create a beautiful result. Skill, know-how, and persistence may make up the difference. On the other hand, the raw materials may be good and the finished product an unsightly mess. I heard Albert Ellis tell a group of marriage counselors that most divorces were the result of "goofing" or "drifting." That makes good sense. Goofing is performing poorly, making too many mistakes, playing one's role awkwardly, behaving badly, and just plain "blowing it." I have heard many a dejected spouse say that to me, "I had a good thing going, and I blew it." Drifting is taking a marriage for granted and letting it take its course with little planning or effort. We know that marriages deteriorate or fail because of neglect. Neglecting one's spouse, neglecting the home and children, or the responsibilities of the role of husband or wife, can be dangerous.

A spouse may lack motivation, enthusiasm, endurance, persistence, courage, energy, thoughtfulness, or creativity. Some of these qualities are necessary if one is to become skillful and dedicated in his work of building a marriage. Lose them and you may lose the marriage.

Tim loved Trudy very much. They seemed well matched, and the marriage counselor thought they had the ingredients of a successful marriage. But the marriage wasn't working. Trudy complained that Tim didn't pay any attention to her anymore. He didn't compliment her cooking artistry, her good looks, her attractive clothes, or her management of the children. They rarely went places together because Tim felt he was too busy to take the time. Trudy decided that something had to be done about it. "Look, Tim," she said over the breakfast table, "something has to be done or our marriage is going down the drain." Tim was shocked. He knew that there were problems, but he was fairly content. But he agreed to face the reality of what was happening to the marriage. The decision they reached with the marriage counselor was to apply some planned effort to improving the relationship. Tim would take Trudy out one night a week regularly. They would have some vacations together at places conducive to their getting to know each other again, and do just the things they enjoyed together. Tim would be more thoughtful and attentive to Trudy's needs each day. Trudy agreed not to nag or complain, to display more good humor and optimism, and to be a more enjoyable companion for Tim. Check-ups during the following year proved that their resolves, faithfully carried out, produced fruit. What once seemed to be a marriage "going down the drain," now appeared to be one running smoothly on its course.

Bill and Debby were not so fortunate. Debby, a school teacher, approached matters with calmness and thoughtfulness. Bill was a young attorney, aggressive, bold, and, according to his way of thinking, very masculine. Debby had a great need to talk over problems and plans at the end of the day. Bill was impatient and felt that talking was a waste of time. When Debby forced him to talk, he became upset, angry, unwilling to negotiate. The marriage counselor felt there was an inability to communicate in this relationship and suggested that they devote some time to working on this skill. Bill made a feeble effort, but relapsed to his old ways, "We'll talk about it later." Perhaps he felt unable to match wits with his intelligent, rational wife. Matters grew worse, and Bill and Debby seemed increasingly unable to settle anything. A year later, Debby applied for a divorce.

Many parents have trouble with each other because they disagree about child nurture or discipline. Many of them don't know enough about child care to do an adequate job. In such cases, children are allowed to become such a disruptive force in the marriage that the parents separate because of it. Lack of knowledge and skill in nurturing children can be damaging to a marriage.

It is not uncommon to see a person dismissed from a job because of a lack of the knowledge and skill needed to accomplish the tasks the job called for. As we have said repeatedly, marriage is a vocation requiring knowledge, skill, and hard work; without them, divorce appears to some couples as a preferable alternative.

4. *A marriage in which situations militate against the successful functioning of the marriage.* To what extent does the context in which a marriage operates cause it to fail? Are there special circumstances that can cause an otherwise good marriage to end in divorce? I believe that in some marriages, a change in certain situations would have prevented a divorce.

After World War II, the divorce rate reached the highest point in the nation's history. How many of those divorces would not have occurred if the war had not disrupted them? I am sure a reasonable percentage of them could have been prevented.

We know that the casualty rate is great for marriages in which the couples are under age twenty. If these same couples had waited until they were twenty-one or twenty-two, would some of these marriages have lasted? If the young people had waited, many of them would not have married at all, but I believe that a considerable number of these marriages, if they had taken place at a later time, would have survived.

Jill and Hal married after a lengthy courtship and a careful consideration of what marriage meant for both of them. Most people looking at the marriage objectively would have said that the chances of success were good. Both parties seemed to have the personal characteristics that help to make good prospects and they were very much alike in their interests and values. They were unconventional, informal people and easy to get along with. But after marriage, Hal couldn't seem to decide in what direction he wanted to go. Jill knew exactly what she wanted to do. As a result of this, Hal only picked up odd jobs here and there. There was little money with which to operate their home, except what Jill brought in from part-time work. As Hal continued to flounder, Jill became increasingly impatient. She didn't want to force Hal to decide on his life goals, even though she felt he was old enough to do so. Finally, in desperation she left him, thinking that a separation would bring him to action; but he continued to drift. After a long separation came a divorce. Two years later Hal did "get his head together" as he put it, and now seems to be moving with a sense of direction. He wonders if his marriage might have been saved had he been able to do this sooner.

Most marriage counselors have seen couples struggle through financial difficulty, problems of health, interference from in-laws, attempts to complete an education, living in poor housing conditions, and having children too soon and too often, and they wonder if the marriages might have been different had the situations been different. Some couples pull through and avoid the divorce, but the marriage may limp along for a considerable length of time and never quite recover because of circumstances that no longer exist.

According to statistics for divorces recorded in the year 1968, the median age of the husband was about twenty-four when he married and thirty-four at the time of the final decree. The median age of the wife was about 20.5 when she married and 30.5 at the time of the decree.[4] The time span between the median age for marriage and the median age for divorce was ten years. The most critical year is considered to be the first year, and the second year is the next most critical. If trouble is to appear, it is apt to appear within the first two years.

Couples do not, as a rule, rush out and get a divorce, even when trouble becomes quite pronounced. They try as best they can to work it out or to endure it. An educated guess might be that the average person waits about two years after deciding to get a divorce before actually getting it. Yet a large percentage of divorces occur within the first seven years of marriage. In California in 1968 there were 75,410 marriages. According to available records, 36,880 of the couples married in 1968 were divorced before the end of the seventh year. Is it possible that the situations that exist in the early years of marriage are least favorable for the success of the marriage? The divorce rate seems to fall off appreciably after the seventh year. If couples could be helped to ride out the storms of the first seven years of marriage, would it be possible to avoid a great number of divorces that occur during that period? I believe it would. Situations can be changed or altered over a period of time, but patience, courage, skill and, often, outside help are needed.

Thus, it seems that the general causes of divorce can be seen in marriages that fall into one or more of the four following categories: (1) those in which there are personality or character disorders in one or both parties; (2) those in which there is a general state of incompatibility between two married people; (3) those in which there is a lack of ability or an unwillingness to develop the necessary skills and accomplish the expected goals that could make the marriage function; and (4) those in which unusual situations develop that militate against the successful functioning of the marriage.

Having discussed the *general* causes of divorce, let us move on to the *contemporary* causes that seem to affect the stability of marriages currently. It should be clearly understood that many developments in modern life that have enhanced the welfare of people in general have also increased the number of divorces. It is somewhat analogous to the fact that we have all enjoyed the benefits of high-speed transportation, particularly the automobile, yet the introduction of the automobile has increased the accident and death rates far above what they were in the days of the horse and buggy. Along with progress has come the increased risk of being hurt or killed. To live in the urban-industrial world of the present, we must pay a price. We must also be alert to learn what adjustments we must make to counteract some of the dangers.

Contemporary causes of the increase in the divorce rate include, I believe, the following:

1. The move from rural to urban life.

2. An increasingly mobile society.

3. Liberalization of divorce laws.

4. Increased independence of women.

5. Increased affluence of our society.

6. Lessening influence of authority sources.

7. Earlier dating.

8. Illusions of love, marriage, and the family created by the mass media.

9. The higher expectation level for marriage.

10. Increased longevity.

11. Rapidly changing ideas and standards affecting people's ability to define love, marriage, and family life.

These causes are referred to as *contemporary* because they have come on the scene, for the most part, in the last fifty years, and have been greatly intensified since World War II. Let us look at each of these causes briefly.

1. *The move from rural to urban life.* America was a rural society at the turn of the century, when the majority of families lived on farms. At one time, more than 90 percent of all families were engaged in rural activities. Today less than 10 percent of our families can be considered farm families. This move has brought about great changes. The family is no longer the self-contained economic unit that it once was, when everyone made a necessary contribution to its economic welfare. If any one member failed to make his or her contribution, the family operation broke down. Also, most of this work was confined to the limited area of the farm itself. I can remember my aunt, a farmer's wife, wanting to give a message to her husband or one of the older children, and going out to the edge of the field where they were plowing, planting, or reaping, and waving for them to come in, or stop as they came around on the plow. It was never difficult to find any member of the family, for they were generally in sight of one another. The children worked hard, but they had a healthy sense of being needed. You may remember Dorene commenting that their young son, who had just come in from helping his father milk the cows, had said "Daddy really needs me, doesn't he?" I am not sure that many children living in cities and suburbs would be able to say that.

The rural family had a feeling of closeness, of needing one another, and staying together for the benefit of one another that the urban family cannot have in the same sense. The farm families in our study felt they had great advantages over city families. Most people who live in cities would not go back to the farm, although currently there is a movement on the part of some of our young married people to go back to the simpler life, as they see it, in areas that are rural or remote. Robert Winch comes to this conclusion:

The moral of this story is that in the modern urban family it is no longer to the obvious economic advantage of all to stay together. In this transition from the early American farm family, which was a self-sufficient economy, to the modern urban family the mutual economic bond has been lost. This appears to be one of the most conspicuous conditions associated with the instability of the modern family.[5]

In some way this failure to feel an essential role in the family may also have added to the identity crisis experienced by teenagers in urban areas who are not sure of their role and importance during the critical years between the ages of 12 and 17. Might this fact also contribute to the disruptive and divisive roles played by many teenagers in modern families, intensifying problems with which parents have to deal and contributing in part to family breakups?

2. *An increasingly mobile society.* My mother and father lived in the same home for sixty-five years, and my father worked in the same office for more than forty years. My wife and I have made five moves and lived in three communities thus far in our married life. Some of the students in my classes report that they have moved as many as fourteen times in the first twenty years of their life with their family. My parents lived within a few miles of all of their immediate relatives. It is not uncommon today to have the nearest relative a thousand miles away. My father and mother knew every neighbor within a radius of about two blocks from their home. Every evening they visited in a common area provided by one neighbor with a large back yard. When there was an illness or death, neighbors carried in food, consoled and took care of one another.

A family living in a large apartment in Chicago told me that after several years they knew only one other family in that apartment complex. It is not uncommon today to find a neighborhood in a city in which the people have lived but a short time, all have come from different parts of the country, and do not intend to stay long. In such a neighborhood, it is hard to put down roots. In my parents' neighborhood, everyone cared, sometimes too much, it seemed, but there were forces that gave people living there a sense of unity, friendship, and responsibility. If a divorce takes place in the apartment complex referred to earlier, does anyone care?

3. *Liberalizing of divorce laws.* For many years, the only convenient grounds for divorce in the state of New York was "adultery." No one felt particularly comfortable using these grounds, so it was customary to

leave the state for a divorce, or stay and endure the marriage. This practice might tend to lower the divorce rate in New York State, although it would have little or nothing to do with the stability of marriages in that state. A low divorce rate does not mean that more marriages in that locality are successful. It may mean only that it is difficult to obtain a divorce. Most states have liberalized their requirements for a divorce so that one may be obtained on the grounds of desertion, adultery, or cruel and inhuman treatment. It is also implied that one party is innocent and the other is guilty, which is almost never the case. If a spouse is dissatisfied with a marriage and wants a divorce, the usual procedure is to go to an attorney and find out which "grounds" can be used most conveniently. Frequently, collusion or perjury or both were involved in getting the divorce. Divorce became a matter of choosing the "right" grounds, taking the appropriate amount of time (in most cases, a year's separation for desertion), and paying the necessary attorney's fees.

But people began to see that this method was often fraudulent and hypocritical, and that making people antagonists in order to dissolve their relationship was stupidity. The state of California in 1970 instituted what has come to be known as the "no fault" divorce law, although it is looked upon as a dissolution rather than a divorce. The guilt or innocence of the spouses is no longer a consideration. If they both declare that the marriage no longer exists and a dissolution is desired, the marriage is declared to be ended. In Arizona, if one party makes a statement to the effect that the marriage has ceased to function and that a dissolution is desired, and there is no objection on the part of the other spouse, within a short period of time, the marriage is declared to be ended. The trend is to make the termination of a marriage easier. It is a more honest way to approach the matter. It also provides the opportunity for a quick ending of the relationship, which may be a disadvantage, for in a longer process, some couples change their minds and decide that ending the marriage is not what they want. In general, however, it would be my judgment that the "no fault" method is to be preferred over the older, more objectionable ways of obtaining divorces. No fault divorce will cause the divorce rate to rise, at least, for awhile. But if we are going to reform marriage procedures, it should be by making it more difficult to get married, rather than more difficult to get divorced, although responsibility should be emphasized at both ends.

It is encouraging to note that along with liberalization of divorce laws has come a new resource for helping people to act responsibly—the family court movement. The movement, which began in Cincinnati, can be found today in most of our larger cities. In many communities, what is known as the "Court of Conciliation" has a sponsoring judge and a staff of marriage counselors and advisers. Already we are beginning to see good results from this resource, which attempts to help couples make wise decisions about their marriages, and in many cases prevents a dissolution where there is a chance for a marriage to succeed. This movement goes a long way toward rectifying a situation described by Judge Paul W. Alexander, a pioneer in the cause to humanize the divorce court and get help to couples who need something more than a quick ending to their marriages:

The divorce court was a morgue where ailing marriages were merely pronounced dead upon superficial examination, and burial certificates were issued in the form of divorce decrees. . . . the new philosophy would be signified by the very titling of the case; instead of it being "John Doe v. Mary Doe," it would be titled, "In the Interest of the John Doe Family."[6]

4. *Increased independence of women.* There was a time when a wife had no alternative to staying with a bad marriage. She could not exist economically, and as a divorced woman, she often was not accepted by the community. The twentieth century has seen the partial emancipation of women from the roles of inferior, dependent females, playing the servant to demanding husbands. The equalitarian family is beginning to emerge. This new status of women has been difficult for some men to accept, and it has caused strife in some marriages. Some studies show poor marital adjustment in homes where the wife is fully employed, because husbands tend to think of a wife who is successful in her employment as a threat to them. Some husbands think of a working wife as one who is not giving proper attention to their children. On the other hand, low happiness scores were discovered in marriages where a wife was denied the opportunity to work or have a career.[7]

Thus, we see that several outcomes of the new independent state of women affect the divorce rate: women who expect to be able to express their independence in working or careers and are thwarted by their husbands; men who are threatened by the fact that their wives want a certain degree of independence; and women who no longer need to stay with a bad marriage because of their complete dependency on their husbands for survival, economically and socially.

5. *Increased affluence of our society.* In times of depression, the divorce rate decreases. People cannot afford the expense of a divorce, and their minds are more preoccupied with survival than with freedom. In times of affluence, there is more money to divide so that two households can be supported. And we might speculate that in times of affluence, people are tempted to adopt a materialistic pattern of values that is not

in the best interests of the institution of marriage, which ultimately depends on deeper spiritual values to bind it together.

6. *Lessening influence of authority sources.* Public opinion has changed its attitude toward divorce. For the most part, divorce is accepted as a necessary alternative to a marriage that is no longer functioning. If one were to conduct a public opinion poll asking how many favored abolishing the institution of divorce, there would be few votes in favor, even from those who would not personally consider applying for a divorce under any circumstances. It is a freedom that everyone has a right to exercise if he so chooses. A divorced person is no longer looked down upon by the public at large or thought of as disgraced.

Institutions that formerly attempted to keep people from getting divorces by admonition or by edict have either modified their positions or lost their place of authority in the minds of their constituents. This is true of public law and the courts, as we have already noted. Religious institutions have changed, also. Up to this time, the position of the Roman Catholic Church has not changed, in terms of church law, which holds that a valid marriage consummated and established as a sacrament of the church is indissoluble. For those whom God has joined shall not be separated by man. But the sympathetic attitude with which most priests attempt to help couples who may feel that a divorce is necessary, indicates a softening of the attitude of the church in general about this whole matter. Divorce is recognized by the Jewish religion and by most Protestant denominations. Although the religious ceremony may include a vow that couples take to remain together "as long as you both shall live," it is recognized that this is qualified by the fact that it is in the "holy bond of marriage" that this permanency is to exist. When it ceases to be "holy," then alternatives to the marriage may be considered.

7. *Earlier dating.* If one were to trace the age at which dating begins, he would find that the curve has moved down year by year since the 1920's. Broderick and Fowler reported that 45 percent of the boys and 36 percent of the girls studied in an adolescent group reported that they began dating in the fifth grade or at ages ten and eleven.[8] Early dating is encouraged by some parents, who give parties for the very young to encourage such heterosexual interests. If the tendency to date at earlier and earlier ages continues, at what point can we expect it to level off? And how will this affect the age at which people eventually marry? Early dating is related to early marriage. After so long, marriage for some seems the only place to go, particularly if they have no long-range goals or college in mind. Lee Burchinal studied this matter and found that girls who married before they finished high school "had begun dating earlier, dated

more frequently, dated more boys, had gone steady earlier, and felt that they had been in love with a greater number of boys" than had other girls who constituted a control group for his study.[9] Since it has been established that the younger people marry, the greater the likelihood of divorce, this trend must be considered a hazardous one.

8. *Illusions of love, marriage, and the family created by the mass media.* The mass media, including motion pictures, television, magazines, and newspapers, have created a romantic illusion about love, marriage, and the family. Even advertising envelops these matters in an aura that is highly misleading. Love is pictured as two people gazing, dreamy-eyed at each other in some ideal setting, which is scarcely an accurate depiction of love as it must exist, day by day, in a marriage. Pictures of beautiful, neat, clean, sweet-smelling babies lying docilely in the arms of a serene mother seated in a room in perfect order is hardly life as it is experienced in the real family. In one way or another, such unrealistic images are created that many young people go into marriage with little more than romantic illusions instead of some knowledge of what marriage and family life are likely to be. A young woman wrote me a letter about six months after her marriage. I had helped her and the young man she planned to marry in some pre-marital counseling. One line of her letter read, "Why didn't you tell me what marriage was *really* like?" It wasn't that she was disappointed so much as surprised. She had not realized that she would have so little free time and so much to do, and this was before children arrived in their family.

When some young people discover the realities of marriage and living with another person day in and day out, they are not only surprised but also disappointed, because marriage wasn't what it was pictured in the media. Disappointment can be a door to divorce.

9. *The higher expectation level for marriage.* If you think back to the time of your grandparents, or your great-grandparents, you will find people whose expectations in marriage were very simple. What did your great-grandfather want in a wife? He wanted a woman who could cook, sew, wash his clothes, be a good homemaker, mother of his children, and a respectable woman in the community. And what did your great-grandmother want in a husband? She wanted a good provider, a man with good character, a competent father of her children, and someone the community held in high regard. Did they expect more than this? Not a whole lot. But what about today? The expectations are much, much greater. Few men would settle for the expectations of your great-grandfather; and few women would settle for the expectations of your great-grandmother. In class, when the students are asked to list the indispensable characteris-

tics of a marriage partner, the list is very impressive. It consists of personal characteristics, special talents and skills, a variety of interests, and physical attractiveness. The requirements their great-grandparents would have listed are scarcely mentioned, probably just taken for granted.

Many marriages cannot meet the expectations of those entering them. Again, disappointment sets in. People become disillusioned and depressed. Is this all there is to marriage? Did I marry the wrong person? If I tried again, could I have a better marriage? When such questions persist, they could lead to an eventual separation.

10. *Increased longevity.* In spite of a high divorce rate, people can anticipate many more years of marriage than their grandparents and great-grandparents did. In 1975, one of the major life insurance companies projected the length of life to be seventy-one years for men and seventy-seven years for women. If we accept twenty-two as the median age for a man at the time of his marriage, he can expect to be married for forty-nine years, if he stays married to the same woman. Forty-nine years is not the average length of a marriage currently, but some estimate it to be between forty and forty-five years, which is a long time to be married. We must say, nonetheless, that the average length of time couples remain together today is a credit to their ability to keep the relationship going. In 1900 the average life span was about forty-nine years. Since men at that time married at a later age than they do now, the average length of a marriage was only about twenty-three years. Today people need to have qualities that will help them function properly in a marriage for about twenty years longer than they did in 1900. Some of the people today are the "sprinters" we talked about earlier. If they had lived in 1900 or earlier, they would probably have died before they got unhappy enough to get a divorce, but in the 1970's that doesn't happen to be the case. They run a short distance, become dissatisfied, and get a divorce.

11. *Rapidly changing ideas and standards affecting people's ability to define love, marriage, and family life.* In any time of transition there is apt to be a state of confusion about institutions and values. Today, articles appearing in books and magazines are titled: "Is Marriage Obsolete?" "Enjoying the Benefits of Marriage Without Being Married." "Would You Like to Live in a Commune?" "How to Live Happily Without a Man to Depend Upon." "Is Old-Fashioned Fidelity a Thing of the Past?" "Children—Who Needs Them?" "How Swinging Can Revive a Sagging Marriage." And on and on. Students are eager to discuss cohabitation and its effects on marriage, or whether it might be preferable to marriage. And the question always arises, "Is it really possible to stay happily married for so many years to the same person?"

While we try to find answers to these puzzling questions, many people are struggling to know who they really are and what they are doing. They are suffering an identity crisis as lovers, wives, husbands, parents, male and female. The norms, standards and beliefs of the past seem vague and irrelevant to them, yet no new ones have appeared on the horizon. In such an atmosphere of moral and ethical relativism, it is not easy to live.

A couple appeared in my office with a severe marital problem. The husband had decided that he wanted to begin a new life style. "I think my wife should allow me to date other women and have affairs with them if I wish. I would give her the same privilege." She replied, "But I don't want to date other men, I am satisfied with you. Besides I couldn't possibly tolerate your doing this and remain your wife." He was determined. We discussed their differences and tried to get them to reach some kind of a compromise that would be satisfactory to both. But he persisted, and so did she. Their lawyer told me that, after some months of turmoil, they were divorced. There may have been deeper problems than their disagreement on the subject they proposed to me, but even if there were, this state of confusion was enough to propel everything into the abyss.

Perhaps we can work through this present state of transition to some firmer ground on which marriages can operate more confidently. Until we do, we will continue to dwell in the realm of uncertainty.

There may be many other reasons why divorces occur. With these *general* and *specific* causes in mind, we should have a better understanding of the anatomy of divorce, and in understanding it, find ways of preventing what most people do not really want when they get married, a parting somewhere along the road ahead.

REFERENCES

1. John Scanzoni, *Sexual Bargaining.* Englewood Cliffs, N.J.: Prentice-Hall, 1972, p. 8.

2. —————— and Letha Scanzoni, *Men, Women, and Change.* New York: McGraw-Hill Book Company, 1976, p. 460.

3. Percival M. Symonds, *The Dynamics of Human Adjustment.* New York: D. Appleton-Century Co., 1946, p. 158.

4. U.S. Department of Health, Education and Welfare, *Vital Statistics of the United States,* 1968, Volume III, Marriage and Divorce.

5. Robert F. Winch, *The Modern Family.* New York: Holt, Rinehart, and Winston, 1971, pp. 91, 92.

6. Paul W. Alexander, *The Follies of Divorce—A Therapeutic Approach to the Problem.* University of Illinois *Law Forum,* Vol. 1949 (Winter Number), p. 707.

7. Mary W. Hicks and Marilyn Platt, "Marital Happiness and Stability: A

Review of the Research in the Sixties," *Journal of Marriage and the Family* (November 1970), pp. 556–59.

8. Carlfred B. Broderick and Stanley E. Fowler, "New Patterns of Relationships Between the Sexes Among Preadolescents," *Marriage and Family Living* (February 1961), p. 28.

9. Lee G. Burchinal, "The Premarital Dyad and Love Involvement," in Harold Christensen (Ed.), *Handbook of Marriage and the Family,* Chicago: Rand McNally and Co., 1964, p. 624.

CHAPTER TEN

A Divorce Takes Shape: Process and Effects

How does it all begin? I have seen divorces start to take shape early in the marriage. I have watched them grow week by week, and month by month, sometimes year by year. Sometimes they grow like a forest fire, a tiny flame at first, which widens to greater and greater areas of the marriage, until all is consumed. Sometimes the fire is extinguished again and again, only to spring up in another tinder-dry spot. Sometimes it grows like a cancer eating from the inside, scarcely noticed until the pain sets in and it is almost too late. I say "almost" because one can never tell. What seems hopeless to the marriage counselor may not prove to be hopeless in the end, which is why marriage counselors should be wise enough never to "advise" a couple to get a divorce. Only the couple, after careful deliberation, can make that decision.

Why do some couples get divorces for certain reasons, while others who seem to have the same reasons, do not get divorces? If we could answer that question adequately, we would be able to tell people about the subtle differences between success and failure, although not all divorces can be termed "failures." Some are, and some are not. If there is the potential for a successful marriage, and a couple does not take advantage of this potential, we could call it a failure. If the match were so poor at the beginning that maintaining it would have taken an effort beyond and above what most people are able to give, then we cannot call it a failure.

When we looked at the eighteen couples in our study of successful marriages, we discovered that they were all functioning very well during the years of our observations. Here was a group of happy people who were very well satisfied with the way their marriages were going. However, when we studied their case histories, we found many instances where deep trouble might have erupted, trouble enough to cause a major break, if proper attention had not been given to it. You may remember the case of Jack and Josie, and the trying times through which they went in their early years, and how Jack said, "We were growing apart—until we decided to do something about it." There's the clue. They did something about it. They did not let the fire spread.

Here we note again the importance of the ability to handle crises as they arise. It is like putting out small fires at the beginning, even larger ones if the crisis is great enough. But immediate attention is needed, and delay is dangerous. Here we recall the wisdom of Albert Ellis's analysis of the causes of divorce as "goofing or drifting." The "goof" is bad enough, and if you put enough of them together, they do a lot of damage. But "drifting" is still worse. And I suppose that is what many couples do—nothing! Something happens. Forget it; maybe it will go away.

It is not easy to trace the anatomy of a divorce, but I would like to try. Of course, the explanations will be greatly over-simplified. Someone said that trying to outline the causes of a divorce is like trying to find the causes of a war. At what point does a war break out? Many things happen, some small and some large; then one day it all comes together in a big bang!

Hal and Veronica met early one summer, when Veronica was engaged to another man with whom she was not getting along well. When Hal came into the picture, it gave her a good excuse to break the engagement. She and Hal dated the entire summer, and late in August, Hal proposed and Veronica accepted. They were married a few months later. Neither Hal nor Veronica came from homes that one could call stable, and there was a great deal of unhappiness in both, although Hal rated his home as more unhappy than Veronica's. Veronica's parents experienced severe financial difficulty, which she believed affected the marriage adversely. Hal's parents also had financial difficulty, but he describes his mother as one who complained, criticized, and nagged constantly. Hal's mother died early, but his father lived a long time, and Veronica hated him intensely.

Hal and Veronica thought they were "madly in love" when they married. Veronica was extremely attractive physically, and Hal felt this was very important. Their sexual life was delightful for the first few years of the marriage. It seemed to keep them close and was a convenient way to end arguments and disputes.

I will now attempt to draw a space diagram representing distance and closeness in the marriage. It is impossible to do this in detail for the entire marriage, and I shall attempt only to show general trends. You will notice that Hal and Veronica lived together twenty-five years before the divorce finally came about. Why did the marriage last this long when there was so much trouble all along the way? Neither Hal nor Veronica ever thought they would experience a divorce. They had accumulated a rather large estate as the marriage progressed, and they didn't want to break it in two. They both had concern for their four children and felt that a divorce might be harmful to them. The children, in turn, did not want them to separate. As it turned out, they did not get the divorce until the children had all left home. The complaints they made about each other, in the order of their importance, were as follows:

Hal's complaints about Veronica:
1. Critical of me.
2. Complains a great deal.
3. Interferes in my business.
4. Nags.
5. Selfish, inconsiderate.
6. Disagree with her disciplining of children.
7. Quick-tempered.
8. Narrow-minded.
9. Insincere.
10. Intolerant.
11. Jealous.

Veronica's complaints about Hal:
1. Touchy.
2. Nervous and impatient.
3. Critical.
4. Unaffectionate.
5. Selfish, inconsiderate.
6. Rude.
7. Complaining.
8. Bad temper.

Hal elaborated on some of his feelings this way.

Negative:

Veronica doesn't give me any support. When I make a decision she won't back me up. She lacks tolerance. Doesn't like my recreational needs, and criticizes me for watching TV. We can't agree that security means sensible, systematic, financial planning rather than "money-madness." I am accused of being unattentive, especially after her operation and after pregnancies. We have different ideas about home life in that I believe in reasonable tidiness and a loose schedule, not slavishness to neatness and a time table. I am not much of a dresser and I get criticized a lot for this, and I guess I am not as social as Veronica would like for me to be. We can't agree on going to bed at the same time. I have felt that Veronica should have gotten a job early in our marriage

THE ANATOMY OF A DIVORCE

A Closeness-Distance Diagram of the Marriage of Hal and Veronica

MARRIAGE

5 years | 5 years

Veronica

Trying to please each other in every way.

Settled by having two accounts. Veronica is satisfied.

Veronica likes to travel and enjoys the companionship.

Veronica is disturbed by these trips and that Hal enjoys watching girlie shows.

She feels better.

Veronica upset about her small allowance.

She feels relieved about the new budget.

Work on communication with the marriage

Hal

First married. Feel close.

First disagreement. Hal objects to joint checking account.

Planned trips together help reinforce happiness. These occur frequently.

Hal takes a trip by himself to Mexico.

When Hal returns, he is very good to Veronica.

They work out a new budget with marriage counselor.

Hal complains that Veronica won't communicate.

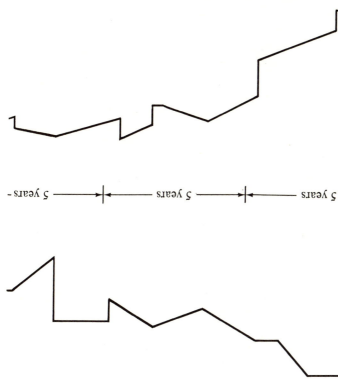

counselor. Slight improvement.

Veronica enjoys walks.

Veronica is very permissive. Hal is strict.

Anticipating trip helps.

Hal is tight with money.

Veronica has adequate money now.

Veronica loses interest in sex.

Veronica is angry about lack of companionship.

Veronica builds a world of her own.

Veronica says she would leave if it weren't for children.

Veronica gives up. Not interested in saving the marriage. Children gone now.

— 5 years → | ← 5 years → | ← 5 years → |

DIVORCE

Try taking walks together at night.

Trouble over discipline of children.

Plan a trip to Europe together.

Trip disappointing. Argued a lot.

Increase in income helps ease situation.

Increased bickering.

Don't do much together.

Resentment toward each other grows.

Hal stays away from home much of the time.

Hal does not want a divorce. Tells marriage counselor he will do anything within reason to save the marriage.

to help out financially but she would never agree to this. She won't compromise—has a strong will and will never give in. She calls me a hypochondriac, but I just want to take good care of my health; she never takes care of herself.

Positive:

She is physically attractive. She is tidy, a good housekeeper, cultured, ambitious. She is educated and intelligent and can carry on an intellectual conversation. She has high moral and religious standards. She is faithful, good to the children. I am satisfied with our sexual life most of the time, although it gets bad when we quarrel. We take walks together late at night.

Veronica's feelings about Hal:
Negative:

I become irritated over an accumulation of things, like when I make a remark, "Hal, I wish you would (or wouldn't) do this. . . . Then he blows up. We have a quarrel, and in a few minutes my temperature is down, but it's too late. He may stay mad for days. I apparently get on Hal's nerves, but I like to have him around when he isn't mad at me. If we work on something for me, we have to do it his way. If we do it for him, it has to be his way. Yet he says I won't cooperate. I believe a housewife should have something to say about something other than how the housework is done. Financial security seems to be his only goal. He is trying to get ahead too fast. He thinks I expect too much by trying to arrange for all to sit down to the evening meal together. A five-minute warning doesn't seem to help. He may be on the telephone with a business conversation, and he won't break it off; or if he is watching a TV program that interests him, he wants to stay with it to the end. I don't like it when he goes out of town, especially the time he spends in those night club shows watching the pretty girls with very little on. We disagree on how to discipline the children, and he doesn't seem to understand teen-age self-assertions. We don't do enough together in the way of outside activities. It seems I always need more money than he gives me.

Positive:

He is ambitious. Doesn't drink or smoke, and doesn't use dirty or profane language. He loves our children and is a good provider. When he is not angry he is a pleasant companion. We have had some good times on family projects we have done together. On evenings after the children have gone to bed, we have taken walks and visited over cokes in a nearby restaurant. We have had some fun with our children, and we are both thankful they are healthy and intelligent.

Mutual Interests. We discovered that Hal and Veronica scored low on their mutual interest inventory. They had said that they did not do enough to get to form a solid companionship, and this was partly true because they did not have a great many common interests to share. When they found something they both liked very much, such as travel, however, they disagreed on how to do it successfully, so their traveling together did not do much for the marriage.

Personality Problems and Conflict. A great amount of tension here. It seemed that every time they tried to talk over a problem, it ended in an argument. The clash of personalities in their marriage was very obvious. Veronica indicated that she tended to be pessimistic, and often unhappy under adverse circumstances. She was easily disturbed by trouble, and did not share her feelings with those close to her. Hal admitted that he lacked confidence. He tended to be moody at times. Neither Veronica nor Hal displayed a very pronounced sense of humor. Both tended to be somewhat stubborn and hesitant to give in to each other on occasion. Both had volatile tempers: Veronica's explosive; Hal's coming through in a slow burn.

Value Systems. In testing their values, we found them to be very much alike theoretically. Yet there *was* a value conflict in their marriage. Perhaps it was in the method each chose to express his or her values. Hal tended to be very frugal, methodical, and careful in financial planning. Veronica was impatient with these methods of handling money, and felt they should be more "loose" and carefree. Each had come from family backgrounds where money was scarce, but they reacted differently to handling money in their own home.

Role Concepts. There was considerable disagreement on roles in marriage and family relationships, in spite of the fact that Hal thought Veronica was a good homemaker, and Veronica thought Hal was a good provider.

Meeting Each Other's Needs. Again it seems that many of their basic needs were met, yet emotionally they did not seem to contribute to one another adequately.

What Did They Think Could Be Done? Veronica in a self-criticism indicated that she really didn't understand herself. She didn't understand Hal either. Also, marriage bothered her in that she didn't seem to get out of it what she expected to. She felt she lacked patience and self-control, but was willing to work hard to save the marriage. Hal admitted that he did not understand Veronica and that she was an enigma to him. When they had quarrels, he found it difficult to forgive and forget. He thought that they could get along, if they could only learn to communicate rationally. Theirs seemed to be the case of a couple who couldn't live together, yet who couldn't live apart. Until the last, they did not give up hope. Even then, I believe Hal would have been willing to go on, but Veronica finally said she had had enough and could tolerate the situation no longer, especially now that the children had departed. Before it was over, Hal wrote a letter containing these words, "I am, of course, still bewildered for the most part as to what Veronica wants (within reason) and whether she, under any condition, would be a loyal and loving wife."

Veronica responded to this in a counseling session in which she said:

Living together would only be possible if we could settle our "blowups" and get them over without letting them hang on for so long a time. I know I do things that make Hal furious, but I have to find ways to solve this. I can't change completely. Living together isn't impossible, but the problems are very great. The biggest problem is "temper." It seems that after we argue for awhile, then we blow up, and then it goes on for hours, days, or even weeks. This is something which I simply can't take any longer. I believe Hal is trying. Sometimes he surprises me. He took out the trash recently and it was a surprise to me. I don't know how to stop things after they get started. I can't stand being "bawled out." Then I start doing things to hurt him and to get even. These long sessions of anger, resentment, and icy hostilities are too much. I can't seem to take it any longer. We need to be able to talk things over in a very calm and objective way. This we have not seemed to have been able to do. It always ends up by our getting angry with each other.

We need to do things together, such as bicycle riding, dancing, bowling, walking in the woods, swimming, picnics and so forth. We would have to find something we could do together that is more active than going to the movies. There doesn't seem to be much real love expressed. We have got accustomed to one another and are dependent on each other, but we have not been able to accept each other. Our relation is too businesslike. There is no tenderness. We need more demonstration of affection. Little things count so much. We need more of this.

This marriage seemed to have something in common with that of George and Martha in *Who's Afraid of Virginia Woolf?* They express bitter conflict, anger, accusation, and criticism, yet from time to time they reveal a wistfulness that seems to say, "This is not the way it should be; we could do better, and perhaps we will." Each sees some things that are objectionable but could be corrected. Each sees outwardly a relationship that is being handled badly. It is sad, tragic, because it does not have to be that way. Martha speaks to Nick about George in a way that expresses the deeper feelings of many couples who are performing badly in their marital relationships:

. . . George who is out somewhere there in the dark. . . . George who is good to me, and whom I revile; who understands me, and whom I push off; who can make me laugh, and I choke it back in my throat; who can hold me, at night, so that it's warm, and whom I will bite so there's blood; who keeps learning the games we play as quickly as I can change the rules; who can make me happy and I do not wish to be happy, and yet I do wish to be happy. George and Martha: sad, sad, sad.

NICK: Sad.

MARTHA: . . . whom I will not forgive for having come to rest; for having seen me and having said: yes; this will do; who has made the hideous, the hurting, the insulting mistake of loving me and must be punished for it. George and Martha: sad, sad, sad.

NICK (Puzzled): Sad.

MARTHA: . . . who tolerates, which is intolerable; who is kind, which is cruel; who understands, which is beyond comprehension. . . .

NICK: George and Martha: sad, sad, sad.

MARTHA: Some day . . . hah! some night . . . some stupid, liquor-ridden night . . . I will go too far . . . and I'll either break the man's back . . . or push him off for good . . . which is what I deserve. . . .[1]

And so it is—a very sad story. What each of us wants to be personally and what we would like our relationship to be with others, especially our "significant" others, are not what we see happening. How do we bring into agreement our wistful longings about what should be and what actually happens in our marriages? This is the question we will have to continue to try to answer, if what comes after we say, "I love you," is to be a rewarding and productive experience.

When two people such as Hal and Veronica have joined their lives, raised a family of four children, gone through countless experiences together—with tears and laughter, accumulated a sizable estate, made numerous friends, shared twenty-five years of memories, good and bad, and then break the ties and say, "it is finished," a very complicated and traumatic situation lies ahead. What is the anatomy of this kind of separation as it is reflected in the lives of the people who experience it? Paul Bohannan has attempted to describe it in what he calls the "six stations of divorce."

The complexity of divorce arises because at least six things are happening at once. They may come in a different order and with varying intensities, but there are at least these six different experiences of separation. They are the more painful and puzzling as personal experiences because society is not yet equipped to handle any of them well, and some of them we do not handle at all.

I have called these six overlapping experiences (1) the emotional divorce, which centers around the problem of the deteriorating marriage; (2) the legal divorce, based on grounds; (3) the economic divorce, which deals with money and property; (4) the coparental divorce, which deals with custody, single-parent homes, and visitation; (5) the community divorce, surrounding the changes of friends and community that every divorcee experiences; and (6) the psychic divorce, with the problem of regaining individual autonomy.[2]

Many people who get divorces anticipate them for a considerable length of time before they become final, and yet find themselves ill prepared to face the realities of the complex nature of divorce. There is a new emphasis on "divorce counseling," which attempts to help people adjust to the changes that divorce brings in many areas. We might anticipate certain effects of each one of these "stations" suggested by Paul Bohannan:

1. The emotional divorce. Feelings of growing apart; not being loved or supported emotionally; frustration and disappointment set in. Resentment grows.

2. The legal divorce. By order of the court the marriage is declared to be over, and the right to remarry is established. The financial cost is sometimes more than anticipated.

3. The economic divorce. The couple owns property together. How this is to be divided is not an easy matter even in states where the "no fault" law is in effect.

4. The coparental divorce. When there are children, their future must be decided; with whom will they live? How will they be supported? Who will give them guidance and help them make decisions? What kind of relationship will they have with their father and mother who are no longer together?

5. The community divorce. Will the community approve or disapprove? Which friends will be related to in the future? Will the divorced person be able to relate to the same clubs, social organizations, church? Will it be embarrassing to be seen at the same functions with the ex-spouse? How should one relate to former in-laws?

6. The psychic divorce. Marriage brings two people together mentally, emotionally and physically. How will each party regain individual autonomy and identity? How will it be possible to change from thinking in "couple" terms to "single" terms? How does one learn to live alone without the pangs of loneliness?

Successfully negotiating these six stations can produce a real feeling of achievement, but it is not an easy matter. Help from a counselor is advisable, because, for example, failure to work through some of these stations might propel a person into a quick remarriage. Keeping a sense of balance and learning how to deal with resentment, guilt, regret, angry feelings, frustration, and insecurity are a part of the challenge that faces the divorcee. Some meet the challenge well, while others fail miserably.

Perhaps tracing the anatomy of divorce, and one divorce in particular, will help us to understand the pitfalls of marriage and how to avoid some of them that might lead to a divorce. If a divorce seems unavoidable and necessary, it may help people to know what is involved, and what they must be prepared for if they are to meet it in a productive manner.

REFERENCES

1. Edward Albee, *Who's Afraid of Virginia Woolf?* New York: Simon and Schuster, 1962, pp. 190, 191.
2. Paul Bohannan, *Divorce and After.* New York: Doubleday and Co., 1970.

CHAPTER ELEVEN

The Fear of Love and the Flight from Intimacy

The inability of some people to live in intimate relationships with others is caused by their almost unrecognized fear of close involvements. Mature love calls for mental, emotional, and physical closeness. When people are incapable of such closeness, their interpersonal relationships and their marriages will suffer. Empathy, a state in which two people understand each other and participate deeply in each other's thoughts and feelings, cannot exist in the chill of the fear of loving.

Larry was three years into his second marriage and becoming increasingly dissatisfied with it. He felt that it would have been better to have stayed with his first marriage. There were many good things about the first marriage that he could appreciate now, but which he hadn't been aware of at the time. What bothered him now was his feeling that he might not be successful in any marriage. His current wife, Jane, seemed to have the qualities he wanted in a wife, but Larry was not relating to her satisfactorily. What seemed to be the matter? Larry explained that he was never able to feel close to his first wife, and he had this same feeling about Jane. Then he elaborated by saying he could not feel close to anyone really, and this had been a problem all his life. He described his home life, his cold-natured father, and how he felt unwanted and rejected by his parents. He had never known love in the sense of a close, warm relationship with anyone. At intervals during his first marriage he had had brief affairs with secretaries, and a more serious one with a single girl who had visited frequently with his family. He had thought this affair might develop into something serious, but she moved away and quickly forgot about him. He felt jilted and hurt. Could anyone ever love him as he wanted to be loved? His life story was that of a search after the elusive experience of loving and being loved. Now he began to doubt that he would ever find it, or if he did, whether he could sustain such a relationship.

To test a hypothesis about his difficulty, the marriage counselor gave him a book to read entitled, *Your Fear of Love*. A few days later he called the counselor on the phone to exclaim almost jubilantly, "This is it. This is a description of my life. I now know what my trouble is: I am afraid to get close to other people and I am afraid to let them get close to me." This insight provided a new platform of understanding on which counseling could continue to operate. From this point on, Larry began to show slight signs of improvement. What had he discovered in this book that opened a new door of hope?

The author of the book, Marshall Hodge, describes it this way:

It is one of the more puzzling facets of human existence that we often avoid those experiences that we most desire. We long to give and receive expressions of love, but at the critical moment we frequently back away. And in a similar way we frustrate ourselves in many of our strongest desires, such as our wish to be free and spontaneous in our actions.

Our avoidance of longed-for experiences is rooted in fear. We are, as we shall see, afraid of freedom, afraid of sexual enjoyment, and afraid of being ourselves with other people. And the most basic of all these fears is our fear of emotional closeness with others; in a word, love. . . .

At first glance the idea that we are afraid to love does not seem to make sense. And while it may not be easy to understand it intellectually, it is even more difficult for many of us to become emotionally aware of this fear within us. Yet there seems to be no better explanation for the fact that moments of feeling very close to another person are rare and short-lived.[1]

Most of us have experienced this in our own relationships with family and friends. After some very intimate moments, we may feel distant and withdrawn. We may have shared a warm, friendly period with someone, only to have it interrupted by an argument or a careless word. Do we cause these interruptions to happen because we are afraid we are getting too close? It is possible.

It seems that in the case of Pat and Alan, which will be discussed in detail in Chapter 12, there was a reluctance on Alan's part to cultivate an intimate relationship with his wife. She was a very affectionate person and invited a closeness, which he seemed to avoid by being too busy, regarding it as overly sentimental, or just neglecting it. It wasn't that he did not love her. He always affirmed that he loved her deeply. But intimacy was something he did not seem to be able to handle. Pat noticed this. Why didn't he touch her more, hold her hand, sit close to her on the sofa and say loving things to her? It was only in bed that they were close physically. That didn't seem right to her. If they loved each other and if they had joined together as husband and wife, why couldn't they express this throughout the day?

Some people use sexual intercourse as an escape from emotional intimacy. This may be noted in the premarital state quite often. As Hodge points out:

One of the most interesting but often unrecognized facets of the relationship of sex and love is that physical intimacy is often used as a way of avoiding emotional intimacy. Since we long for love but are afraid to express caring, we often use sexual relationships either as a substitute or counterfeit for the experience of love. . . .

One problem of many engagements is that the couple mistakes physical intimacy for emotional closeness. Many couples become so enthralled with the excitement that goes along with the physical closeness that they feel they love each other. Often their feeling for each other is based on only the vaguest knowledge of one another.[2]

Love as emotional closeness can be enhanced by physical expressions of love-making and sexual intercourse, but never replaced by them. It is a well-known fact that physical intimacy, though it may be very gratifying and stimulating, reveals very little of the inner thoughts, ideas, and emotions of the person expressing it. And it may be used as a shield by one who is afraid to express love freely and openly.

What causes the fear of love, and why do we see it creep into a marriage and begin to stifle the relationship between husband and wife? How many divorces begin when the participants in a marriage start to back away from each other because they fear, consciously or unconsciously, the eventualities of love? And what is it they fear? Let us begin to try to answer these questions by saying that to love, in the deepest sense, is to become extremely vulnerable. This vulnerability is one of the implications of love, both to the one loving, and to the one being loved. It arouses expectations of responsibility, giving, trusting, feeling, involvement. These things come after one says, "I love you!" If they do not, one might have cause to doubt that there was any love there in the first place. If I tell someone I love him, is he not likely to expect that I might be willing to help him when he needs help? If one needs assistance, reinforcement, empathy, that he cannot supply himself, is it not likely that he will turn first to someone he thinks loves him to help meet these needs? Yes, indeed. If you do not want to do anything for another person, do not tell him you care for him, because caring implies availability of your time, attention, feeling, and energy.

Not all people are willing to become this vulnerable. Sometimes these people get married and find out what it means to get into a situation in which they are subject to another's needs. They may feel panicky or trapped or anxious about what might be expected of them. They may begin to withdraw, fearing that closeness might be more than they could negotiate. In our study of couples in our select group of well-functioning marriages, we discovered that in some cases there has been an illness on the part of a husband or wife which has required long, patient care on the part of the other. This is a demanding situation that cannot be met by one who fears being involved in the pain and suffering of another. If, when one says he loves another, he means that the interests of the other are as great as, or greater than, his own, he has assumed an obligation to meet needs that may require a considerable amount of his life energy. If one knows in advance what love means in terms of vulnerability, then the surprises are not so great later. If one does not know, then he may be frightened once the realities of love become apparent.

Within all of us there is the temptation to be preoccupied with self-interest. When we discover that love does not thrive when we become too self-preoccupied, we may back away from love. We may measure just how much distance we think we must keep from others or another in order to be safe from too much involvement. A husband may attempt to make his wife angry so that she will not ask him to help her with the housework or children. A wife may initiate a disagreement with her husband so he will not attempt to make love with her that night. There are ingenious ways of keeping our distance from another, of avoiding the emotional intimacy that so frightens us or makes demands on us.

Hodge believes that many people attempt to escape a love relationship out of a feeling of low self-esteem.

The cycle of rejection and the need for escape from intolerable self-hatred is also the origin of our fear of love. Out of the experience of feeling rejected, with subsequent feelings of worthlessness and self-hate, comes the child's feeling that love is risky. He probably never puts this feeling into words, even to himself, but the child's emotional logic must run something like this: "Since I hate my real self and know it to be worthless, I dare not be myself with others. If I am open and direct with people, they will see me as I am and hate me. If I love, I will only be hurt in return. I have had enough of that already, so I will find some other way of dealing with people."

The escape hatches not only provide a way of avoiding full awareness of self-hatred; they also help the person bypass the anticipated dangers of intimacy. And because he has feelings of worthlessness, the individual desire to avoid the risks of love are increased because he lacks confidence in his ability to cope with emotional hurt when he experiences it.[3]

This cycle of rejection begins with feelings of rejection that lead to feelings of worthlessness, to self-hate, to an attempt to escape through bullying, bragging, physical or mental illness, alcoholism, hostility, delinquent behavior, etc., which make the person feel even more rejected, and starts the cycle all over again in an intensified fashion. This is very unproductive behavior and it leads to self-defeat on the part of the persons who engage in it, yet it is frequently practiced. One can readily see how devastating this can be to a marriage. Suppose that, because of a feeling of low self-esteem, a spouse fears that he cannot be loved, so he turns to alcohol. Drinking makes him even less acceptable to his spouse, who rejects him and in turn makes him feel even worse than he did before. The marriage counselor has repeated opportunities to observe cases in which one spouse or the other seems to be deliberately trying to create estrangement when there is no apparent reason for it. Often the offending party is very sorry for what he or she has done. The irrationality of the act indicates there must be some deeper cause than that which meets the eye. The cause may be the fear of love and intimacy that constantly creeps into so many marriages.

Paul Tillich has suggested another factor that may have a subtle effect on some marriages. He believes that love exercises its greatest power when it is overcoming the greatest separation and brings together that which has been estranged. Love strives most to unify that which is separated. Perhaps this is why young lovers say they enjoy a quarrel, because making up is so sweet and satisfying. In marriage, the novelty of the lover's quarrel and the aftermath of making up lose some of their attractiveness over a period of time. Yet one cannot deny that in a reunion of the separated there is an emotional peak. An enforced separation brought about by the husband's being away on business, or a wife's visit to a sick parent, often results in an exceedingly pleasant experience of reunion. The reunion may bring about an emotional high that cannot be sustained for a long period of time. So Tillich writes:

In man's experience of love the nature of life becomes manifest. Love is the drive towards the unity of the separated. Reunion presupposes separation of that which belongs essentially together. . . .

The ontology of love is tested by the experience of love fulfilled. There is a profound ambiguity about this experience. Fulfilled love is, at the same time, extreme happiness and the end of happiness. The separation is overcome. But without the separation there is no love and no life.[4]

Is it possible that we may fear the love that brings us together with the person we love, yet threatens to end the separation that motivates us to love in the first place? There is an old saying that some people cannot stand prosperity, perhaps because it seems to be an achievement rather than a challenge. Is it also possible that some people cannot tolerate loving and being loved because they fear there is some kind of ending in sight?

This strange and frightening matter of the fear of love and the flight from intimacy will remain something of a mystery. It is a part of life, and many do not seem to be able to cope with it successfully. Others are able to accept it and work through the periods when it enters the scene and invades a relationship for what is, one hopes, only a brief moment.

If "perfect love casts out fear,"[5] then it behooves us to work toward this kind of perfect love that will safeguard us from the fears and flights that would separate us from that which we want most of all.

REFERENCES

1. Marshall Bryant Hodge, *Your Fear of Love,* Garden City, N.Y.: Doubleday and Co., 1967, pp. 85.

2. *Ibid.,* pp. 152, 153.

3. *Ibid.,* p. 30.

4. Paul Tillich, *Love, Power and Justice.* New York: Oxford University Press, 1960, pp. 25, 27.

5. I John 4:18, Revised Standard Version of the Bible.

CHAPTER TWELVE

Don't Say Goodbye
to Love Too Soon

In the motion picture, *Butterflies Are Free,* the young lady says, "I was married once for three weeks. I guess I liked getting married better than being married." So it would seem for many, though three weeks is a bit short even for the shortest of "sprinters." After a couple says, "I love you," to each other and decides to get married, one would expect the marriage to last awhile on the impetus of the initial emotion alone. It is not uncommon, however, to see one or both parties in a marriage give up rather easily, saying, "It just won't work."

Larry, referred to earlier, always thought that some day he would find a marriage that would work—some woman who would be just right for him. Some spouses give up their first marriage without trying to make it work, or finding out whether or not they really want it to work. I suspect that the reason a second marriage is frequently no more successful than the first is because all marriages have a certain set of problems that must be worked out. The problems may be different, but they will be there. If one entertains the illusion that there is a perfect marriage in the future with no problems, it may tempt him to give up easily in order to keep searching for something that isn't there. So we say, "Don't say goodbye to love too soon," because your first love may be the best love for you, if you give it the attention and skill it needs to function well. Looking for that second love that will be everything you always wanted, may be searching for a "will o' the wisp."

The story of those who *almost* gave up is an interesting one to study. In Chapter 5 we made a brief reference to Pat and Alan. Theirs was a case in which Pat almost said goodbye too soon. Pat and Alan lived on the campus of a large state university. Alan was a graduate student working for his Ph.D. degree in a scientific field. Pat had graduated from a college in another city earlier and now worked to support Alan and herself while he finished his graduate studies. Both were twenty-three when they first came to a marriage counselor. They had married when both were nineteen. They had dated for seven months, been engaged two months, and then married in a church in their hometown in the South. They were graduated from college a year after their marriage. Both were rather inexperienced in relating to the opposite sex—Pat had engaged in steady dating but twice, and Alan but once before their marriage. When they announced their plans to get married, both parents objected and asked them to wait.

Pat and Alan were determined to go ahead, so the parents gave their consent. After graduation from college, they came to a large state university where Pat secured a job and Alan became deeply immersed in his graduate studies. Two years elapsed, and the marriage settled into a routine in which Pat went to work each day to make enough to keep them going, and Alan spent a twelve-hour day in the classroom and lab. Pat spent many an evening alone, and Alan was too exhausted on the weekends to suggest anything very entertaining to offset her loneliness and boredom. It seemed to Pat that Alan was too preoccupied with his work to communicate with her about things she thought should be brought into the open about their marriage. In spite of her protests, the situation did not change. Pat began to feel increasing dissatisfaction with the marriage. Although Alan noticed this, he did not change his ways or attempt to discuss the problem with Pat. As he stated later, "I know that the situation wasn't good, but thought it would work itself out in the course of time when I would have my degree and a job. I also knew that all marriages had problems, especially at first."

Out of desperation, Pat came to a marriage counselor in October. After several sessions, Alan decided to come with her to see what could be done. By this time, Pat had decided that she could no longer live with Alan, so he agreed to move to other quarters. It was also agreed that they would continue seeing the marriage counselor separately and, after awhile, together, to see if the marriage could be mended.

Pat made her position clear, "I simply have no feeling of love for Alan anymore. What was once very warm and significant is now gone—absolutely gone. I have a great deal of respect and admiration for Alan, but I do not love him anymore and I am afraid I never will. All I can say is that I want to do everything I can before giving up. That's the least I can do. When I married I said I never would consider a divorce, but now it all looks different. I'll try, but it looks hopeless." Alan felt quite differently about it. He maintained consistently that he loved Pat and wanted her for his wife more than anything else in the world, including his graduate degree. Her separating from him shocked him into a state of desperation and willingness to do anything in his power to save the marriage.

During the first months, the marriage counselor spent considerable time helping the couple make a detailed analysis of their marriage to discover what had gone wrong and where the major complaints were. Pat and Alan both talked about their family backgrounds. Pat came from a home where culture and good breeding were stressed. Pat's father and mother were college educated, highly respected in their community, active in church life, and successful in business and social activities. Pat had a brother five years younger and a sister one and a half years younger with whom she related fairly well, in spite of some jealous feelings on her sister's part. Their home was full of gaiety, courteous attention one for another, family activities in which all participated, and a noticeable demonstration of affection.

Alan came from a sound home in which parents believed in firm discipline, the importance of education, and achievement as a necessary goal in life. Alan felt that nothing had ever been denied him and that this "spoiled" him to the extent that he was never taught to deprive himself or to share. He had a sister two years younger. The members of the family were kind and thoughtful of one another, but not especially warm or affectionate. Pat felt that Alan's mother resented her for "taking her son away from her." Pat's home gave more of an appearance of being a happy one than did Alan's. In this atmosphere she grew up to be a happy, cheerful, sociable person. She wanted to be active in school life, the social life of the community, and in the religious life of her church. She might be thought of as a sentimental person saying that she liked to do romantic things such as going to candlelight dinners with music, soft lights, and a dreamy atmosphere. She acquired a number of friends wherever she went and maintained these friendships with careful attention. She admitted a tendency to talk too much and to become overly effervescent in social gatherings. She was a deeply sensitive person whose feelings could be hurt easily.

Alan developed into a serious, hard-working intellectual. He had friends whose interests he could share, but he was not noticeably friendly. He communicated with effort and was reluctant to engage in small talk. While Pat always looked like she had stepped out of a shop window with the latest feminine attire, Alan took little interest in his personal attire and often appeared on the campus in a well-worn sweat shirt and dirty slacks. He was brilliant and took pride in that fact. People who were not intellectually inclined were of little interest to him. He was dedicated to science and came to feel that religion was for the weak, dependent, and naive. He thought of himself as hard-headed, and void of sentimentality and displays of emotion. If Pat laughed too much or cried too much, he looked on her with an air of disdain. He also chided her about her religious beliefs and feelings and was quite willing to let her go to church alone.

Pat had a great many complaints to make about Alan. He was unaffectionate and seemed reluctant to say kind and loving things to her, to surprise her with thoughtful and generous acts, or to touch her affectionately except when he was trying to get her into bed with him. "If he loved me, wouldn't he show some interest in me? I believe that sex is very important, but when you separate it from affection it is nothing. He doesn't seem to want to be home, preferring to work late in his lab. And there are so many things we should talk about and problems we should be trying to solve, yet he is unwilling to talk and keeps telling me these things are unimportant or that we can talk about them later. He acts as if he is superior to me; I think he is a conceited person. I guess I don't like him anymore."

Alan admitted that Pat was right in most of her complaints, but he maintained that she tended to be too sensitive and overly critical. "I have to be so careful because her feelings can be hurt very easily. I really believe she is narrow minded and in some ways is not liberal and up to date. About my not being willing to talk—she seems to enjoy arguments, and I do not like to argue. And she can lose her temper easily, too, and that bothers me. I may not be as warm and affectionate as she wants but I don't see her as one who is very responsive sexually and that makes a difference."

Pat and Alan were different in many respects. They were asked to evaluate each other on a personality inventory chart, and the results show some of the differences in their perceptions of each other. Alan saw Pat as neat and methodical, while Pat saw Alan as somewhat careless. Pat thought of Alan as calm, while Alan saw Pat as emotionally tense and nervous. There were other critical differences in the degree to which each assumed responsibility, desired to be thought important, was interested in religion, enjoyed home life, and communicated. Both rated the other as not being willing to admit it when wrong, susceptible to being hurt easily, and not willing to take suggestions. One would assume from this evaluation that Pat and Alan were temperamentally incompatible. Certainly there was a dispositional clash.

On a religious test Pat was shown to be a religiously conservative person, while Alan rated on the opposite end of the scale—almost beyond the point of showing any interest in religion at all. They used a rating

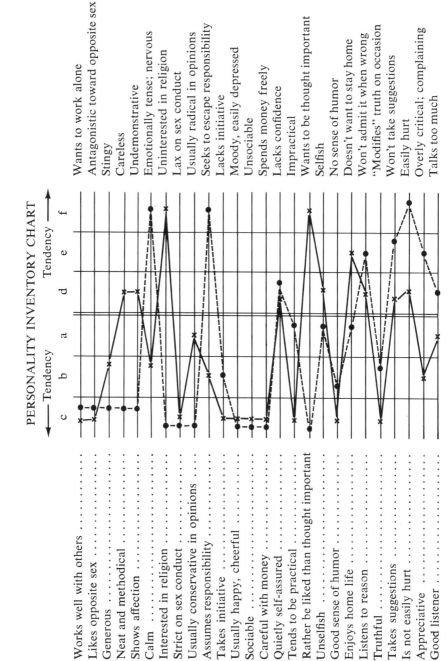

PERSONALITY INVENTORY CHART

← Tendency   Tendency →

c   b   a   d   e   f

1. Works well with others ....   Wants to work alone
2. Likes opposite sex ....   Antagonistic toward opposite sex
3. Generous ....   Stingy
4. Neat and methodical ....   Careless
5. Shows affection ....   Undemonstrative
6. Calm ....   Emotionally tense; nervous
7. Interested in religion ....   Uninterested in religion
8. Strict on sex conduct ....   Lax on sex conduct
9. Usually conservative in opinions ...   Usually radical in opinions
10. Assumes responsibility ....   Seeks to escape responsibility
11. Takes initiative ....   Lacks initiative
12. Usually happy, cheerful ....   Moody, easily depressed
13. Sociable ....   Unsociable
14. Careful with money ....   Spends money freely
15. Quietly self-assured ....   Lacks confidence
16. Tends to be practical ....   Impractical
17. Rather be liked than thought important   Wants to be thought important
18. Unselfish ....   Selfish
19. Good sense of humor ....   No sense of humor
20. Enjoys home life ....   Doesn't want to stay home
21. Listens to reason ....   Won't admit it when wrong
22. Truthful ....   "Modifies" truth on occasion
23. Takes suggestions ....   Won't take suggestions
24. Is not easily hurt ....   Easily hurt
25. Appreciative ....   Overly critical; complaining
26. Good listener ....   Talks too much

————— Pat rates Alan   ------------ Alan rates Pat

scale that would help reveal what they had in common by way of hobbies and leisure-time activities. Their score was fairly high, indicating seventeen areas in which they might enjoy interests they had in common. However, Pat's comments in the margin were interesting. Where Alan had said he liked picnics, Pat had noted, "never interested unless with a group." Where he indicated he liked parties, she wrote, "he never suggested any and I would have to beg to go to one." He indicated that he liked tennis, but her remark was, "we only had one racket and he played with the boys." Alan said he liked going out to nightclubs, but Pat commented, "he seldom ever asks me." And where he checked stamp collecting as a hobby, she wrote, "he hasn't showed any interest in years and has no hobby." Theoretically, they had a number of hobbies and leisure-time interests in common, but in reality they spent little time pursuing them in their marriage.

In stating their goals, Alan indicated that he would like to have a happy home, but Pat noted, "he would like to have a happy home without joining in to make it that way." When he said a goal in his life was to cultivate common friendships in the marriage, Pat said, "he has always been critical of friends that I found for us and he very seldom made friends that we both knew together." When Alan indicated that he was generally happy in spite of circumstances, Pat countered with, "he hasn't acted happy around me in months." And when he rated himself as doubtful about being affectionate, she noted, "affection is a waste of time to him and he doesn't understand it."

One might conclude here that the couple had important goals that were not shared, and that there was a failure to meet each other's needs, especially Pat's.

In the counseling sessions beginning in middle November, Pat, Alan, and the marriage counselor tried to discover why the marriage was not functioning and what might be done about it. It became clear that certain areas must be worked in if improvement were to become possible.

1. *Personality compatibility.* Pat and Alan were different in terms of personality traits. In some ways, these traits clashed rather than blended. Could they accept some of these differences and learn to live with them? Could each modify certain characteristics that were particularly objectionable to the other? Pat tended to be nervous, impulsive, impatient, restless. Alan was calm, patient, almost lethargic at times, and preoccupied with his intellectual interests. Pat was impatient with Alan's lack of emotion and slow movement. Could she become more patient, develop a more relaxed attitude, stop worrying about little things, and take some of her emotional pressure off Alan? Could the idealistic Pat and

the practical Alan become compatible? Alan commented: "Our personalities differ in some instances. Pat is aggressive; I am reserved. Pat is emotional; I hide my feelings. Pat holds a grudge; I tend to forget. We both are very sensitive and hurt each other when we argue. I feel these differences can be made to complement each other, but at present they clash."

2. *Role concepts.* Pat felt she worked hard all day to support Alan's educational pursuits, but received little appreciation by way of help in cooking meals, washing dishes, or keeping the house clean. She added: "I handle all the finances and pay all the bills as Alan doesn't want to bother. I do most of the shopping—even buy his clothes and shoes." Alan admitted he needed to take a greater interest in money management and household operation. Alan had not helped his mother at home, so he did not consider those tasks as a part of a man's role. Pat's greatest objection was to Alan's seeming lack of interest in the home and in having children, which she said he never talked about. Since Pat was the domestic-type wife, could Alan motivate himself to take a greater interest in family life and in helping his wife with household tasks? Would he welcome children into their life in the course of time?

3. *Companionship.* Pat was lonely. She needed a husband who would take her places where they could enjoy themselves. They needed to cultivate common interests and make friends they could share together. The lack of this companionship caused Pat to begin to make friends of her own, go her own way, and build a world of her own. Their tests showed that they shared a number of interests in recreational activities but did not participate in them. Could Alan find the time to revive interests they could share together, or would they need to wait until he was through with his graduate studies? Pat summed up her feelings this way: "He shows little interest in anything but his work, reading magazines, T.V. and movies. I made a list of thirty-five things that we might do together, but when he looked at them, he got mad. Part of my list was movies, dancing, cards, picnics, friends, out to dinner, make something together, walk, swim, bowl, learn golf, fix home together, develop hobbies, discover amusements. . . . Marriage is doing things together."

4. *Communication.* Pat complained about the lack of communication in their marriage. She enjoyed talking; Alan was the quiet type, and he thought Pat talked too much. He said: "She talks a lot, but is very hurt if I don't feel like talking. Unfortunately I haven't taken enough time to listen. She becomes very emotional when we talk over our problems, thus talking doesn't do any good. Right now she won't even talk." Pat replied:

"I only become emotional when he says he doesn't care or refuses to comment, or pretends not to hear." Was this difference too great to bridge? Pat worried about matters that seemed trivial to Alan. He seemed unconcerned or procrastinating about problems that were in urgent need of solution for Pat. In her frustration she pressured Alan to talk—to do something. He rebelled at this tactic. The distance between them widened. It was suggested that training sessions in communication might help them.

5. *Alan's good qualities.* In the period when Pat felt particularly neglected, she had almost forgotten about Alan's admirable qualities and his excellent potential. He was a diamond in the rough in urgent need of polishing. He lacked the social graces Pat wanted in a man. He was neither thoughtful nor attentive, but Alan seemed willing to make changes here. He had a promising future, because his knowledge and skills were in great demand by industry. In time he would command a more than adequate income to give his family financial security. He was steady, trustworthy, dependable, and could provide emotional stability for the less stable Pat. In the counseling sessions, Pat needed to rediscover these good qualities. Her comment was: "I need to understand my husband more. I am not sure what I can change. I tried hard to find out what I could change before my separation and was unsuccessful. I am an outgoing person, and I love to do things for anyone close to me. I like to show an interest in all of their activities and give as much of myself as I can. This makes me happy if I can make someone else happy. I can't change this. I am willing to learn to understand Alan. I need a greater sense of understanding of his good qualities. I need to become more patient and tolerant."

6. *Religious differences.* Pat and Alan were poles apart on their attitude toward religion and the church. Pat not only felt the solid impact of this difference but also was humiliated by Alan's ridicule of her beliefs and devoutness to her church. He often called her a "do-gooder." She was particularly embarrassed when Alan would try to shock her religious friends by his radical notions, which she felt he exaggerated for effect. Pat was not about to change her position or leave her church. It would be unfair to ask Alan to start going to church with her or accept her beliefs unless he genuinely wanted to. Regardless of what position he might take in the future, it was obvious that Alan needed to modify his attitude in some respect to give Pat a greater feeling of security in what was so meaningful to her. Some of their comments were as follows: Pat said, "We do not agree on this at all. I need religion and wish to have it as part

of my life. Alan has no religion and mocks me for needing it. He said it was for weak people who needed something to lean on—and he needed nothing other than himself. I miss the discussion of religion and having prayers at home." *Alan:* "Because I don't believe, there is some difficulty, but I don't feel this is a major problem. There is no disagreement as to the importance of religion when we raise children."

7. *Pat's need for affection and encouragement.* In the course of time, Alan's disdain for Pat's beliefs, romantic inclinations, and gay manner lowered her self-esteem to a point at which she began to feel a deep sense of insecurity. She needed and would always need more than an average amount of positive reinforcement. She was starved for affection—loving words and touches—someone to tell her she was loved and needed. A portion of their comments in this area were: *Pat:* "When I want attention I have to ask for it." *Alan:* "Pat feels the marriage should be as romantic as the courtship, but I feel your attitude changes as you get older. I know I have much improvement to make in this area." *Pat:* "He doesn't say, 'I love you,' and I have to initiate the goodbye kiss. He never brings me anything except at Christmas and on my birthday." *Alan:* "I will show the love that I have for Pat and work hard to give her the love, understanding and affection she needs. I want to improve our method of communication. I need to show Pat how much I love her and show her I'm interested in what she does and that I need her very much. I need to accept more of the responsibilities of the marriage. I know now better what it takes to satisfy my wife. I will try not to judge so quickly when I feel she is in error."

These were the critical areas agreed upon in the counseling sessions. They were discussed thoroughly, and Pat and Alan understood what they meant and their implications. It seemed that the scales were tipped in favor of Pat. It must be remembered, however, that it was she who was dissatisfied and unhappy about the marriage. Alan knew the marriage was not functioning as it should, but he would not have demanded a separation and he never said he had ceased to love Pat. The counseling process was difficult for both of them. Pat was motivated only by a sense of duty. She said, "I feel blank. I don't want to be married now. The door isn't shut to a reconciliation but it can't come now." She tried to outline what was good about the marriage for the counselor.

Alan is a hard worker in his field of interest and strives for the best. He has a nice personality. He is generous, honest, considerate of people in general. He is law abiding, he is very intelligent and has great goals in life to accomplish in his field of work. Before marriage we took walks, watched T.V. together, loved to dance, went to all sports, etc. After marriage we got some enjoyment out of going to parties, playing bridge, going to dinner—but we have had so few experiences where we were happy together in the last two years that I can't list any. I am not sure that our marriage has been a success in any way. We have nothing in common together so therefore I feel that nothing is successful. We look nice together and we are an attractive couple and I think we both felt this. I think now that we were only reasonably happy for the first nine months of our marriage and from that time on we lost companionship and happiness. I think that Alan realizes what the problems have been in our marriage but not how deeply they affected me. If you compare our marriage with others, I'm sure you will find many are worse. But what is most important to me in a marriage cannot be found in ours.

In middle November, Alan wrote this in his evaluation of the progress during the first month when each visited the counselor separately.

I feel progress has been made since now she at least speaks to me, but we have lots of things to work out. I feel like a man hanging on to a rope over a cliff and Pat is standing on the cliff with a knife. If I say anything wrong she will cut the rope; however, she might cut the rope anyway. It's a perplexing situation. I love her very much and I don't want to lose her. I know I have several areas for improvement and I am willing to work hard to be a better husband. We do have different personalities and we both need to accept our differences. I can accept Pat as she is but I don't think I could become as "bubbly" as she is. I know I have to change some, but don't you think we both need to change?

In Pat's evaluation of the situation after the first month, she wrote:

After reading what we have both written I feel maybe a little bit more unhappy than before, for I feel that we have lost so much that we could have made a wonderful life on. Alan seems to see more of the problems than he ever did before. I do feel that he is not mature in many ways and that this hasn't changed up to now. He shows that he would like very much to undo things that have been wrong and I am glad that he sees many of these things. I don't think he fully understands my feelings and I don't think he really wants to. The times I have talked with him on the phone he sounded like a very immature, lost young man.

As for the way I feel—I would give anything if I had believed I could have gone to a marriage counselor a year and a half ago. At that time we had enough understanding between us that I think it would have done wonders. I loved Alan very much but slowly he pushed me away and little by little I feel he killed the love I had for him. I have had a very empty feeling for about three months and feel nothing but emptiness and unhappiness at this point. I could never live the way I did again and right now I don't feel anything toward Alan but sorrow, hurt, and like I have lost an awful lot. I do not feel any anger or bitterness but I do not feel love, either. There is just nothing and this is a horrible experience for me. In church today the minister asked us to stop and pray for one thing that we really wanted—and in my mind there was nothing except the desire for happiness—but I couldn't pray for something when I don't know any longer what I want.

If the love I once had for Alan could be restored, I don't know it right now.

It would take a long time and he is in a hurry for he does not yet understand. He has called several times and he doesn't realize how I feel when he calls. He is grasping for something I don't have to give and I become very upset for to me he is a wonderful person and I remember my love for him and feel much loss and sadness.

After he understands this, I would be willing to meet with him for counseling in your office. I will be leaving for Thanksgiving on a Wednesday morning and if you think we should get together before then, I will. I know it will be an upsetting experience for us both and I don't want to hurt him for we both feel that now.

Pat and Alan came to the counselor's office near the middle of November. After discussing what might be done in the months to come, Pat made it known that she needed a number of sessions apart from Alan, and he agreed. Pat felt that she was in no way ready to discuss matters with Alan, as she had so much to do to get her own mind and emotions straightened out. A problem that Alan had as a result was that of maintaining patience. He couldn't understand why it had to take so long, but there was nothing he could do about it—Pat was determined to take her time.

Pat made it clear in her first sessions with the counselor that the marriage hadn't always been this way. In answer to the question, would you marry him if you had the opportunity to do it all over again? she replied:

We were head over heels in love and if I felt that way again, I guess I would marry him again. He is a different person to me now. After marriage he seemed to think that romance was over, that kissing except in bed was silly—that he shouldn't hold my hand or put his arm around me, or do something special once in awhile. These were all things he did before marriage and he began slowly to live the way he does now. I guess we got married too quickly and we were too much in love to see things that have come up since, but I feel that there has been a definite change in him. At the time of our marriage I felt sure I should marry him.

Apparently the brief courtship and engagement did not give them the opportunity to know each other and to test the relationship adequately. Albert Ellis's words, "goofing" or "drifting," describe accurately what happened in the first years of their marriage and eventually brought them to a real impasse.

Pat seemed to need to go back and relive some of the experiences of the past and try to understand them. Why had Alan changed, and why had she changed? At what point did love disappear? The counselor helped them make the analysis of the marriage, examine the complaints each had made and the needs each expressed, which eventually led to a better understanding about what had happened. It appeared that a healthy kind of objectivity was developing in both of them. They reacted to their individual discussions with the counselor with an increasing amount of understanding and maturity.

Although Alan was ready long before, it was not until March that Pat announced that now she could feel comfortable with Alan in the remaining counseling sessions. Working together, Pat, Alan, and the marriage counselor made a thorough review of all the work done separately and discussed what each felt was important. It was interesting to note the changed attitude each had toward the other. From this new perspective, Pat had come into a new appreciation of the fine qualities her husband possessed. Perhaps their personality characteristics might blend in a complementary fashion now. By April 5th, Pat was able to say, "During the last four weeks I feel I am beginning to love Alan again. But I am scared about the future a little. Suppose we got back together again and the same things happened to our marriage as before!" In the sessions to come, it would be necessary to restore Pat's and Alan's trust and confidence in each other and in the relationship. It was interesting to see the revival of love that Pat had declared earlier had vanished, leaving her blank and empty. Here is evidence that a person may feel that love is gone, when in reality it is waiting only to be reawakened with the proper stimulus. This may not happen in all cases, but it did in this one.

Following is a summary of work done in specific counseling sessions.

April 5. During this session, Alan's negativism was the main topic for discussion. Alan had a tendency to say, "No" as his first response to any suggestion. It was agreed that in the future, if he had doubts, he would respond to a suggestion that Pat might make by saying, "I would like to think about it." When going to a party, Alan would tend to complain and say he didn't think he was going to enjoy it. In the future he would take an attitude of "I might enjoy this party." Since, in the past, Pat had made nearly all of the suggestions about what to do and where to go, in the future Alan would assume at least half the responsibility for suggesting things in which they might participate together. His taking the initiative would relieve him of the pressure of having to respond to so many suggestions, and make Pat more comfortable in not having to feel she was doing all the suggesting. Alan's favorite expression for Pat and her idealism, "You are just a 'do-gooder,' " infuriated her. It was agreed that from now on he would try to understand her desire to help others as an admirable quality from which he as well as others would benefit. The contracts Pat and Alan made at this session helped to enhance the relationship.

April 28. During this session, Pat's tendency to be too busy was discussed. Pat responded to the discussion by suggesting that she could calm down a bit and not give Alan the feeling that she was continually restless and wanting to go someplace for activity or entertainment. Pat's energy and emotional nature motivated her to be overly aggressive, intense, talkative, and desirous of being continually active. She agreed to watch this tendency and attempt to be more relaxed, a better listener, and more rational in her approach to matters arising between Alan and her. It was noted that Pat had an adventurous spirit which caused her to want to try new things and delve into unexplored areas. Alan was conservative and satisfied with the status quo.

After considerable discussion, an agreement was reached on how to compromise this difference.

Late in March, arrangements had been made for Pat and Alan to see each other in settings other than the counselor's office. Perhaps the relationship could be reconstructed in part by their starting to date as any couple might after their initial meeting. With the counselor Alan planned the first date. Since Pat liked good food, soft lights, and sweet music, plans were made to go to a very nice restaurant with plenty of atmosphere. The next day they reported that they had had a miserable time, finding the situation strained and communication difficult. It was then decided that a less formal atmosphere was more conducive to getting to feel comfortable together. Short sessions over coffee met the need more satisfactorily. Gradually this procedure evolved into situations where they danced together, had fun, laughed together, and became increasingly friendly.

In the meantime, they worked with the counselor on personality compatibility, a difficult matter in their marriage. An effort was made to preserve the best qualities of both, so that they did not feel they were losing their individuality. A better understanding of each other was developed, together with agreements for modification of objectionable characteristics.

A matter of considerable encouragement to both Pat and Alan was the fact that each was making an all-out effort to meet the other's needs. Alan came to realize that he must give more attention to Pat's need for affection and encouragement. Even though he was not completely convinced that a husband should be attentive and affectionate to the point of carrying on a "courtship" relationship with his wife, he decided to change his time schedule in order to spend more time with Pat, engage in some of the activities in which she was especially interested, and begin to learn to appreciate the kind of person she was. Table conversation was considered. It was Alan's habit to eat his meal in ten minutes and then get to the newspaper or television. It was agreed that mealtime should be enjoyed in a leisurely fashion with pleasant and unhurried conversation. Pat, in turn, came to see that Alan tended to be a practical person who was prone to neglect such things as manners, compliments, little assurances, and the opportunity for relaxation and informal good times. She would try to be more patient and less demanding, and make it easier for him to be a companion to her.

Pat recognized that she had withdrawn from Alan in order to construct a life of her own more acceptable to her idea of what life ought to be. In this way, she shut Alan out of her life and locked the door. Their life together would have to be rebuilt, first in small ways as the months went by. During their months of separation, Pat had had an opportunity to see Alan's positive characteristics in a new light, and to see possibilities in the relationship that eluded her during the last months they had lived together. The "dates" they were having created a new climate in which good feelings of the past were revived and new positive feelings were generated. Hope and trust were revived in both through these get-togethers.

Religion was discussed after Alan had read some recommended books on the subject. Alan found in his reading that the best in science and religion are not incompatible, and that there are values in religion quite beyond that of supplying reinforcement for the weak. Pat came to better understand the way a person thinks from a scientific orientation and how articles of religious belief need to be tested by rational thought and historical perspective.

They did not feel that the malfunctioning of their sexual relationships in the latter months of their marriage would be a great problem when they reunited, because it was caused, for the most part, by the poor interpersonal relationships which had developed. Both were interested in reading more about sexuality in marriage and discussing it together for suggestions for improvement. If everything went well, they said, they would consider having their first child in the near future.

Pat's sensitivity had been a problem, particularly in view of Alan's tendency to be critical of everything, which he thought was the proper stance for a person in the scientific field to take. Did he tend to over-intellectualize, forgetting that the "heart has reasons that reason knows not of"? An agreement was reached that Alan would use his critical faculties with restraint around Pat, and she would learn how to take honest and frank criticism without feeling hurt or threatened, or harboring resentment afterwards.

Counseling sessions continued with ever-growing signs of progress and productivity. Once Alan believed there was hope for reunion, patience became easier for him, and he worked with renewed energy and enthusiasm. Pat responded with new affection for Alan. Near the middle of May, Pat and Alan approached the marriage counselor and expressed the hope that he might encourage them to go back to living together within a few days. The counselor countered with, "You are very nearly ready, would you be willing to wait just a few weeks more?" They were surprised at this request, but willing to comply with it. In the remaining sessions their efforts were stimulated and intensified to do everything they could to make the reunion the best possible. In the first week of June, they again approached the counselor with the suggestion that they go back together on June 16th. He agreed that this was a good idea. They then asked if he would arrange a wedding ceremony for them, so they could renew their vows to each other in a meaningful way. June 16th was a happy day for three people, at least: Pat, Alan, and the marriage counselor.

What about this marriage—would it work? It would and it did. Several years later the counselor received a letter from Pat telling how happy they were, and how grateful they were for help in getting their marriage functioning again. They were continuing to work on the marriage to improve it, and the relationship was getting better all the time. And she added, "I'm pregnant, and that ought to tell you something."

What caused the problems in this marriage to develop to the extent that the marriage almost ceased to function? Perhaps the greatest reason was the immaturity of the couple at the time of their marriage. Alan was nineteen years and nine months old, and Pat was nineteen years and eleven months. They were not ready to negotiate the numerous obstacles in their path. They were different kinds of people, and if their differences were to be bridged, it would take a considerable amount of skill, maturity, and ability, none of which were present in sufficient amounts to keep the relationship functioning and the marriage stable. So, because of the many mistakes committed, compounded by neglect and poor communication, the marriage took a downhill course.

Should they have married in the first place? Who is to say? There is a division of opinion on the part of various persons who have studied the case history. Most agree that they should have waited. Pat and Alan agreed that they were right in marrying each other, and if they had to do it all over, they would have chosen each other. Many things they would have done differently, however. They would have waited until they were several years older, then married with a deeper understanding of who they were and how best to relate the qualities and characteristics they brought to the marriage. They recognized that a sound, healthy marriage is not something that just happens. It is the product of two dedicated creative artists working together day by day with love and care upon a design ever changing, ever incomplete.

And now they have that opportunity. And they will always be grateful that they did not say *goodbye to love too soon.*

Before you say goodbye to love (and get a divorce), consider the alternatives. Is a divorce what you really want? Divorce is an unpleasant and often devastating experience. It leaves a lasting effect on you, your family, your friends and community. Would salvaging your marriage be a preferable alternative?

Find out what is wrong with your marriage. Many people are unhappy but don't know why. Be willing to face the facts.

No marital problem is caused by one partner only. Both are at fault, though one may be more at fault than the other. But blaming your partner is unproductive. Ask where you are at fault and begin to work on that. At least you can stop being a problem and start being a part of the solution.

Be skeptical about the possibility that a divorce will solve your problems, or that in another marriage you will find the perfect partner and the happiness of which you dream. Remember that all marriages have problems and conflicts. There is no perfect marriage or perfect marriage partner. If a marriage is to function well, it will do so because two people have learned to meet difficulties and differences successfully, and have carefully nurtured love and companionship.

In some instances two people formerly married regret their divorce and wish they might marry each other again. Second marriages are frequently disappointing in that one trades one set of problems for another.

Make up your mind that you will not act hastily. Some people move toward a divorce after a major quarrel. What you decide to do needs to be done carefully, intelligently, and over a considerable period of time.

Most people think of a marriage that is not functioning properly in terms of all the unpleasant factors. Make a list of the good times you have had with your spouse, beginning with the wedding day. Your spouse has some positive and admirable characteristics. Make a list of them. Have you tried to encourage these characteristics, or have you sometimes kept them from functioning?

If life is too unpleasant in the marriage, consider an agreed-upon separation. Try living apart long enough to regain your perspective on the marriage. Perhaps then you will see yourself and your partner in a different light and will be better able to make the adjustments necessary for a more compatible relationship.

If after living apart (consider six months or more), and getting help from a competent marriage counselor, you find the relationship has not improved, then you might consider a permanent separation. You will need assistance to help get the most satisfactory divorce available to you both, leaving as few injuries and scars as possible. Don't let the divorce proceedings develop into a contest between two antagonists. A "no fault" dissolution is preferable, if the state in which you live allows it.

When you are not feeling well physically, you go to a doctor for a diagnosis and help that will restore you to health. If your marriage is ailing, why not do the same? Consult a minister, rabbi, priest, marriage counselor, family counseling service, or conciliation court, and ask for assistance in dealing with your problems. Go together as a couple, if at all possible. Follow the suggestions of your counselor as you would those of a physician.

The marriage counselor. Who is he? In what way is it possible for him to help you?

He or she is a professional who has met rigid educational and competency requirements, and where the law requires it, is licensed by the state. He has had training and experience in the areas of human relations, family interaction, and the dynamics of behavior. He is skilled in the techniques of marriage and family counseling. He has had adequate experience in his vocation and is committed to a code of vocational ethics. He is a member of a professional organization of marriage and family counselors. If you wish, he will explain his background and experience, methods of counseling and fees.

He will not tell you what to do nor will he make decisions for you. He will help you make your own decisions in the best possible way.

He prefers to work with husband and wife together. Some sessions may be held with each spouse separately, but do come together for the first meeting if at all possible.

First, an attempt will be made to find in what ways the marriage is not functioning and the causes.

The counselor will want to know how willing each spouse is to work to get the relationship functioning.

If both want to work, then the counselor will discuss a plan to assist the process of restoring health to the marriage.

He will help reduce tension and conflict in the relationship in order that the process of understanding and reconciliation will have a greater opportunity to function.

He will help you modify certain personal characteristics and behavior patterns that may be hindering a relationship from functioning properly.

He will work with you to improve communications.

He will help you to develop new patterns of relating, loving, understanding, and meeting each other's needs.

He will help you make contracts with each other for new ways of helping the marriage to function more smoothly and more efficiently. He will aid you to improve your sexual relations, financial management, nurturing of children, and relating to friends and relatives. He will also refer you to other resources for help, if necessary.

If you decide after careful evaluation that the marriage will not work, he will assist you in considering and attaining the best possible alternative.

If you wish assistance in obtaining competent marriage counseling, consult your clergyman, physician, family counseling agency, or write: American Association for Marriage and Family Therapy, 924 W. Ninth, Upland, California 91786, (714) 981-0888.

PART V

Interlude

CHAPTER THIRTEEN

Let's Love Each Other
in an Unconventional Way

Jenny had dated Rob for less than six months when he proposed that they live together. Neither had made much of a commitment when they moved in together. Rob had told Jenny that he was very fond of her and that living together would be a way of making their relationship closer. She hoped that it might lead to a marriage later on, but she didn't feel that she ought to press the issue at the beginning. As months passed by, Jenny became uneasy because Rob made no mention of marriage. He made it clear to her that he did not consider their relationship exclusive and that each should be free to date others. When Jenny discovered that she was pregnant, the situation became more complicated. Rob said he was willing to marry her at that point, but that he was not sure that he would stay with her permanently. Also, Rob seemed to be developing an interest in another woman whom he was seeing frequently. Jenny had a miscarriage in the second month of her pregnancy. Soon after this, she left Rob, feeling that there was no future for her in such a relationship.

What comes after you say, "I love you"? Not always a marriage. Some unconventional arrangement may be suggested to carry out the implications of love for the couple. Or there may be an unconventional marriage. Some feel this is the only answer to the large number of divorces taking place in our culture. Some feel that the traditional marriage and family as we have known them have outgrown their usefulness and can no longer function in modern society. Mervyn Cadwallader writes his opinion on this matter:

Contemporary marriage is a wretched institution. It spells the end of voluntary affection, of love freely given and joyously received. Beautiful romances are transmitted into dull marriages; eventually the relationship becomes constricting, corrosive, grinding and destructive. The beautiful love affair becomes a bitter contract.[1]

Freddie and Rose came to their marriage counselor with an unusual problem. Freddie had been reading a book on open marriage, and a chapter had motivated him to suggest a new style of living to Rose, who became furious at the suggestion. Now they wanted to discuss it with the marriage counselor. Freddie outlined his proposal. Why not have an arrangement in which they would live together as husband and wife, yet agree to have affairs with others as the occasion might arise? He felt a strong affection for Rose, but other women attracted him also, and he said he would like to establish relationships with them. He could see no reason why this should disturb his marriage with Rose.

Rose felt differently. Two people in a marriage should be intimately related only to each other, she felt. "I could not tolerate any other women relating to Freddie. Besides I have no desire, nor will I ever, to have an affair with another man." For the moment, at least, there was an irreconcilable difference between the ways they wanted their marriage to go. Freddie wanted to develop an unconventional marriage, while Rose wanted to maintain a traditional one.

Jed and Andrea had been living together for six years. They enjoyed being together and their relationship functioned smoothly. Both were in their late twenties, and they discussed the possibility of having a child. They agreed that they would be uncomfortable having a child out of wedlock, so they decided to get married. The wedding and the ceremony were conventional in every way, with friends and relatives present.

Roxanne and Mark agreed before they were married that Roxanne would retain her maiden name. She would have a career and finance the home they would establish. Mark would stay home most of the time and do the cooking and housework. He also has some desire to write. There are some legal problems about using different names and there is confusion in doing business, but they are trying to work out these matters. Both seem to enjoy the arrangement, and Mark does not object to his wife's name being different from his. He admits that his role as a husband is a bit unconventional, but he is comfortable with it.

Little by little, couples are beginning to enter into unconventional ways of saying, "I love you." In this way, some hope to save themselves from the routine boredom into which so many marriages subside. Others feel that they must find ways of relieving women from a traditional marriage in which they are enslaved by housekeeping duties and meaningless routine. Will deviations from the traditional forms of marriage and family slow down the rapidly accelerating divorce rate? What sort of changes might make marriage more compatible with contemporary conditions? Certainly, marriage roles need to be more fluid. The rigidity of our traditional notions of what is appropriate for men to do, in contrast to what women do, in performing their marital roles, needs to give way to more flexible concepts. Society should not frown on what a husband and wife feel contributes to the welfare of their marriage, even though it differs from the more conventional forms.

A dramatic change has taken place already in the shift from the extended to the nuclear family. From the beginning of this century to the present, we have changed from a nation of rural families to one of city-dwellers. When people lived on farms and in small towns, their families might well have consisted of husband, wife, children, a grandmother, grandfather, or both. Aunts and uncles lived nearby and cousins abounded. When sons and daughters married and moved, they did not go far. When the migration to cities began, the extended family started to disappear. Today we have, for the most part, the nuclear family, consisting only of father, mother, and children. Other relatives may be many miles away.

Whether this change is an improvement or not is a matter of controversy. If members of an extended family related well together, there must have been advantages in the mutual support and satisfying fellowship they shared. If they did not get along, or if there was interference or an attempt to dominate on the part of some members or member, then distance from them would have been beneficial. Speaking from my own personal experience, I would say that I miss the experiences I had in a modified extended family in my youth. My wife and I now live at considerable distances from our relatives, who are scattered all over the country. No one of our three children is closer than five hundred miles. A great number of communal groups have sprung up in this country in the past decade. Perhaps this is the result of people turning away from mass society and a depersonalized world to a more intimate setting, where they do find the support and close relationships they desire.

We should not close our minds to innovations in marriage and family forms if they result from the efforts of serious people seeking a better way of life. Even though we may not want to engage in some of the more radical experiments, we can learn from them, and benefit by discovering what is missing in our more conventional marriages. In this way, conventional marriages can be renewed by attempting to supply missing ingredients that are sought by people engaging in the unconventional forms.

Arthur Bestor begins his book describing some of the early experiments in communal living in this country: "Of all the freedoms for which America stood, none was more significant for history than the freedom to experiment with new practices and new institutions."[2] In the spirit of this kind of freedom let us look at some contemporary attempts to find new ways of expressing the love relationship.

The trial marriage. The trend among young people, college students, at least, is to experiment with living with a prospective spouse to test the relationship. There has been a remarkable rise in the number of women who are willing to have premarital sexual intercourse with the men with whom they have a commitment for marriage. In my university classes in marriage education in 1969, 54 percent of the women said they were willing to have sexual intercourse with the men they expected to marry. In 1975, this figure rose to 82 percent. The willingness of men in these classes to have this kind of a relationship with the women they expected to marry has remained consistently high, with some increase, 75 percent in 1969 and 96 percent in 1975. When asked in these same classes if they would like to have the experience of living with a man before deciding definitely to marry him, if this were socially acceptable, 120 women out of 223, 54 percent, replied in the affirmative in 1972; 151 out of 235, 64 percent, in 1973; 150 out of 225, 67 percent, in 1975. The number of women interested in this kind of relationship has been steadily rising. The percentage of men interested, over the three-year period, has remained consistently above 80 percent.

In a small class consisting mostly of women in a California university in the summer of 1974, 23 out of 24 women replied in the affirmative to the question: "Would you live with someone you are considering marrying if it were socially approved?" However, 20 said they would do so, even if it were not socially approved.

According to the United States census, the number of unmarried couples living together rose from 17,000 in 1960 to 143,000 in 1970. No doubt these are conservative figures, as many such cases go unreported. While marriages rose 10 percent from 1960 to 1970, couples cohabiting without being married officially, rose 700 percent.

Most of the young people who are interested in this kind of cohabitation say that it is an attempt to test the proposed marriage before it begins. They would like to test out the relationship before making a final decision, so that if it does not work out, they can withdraw without having to go through the process of a divorce.

Back in the 1920's, Judge Ben Lindsey suggested the "companionate marriage" as a possible solution to the problems young people were having with marriages ending in divorce. The idea was revived in a more comprehensive form in 1966 by anthropologist Margaret Mead, who suggested the possibility of having a marriage in two steps: an *individual marriage,* binding together two people only; and a *parental marriage* in which children would be born and the couple would be committed to a permanent relationship. She explained:

Individual marriage would give two very young people a chance to know each other with a kind of intimacy that does not usually enter into a brief love affair, and so it would help them to grow into each other's life—and allow them to part without the burden of misunderstood intentions, bitter recriminations, and self destructive guilt. . . . [It] would be a serious commitment, entered into in public, validated and protected by law and, for some, by religion, in which each partner would have a deep and continuing concern for the happiness and well being of the other.[3]

If the relationship grows, and the couple believes they have a marriage that will last and provide a healthy context in which children can live and develop, then the marriage can be taken into the second stage, the *parental marriage*. This stage would be entered by way of a license and a ceremony with vows implying an intended permanent relationship with such children as might come to it. Dr. Mead felt that by the time the couple is ready for this second stage, they would be far more ready for a lasting marriage than they ever could have been at the first stage. They would be more mature, skilled, responsible, and financially secure, and their goals would be more carefully determined. Children born to such a marriage would have an excellent chance of growing in a stable situation in which continuity among themselves, their parents, and grandparents could be maintained.

Although one might expect that a great many of the individual marriages would be dissolved, it is very possible that fewer divorces would occur in the parental marriages. In this case, the tragedy of the broken home would be avoided, and children would not be the victims of the confusion and frustration of trying to relate to parents living apart, and grandparents who are more remote and inaccessible. There is another factor that must be considered carefully. The tendency today among young people is to enter into some form of cohabitation before marriage. There is no reason to believe that this will not continue to grow into a practice for most young couples. In a great many instances, cohabitation is entered into with no ground rules and very little common understanding as to what the relationship means. As a result, many people are being hurt rather than helped by the experience. Would it not be better to enter into such a plan as the two-step marriage, which would be socially approved and protected from many of the hazards of present forms of cohabitation? This question needs to be faced realistically and intelligently, and answered for the sake of a society that is suffering from the devastating effects of broken homes and shattered lives.

Virginia Satir agrees that there is something about the marriage contract as it now stands that does not encourage a periodic review and evaluation, and allow for a socially accepted termination if the relationship is no longer functioning. The present contract

is made with the apparent assumption that the conditions present at its inception will continue without change for eternity. This asks people to be wiser than they can possibly be. It is made at a time in the lives of the respective parties when they have the least preparation in fact with which to make this contract. . . . The current western marriage contract has been derived from a chattel economic base, which stresses possessing. This frequently gets translated into duty and becomes emotional and sometimes literal blackmail. The quality of joy is lost in the game of scoreboard. "Who loses, who wins, and who is on top?" The result is the grimness I referred to earlier.[4]

These are harsh words, but they come from a person who is deeply committed to finding ways of making marriage an institution in which people can grow into human beings free to be creative and loving. Dr. Satir has many suggestions for reform in marriage to make it more enjoyable, satisfying, and productive. This might be done even within the conventional marriage as we know it, if attitudes could be changed and a new sense of freedom and openness could be experienced. She feels that a socially approved apprenticeship might help a couple decide whether their fantasies of each other and of marriage matched reality. She and others question whether many modern couples have the capacity to live together successfully for fifty years or more.

We have used the term "sprinters" and "long-distance runners" in this book to illustrate that some people seem to be able to run only a short distance in marriage, while others can make it for fifty years or more. Should some sort of allowance be made for the "sprinters"? What about a five- or ten-year contract that would expire unless renewed through mutual agreement by both parties in the marriage? While theoretically such a contract may seem to have possibilities, we have found very few college students who would be willing to try it. There is something about the renewable contract that does not appeal to their concept of the way they want to enter a marriage relationship.

Another unconventional form of marriage is that in which a couple participates in a commune. The commune is not new to contemporary society but has existed in one form or another since the early settlers came to this country. There are various types of communes: religious; secular; those in which monogamy is practiced while food, shelter, and fellowship are shared; those involving group marriage, in which all share in sexual relations and produce offspring. The spread of the commune may be an effort to meet the needs of the nuclear family for the close fellowship of an extended family. The commune promises fellowship and a shared community. It is also a part of the back-to-the-simple-life move-ment, in which a group operates a farm or shares in weaving, furniture manufacture, or other craft enterprises. The average life of a commune is short. It seems to satisfy the needs of most people for a short period of time. Albert Ellis feels that group marriage will be desired by a very limited number of people:

In practice, marriage tends to be monogamous (that is, a man and a woman living fairly permanently, though not necessarily forever, only with each other and their own children) all over the world, even when other forms of mating are legally allowed. The chances are that this kind of practice will largely con-tinue, but that a sizeable minority of individuals will devise interesting varia-tions on this major theme or else live in thoroughly non-monogamic unions, including group marriage.[5]

It is obvious that some couples are looking for "interesting variations on this major theme" and are doing so in a variety of ways. James W. Ramey, writing in the *Journal of Sexual Research,* reports on studies he made of eighty couples who were, for the most part, from academic, pro-fessional, or managerial classifications, and all looking for ways of en-riching their marriages through innovations.

It was not necessarily the intent of these eighty couples to form communes or group marriages, although several did result from their activities. They seemed more intent on "hashing out" the actual ground rules and decision structure required for setting up alternatives to marriage at varying levels of complexity. Some couples were content to stop at the level of developing intimate friend-ships. Others were willing to take the additional step of adding propinquity to this relationship and forming some kind of commune, and take the final step of cathectic commitment, i.e., actually establishing multiple pair-bonds. Many couples found that they were either uncomfortable with the level of complexity required or "were still looking for the right people" with whom to become in-volved in some type of relationship more complex than dyadic marriage.[6]

Of one thing we can be quite certain: people now expect much more of marriage in terms of satisfaction and fulfillment than our parents and grandparents did. While they may have settled for a situation in which they could achieve community respectability, financial security, a place to rear children during the early years, and a place to avoid loneliness in the later years, now there is a demand for a situation in which human relationships can be vital and stimulating, there is a strong sense of per-sonal growth and development and, with the passing years, a deep sense of satisfaction that married life has been gratifying and worthwhile. When this level has not been met, people have been disappointed. Some have obtained divorces, and others have looked for new forms in which their expectations might be met. In the years ahead, we shall see much experimentation in the field of marriage patterns and relationships. We shall learn much from these experimentations and the research that will be done on the results. And we hope we shall know better how to bring marriage from its present state of confusion and distress to a point where it can provide stability, satisfaction, and human growth for the families of tomorrow.

REFERENCES

1. Mervyn Cadwallader, "Changing Social Mores," *Current* (February 1967), pp. 52–59.

2. Arthur Bestor, *Backwoods Utopias.* Philadelphia: University of Pennsylvania Press, 1950, p. 1.

3. Margaret Mead, "Marriage in Two Steps," *Redbook Magazine,* Vol. 27 (July 1966), p. 48. Copyright 1966 by McCall Corporation.

4. Virginia Satir, "Marriage as a Human-Actualizing Contract," in Herbert A. Otto (ed.), *The Family in Search of a Future.* New York: Appleton-Century-Crofts, 1970, pp. 62, 63.

5. Albert Ellis, "Group Marriage: A Possible Alternative?", in Herbert A. Otto (Ed.), *The Family in Search of a Future,* p. 97.

6. James W. Ramey, "Emerging Patterns of Behavior in Marriage: Deviations or Innovations?" *Journal of Sexual Research,* Volume 8, No. 1.

PART VI

Keeping the Healthy Marriage Healthy

CHAPTER FOURTEEN

In Love—in Conflict
—a Growing Process

In the earlier chapters we dealt with the basic characteristics of the healthy marriage. We know that each partner needs to express in some measure the qualities of dependability, trustworthiness, warmth and affection, generosity and unselfishness, mental and emotional maturity, honesty and openness, persistence, durability, the ability to meet crises, and the will to succeed. In addition, factors must be present that help the couple to be compatible. They need to admire and like each other. Their personalities need to relate harmoniously. They should share a number of interests, hobbies, and leisure-time activities. Their role concepts should be agreeable to both. Values, goals, and religious beliefs need to be compatible. Other important factors in marital health are the development of marriage skills and the ability to work together to accomplish important goals. These skills and accomplishments involve the ability of the partners to communicate and negotiate, adapt and adjust, meet each other's needs, perform their roles adequately, and attain the goals they have established. Underlying these characteristics are situational factors that affect a marriage: background circumstances, education, economic status, geographical location, health, children, in-laws, vocational status, length of the marriage, and social conditions.

The couples in our select group function well in most of these categories. Our studies show that in certain areas these couples reveal special ability in keeping their marriages healthy. The first of these is their ability to deal with crises and conflict.

Crises are a part of everyone's life and should be expected. Births, illnesses, accidents, deaths, changes in jobs and locations, financial reverses, and critical problems come to all. For some, these present occasional difficulties; for others, they seem to be an almost daily occurrence. Some people tend to think of conflict as something to be avoided. Some couples enter marriage believing that they are going to have a relationship without conflict. Two things need to be said to these people. First, conflict arises in all marriages and should. It represents a difference in points of view, interests, ways of doing things, personalities, life-styles, habits and manners, beliefs, values, and goals. No two people are alike in everything, and life would be boring and uninteresting if it were otherwise. Second, conflict can serve a useful purpose. It can clarify differences that need to be resolved. It can provide a way of settling issues that need to be negotiated. While seeming to divide people on the surface, it may be a unifying factor on a deeper level. It will help people "in love" to arrive at a solution that will serve the best interests of both.

There are times when a spouse needs to protest an action on the part of the partner, or refuse to go along with it. This protest or refusal may be motivated by a smoldering discontent which needs to be aired. There may be a breakdown in communications which a conflict can help get started again. A couple may feel they are drifting apart. Confronting each other in a conflicting situation may bring them closer together—even stimulate love feelings again.

The couples we have studied in our select group have learned to accept and use conflict to improve their relationships. It is not the presence of conflict or problems or crises that destroys a marriage; it is the absence of the willingness or the ability to meet these things constructively.

Karen and Bob, a couple in our select group, were discussing the effect of problems on their marriage. Bob commented that, at first, they thought they were lucky not to have the problems other couples were having. Then they realized that theirs were about the same as those of their friends, but they were meeting them in a manner that made them seem less disturbing. Karen explained it this way: "It's your basic attitude that makes the difference. First we say, 'Let's work on it,' and secondly we know we can find a solution. We go at it knowing we have the ability, the skills and the attitude that we are going to find a solution."

When I asked her, "Why don't you get upset?" she replied, "Oh, we do. And sometimes we get angry, too. But we don't get loud or scream and yell. That's not our style. But we let each other know how we think and feel. If things are real tense, if at all possible, we stick with it until we feel comfortable in leaving each other."

Bob added, "We have hurt each other, but for the most part, we think there are better strategies. We had a round last night that got pretty thick. We stuck with it until we found some resolutions. And even though we were very angry, our overall positive regard and friendship for each other were not diminished or threatened by this." I asked, "How did you do this? What is the process?" Karen answered, "The very first step is getting it out on the table. And that is for me the most important matter. As a child I was not allowed to show anger. So, I had to learn how to express anger constructively. This is one of the growing areas in my life on which I've done a lot of work. I now know how to express my feelings constructively rather than the 'below the belt' kind of thing. It still takes me awhile to get it out on the table. I start out by being very rational and diplomatic. It takes a little while before I can open up the gate and let it out."

"The second step," Bob added, "is what we tried to do last night. We tried to discover what all the issues in our conflict were and bring them together into one. Then we went back and forth until we found a resolution." Karen interjected, "Lately we have been working on some skills to help us do this. It helps to know how to solve your problems. I have a better understanding now about how Bob will react under certain situations when I say or do something and by asking him to tell me how he feels, I am helped to understand. This way, I am more able to deal with Bob where he's really at, rather than on some ethereal plain." I asked Bob, "Do you have confidence now after thirteen years of marriage that you can meet any problem or conflict successfully?" "Yes, we do," he replied.

I have no doubt that they will continue to be successful in communicating and negotiating. As Karen pointed out, they are working on attitudes and methods that will help them transpose problems and conflicts into ways of helping them become more mature and closer together as marital partners. Bob made a point that is so important that it justifies repeating for emphasis. He said, "Even though we were very angry, our overall positive regard and friendship for each other were not diminished or threatened by this." Should not this attitude prevail in all marriages? Should not husband and wife be friends through all events and circumstances? What a difference this alone would make in marital relationships, where husbands and wives too often treat one another with contempt and hostility.

I have some negative feelings whenever *I* see the title of the book by George Bach and Peter Wyden, *The Intimate Enemy*. When one reads the book, one is not so sure that the authors think of husbands and wives as "enemies." But they do believe that intimates must fight.

Verbal conflict between intimates is not only acceptable, especially between husbands and wives; it is constructive and highly desirable. . . . The art of fighting right is exactly what we teach couples who come to us for marriage counseling. Our training methods are not simple and cannot be successfully applied by everyone. . . . When our trainees fight according to our flexible system of rules, they find that the natural tensions and frustrations of two people living together can be greatly reduced. Since they live with fewer lies and inhibitions and have discarded outmoded notions of etiquette, these couples are free to grow emotionally, to become more productive and more creative, as individuals in their own right and also as pairs.[1]

Though the authors picture spouses as "intimate enemies" "fighting" one another, they are very careful to define the nature of the fighting and the rules under which it is to take place. Some counselors and therapists advocate expressing anger and acting out aggressive feelings, believing that in so doing people get rid of inner hostility, bitterness, and resentment. Although no responsible counselor would encourage physical violence between two people in conflict, beating pillows, breaking inexpensive objects, or striking the ground with clubs might be recommended. Yelling, screaming, cursing, or attacking another with words such as, "I hate you," or "I would like to kill you," could be considered therapeutic. Some of the couples who have come to me for marriage counseling have tried these techniques. Not all have found these methods helpful. Much depends on the nature of the couple and their reaction to the particular method tried.

Rudolf Dreikurs thought there was danger in the "fighting" approach to conflict resolution. He writes,

Whenever any conflict arises, the first decision which both parties make—definitely, although unconsciously—is whether to use these incidents as an occasion to fight, for hurting and being hurt, or whether to try sincerely to solve the problem. If the tendency is to quarrel, there can be no solution before one of them checks this inclination. Here we meet one of the most important obstacles to married happiness: the general belief that something can be gained by fighting. So both blame and scold and get excited—and prepare the field for the next fight. They are less interested in finding a solution than in being "right". Winning or losing this one fight will not help. What would help is social feeling—the feeling of belonging together—which would make every conflict a common problem, not a question of what he wants or she wants. Social feeling creates a "we" of which he and she are each only one part. Conflicting interests become opportunities for asserting unity through mutual effort, establishing conditions which both can enjoy together. . . .[2]

Perhaps the current debate over the best method of solving marital conflicts is related to the various concepts of human nature. If one takes the Freudian viewpoint that people are naturally aggressive and need to get their aggressive feelings expressed, then he would be more apt to believe that husbands and wives are "intimate enemies" engaged in a power struggle. If, on the other hand, one accepts the Adlerian viewpoint that social feeling is the natural and potentially ideal expression of a human being, then he would be more receptive to the method of solving conflicts as a friendly confrontation between spouses trying to arrive at a position that would contribute to the best interests of both.

After many years as a marriage counselor observing couples engaging in conflict, I am skeptical of any method of solving conflicts that advocate active fighting, lashing out, cursing, physically hitting objects, letting the anger out without restraint, and uncontrollably ventilating hostile and aggressive feelings. Much damage can be the result of this approach, and the damage may have a permanent effect. A possible exception might be in the case of a skilled therapist working with a patient with severe guilt feelings about letting his true feelings be known by his family or significant acquaintances. Then such a method might break a dam blocking him from being honest and open, and free him to relate more effectively. To encourage most husbands and wives to "let it all out" might eventually increase aggressive behavior and habitual fits of anger in the marriage relationship.

Leonard Berkowitz, professor of psychology at the University of Wisconsin, has studied the phenomenon of aggression for many years. He maintains that when a person is emotionally aroused, he can act in a number of ways. He may fight, or run, or be angry, or sad, or happy. There is no "real" underlying emotion that must be expressed. I have tested this out and found it to be true. Recently, my car stalled on the way to my office early one morning. I was tempted to be disgusted and depressed, but I decided to say to myself, "These things happen and it should be no surprise that it happened to this old car. What should be done about it? Call your wife to meet you with the other car, and call Bob, our mechanic, to come pick up this one." In fifteen minutes, I was on my way with little damage done. Many times I have proved to myself that I can choose my emotion in a time of crisis or conflict. I further discovered that this better emotion tends to prevail when another crisis or conflict occurs. If anyone tells me it would be better to curse my car and get out and beat on the hood, I will simply reply, "Nonsense, I like this other way better." Is it not possible then for two people differing or displeased with each other, to choose the emotion with which to communicate and negotiate? I believe it is. There is an important matter to keep in mind, however: the process must be one in which honesty and openness are practiced.

Professor Berkowitz puts it this way:

The stimulus-response model suggests an important distinction between *verbal aggression* and *talking about one's feelings*. When a person attacks someone verbally (for example, when he curses "you bitch," or screams "I'll kill you" as Lowen recommends for his patients) he provides aggressive stimuli to himself and to his listeners. These stimuli, in turn, can evoke further aggressive reactions. However, if he merely describes his own emotion (saying, for example, "I'm boiling mad"), his remarks constitute somewhat less of an attack upon the other, except through implication, and might therefore be less likely to stimulate other aggressive acts. Telling someone that one is angry can be informative and perhaps beneficial. You let the other person know how he has affected you, and this might cause him to make amends or change his behavior. You give him cognitive feedback so that he is less likely to hurt you inadvertently again. With this knowledge, or better, with learning that he hadn't meant to attack you, you might even feel happier yourself.[3]

Berkowitz is telling us that it is not necessary to act out one's hostile or aggressive feelings, but that it is important to talk about one's feelings and describe one's emotional reactions without attacking others verbally or physically, directly or in fantasy. It is even possible to become mature enough and loving enough to choose what kind of attitude one is going to take in response to his partner's actions. If we look back on Bob and Karen's handling of conflict, we see two people who choose to react to each other, even in highly charged emotional situations, as friends with mutual respect for the dignity each has as a human being. They speak frankly and honestly, but there is never a doubt in the mind of either one about the other's love. Thus, they can stay with an intense and serious situation over a long period of time without suffering any severe damage to their self-esteem and eventually reach what they call their resolution. Having done so, they may enjoy the benefits of their accomplishment, feel closer together, and feel better prepared for any future situation in which they will need to communicate and negotiate again.

The danger, of course, lies in the possibility that a couple may handle conflict and the anger that goes with it in a very unproductive way, as many do. This led David Mace, one of our most competent and experienced marriage counselors, to title a talk given in St. Louis, to the Association of Couples for Marriage Enrichment, "Marital Intimacy and the Deadly Love-Anger Cycle." In his presentation he asked the question: "What is it above all else that prevents marriages from achieving the status most want?" He answered this by stating: "I believe it to be the inability to cope with anger." He explained that married couples formerly were not so intimately related and it was appropriate only for the husband to become angry, which was considered a masculine privilege. In the contemporary marriage, intimacy and equality are expected and practiced, but as couples come closer together in this new relationship, there is a tendency for the situation to "heat up" when there is a disagreement between spouses. If they move away from each other, to relieve the anger, the intimacy disappears. If they stay close together and handle the conflict poorly, the situation heats up more, and there is danger of burning up the love.

David Mace went on to explain that anger in itself is not unhealthy, but what people do with it is very important. Angry feelings do arise in most people from time to time. To suppress them and dam them back inside is painful and unhealthy. To vent them without restraint may summon up more and more anger, thus maintaining tension and making anger habitual. Anger motivates a person to strike. Love motivates a person to stroke. So one must recognize anger as inappropriate; then it may be dissolved or resolved.

Dr. Mace believes that couples should practice the art of managing anger in their marriage relationship. This may be done in three steps:

1. Acknowledge your anger. Say something like: "I'm getting angry!" Explain your feeling to the other person.
2. Renounce your anger as being inappropriate. "I don't like being angry with you." This expression may prevent retaliation and is an invitation to negotiate.
3. Ask your partner for help. "I want you to help me understand the situation and work with you toward a solution." This request for help is not likely to be turned down. It invites understanding and cooperation.[4]

As a marriage counselor, I have helped train couples to meet conflict and anger in a way similar to that described by Dr. Mace, and it does work. Couples learn that dealing with conflict is a part of married life that should be expected and that, when resolved in a mature and loving way, it leads to the growth and development of the couple and the marriage. As Vera and David Mace have written:

. . . it should be clear enough that the difference between a bad marriage and a good marriage is based, more than on any other factor, on whether or not the couple learn the process of mutual adjustment that enables them to resolve their differences and to enter into a close and intimate interpersonal relationship. In other words, learning this process is the key that opens the door to the companionship marriage.[5]

In addition to the proposals made by David and Vera Mace, I would like to add some suggestions for ground rules that might aid couples in the process of communicating during periods of tension and conflict. By observing these rules, a couple can keep the situation cool enough and remain rational enough to arrive at a suitable negotiated solution.

1. Try to keep in mind what the real issue is and confine the confrontation to this issue. Refuse to get sidetracked into other matters that have

little to do with the issue at hand. If you are hassling over finances, don't turn the discussion onto a dissatisfaction about one of the in-laws.

2. Keep your partner's point of view and feelings in mind. Keep asking yourself, if I were in my partner's shoes, how would I feel? This is a place for empathy.

3. Keep an open mind. Don't shut out the possibility of considering a point of view other than the one you have. Don't establish a fixed position from which you are unwilling to move.

4. Avoid using highly charged words or phrases. Don't engage in name calling (for a glaring example of this, see George and Martha in "Who's Afraid of Virginia Woolf?")

5. Don't hit "below the belt." Most people have a level of tolerance below which they cannot accept attacks. Learn what this is for your partner. On the other hand, don't wear your "belt" around your neck. Toughen yourself to be able to accept reasonable aggressive opposition to your ideas.

6. Be conscious of the tone of your voice. Your tonal expression may be more important in communicating your true feelings than the words you use. Your facial expression and body posture are also effective forms of non-verbal communication. Some people exaggerate these forms to a point where they convey meanings that the communicator does not intend, which may block the negotiating process.

7. It has been said that when a person faces an uncomfortable situation, he may resort to fight, flight, or freeze. If you must fight, fight fairly and don't run away, refuse to talk, or lock yourself in your room.

8. Give as much time to listening as to talking. Listening means attentively concentrating on what the other is saying and asking what it means. Let your periods of silence be for more than getting your breath and deciding on how you are going to counter your partner's arguments.

9. The point of your confrontation is not for one to win and the other to lose. It is to arrive at a point you can both live with. The end needs to serve the best interest of both. Little would be gained if you *won* the argument and lost a friend.

10. Show love even if there is no agreement. Agree to disagree, if necessary. Remember there is always time later to continue working on your differences. If you have not arrived at a solution this time, you may be able to do so later.

11. Have patience and continue to work on the art of communication. Bargaining and negotiating make up a skill that no one ever perfects. But as you work to become more skillful, life will become increasingly interesting and fulfilling, and your relationship with your spouse and others will be satisfying and rewarding.

REFERENCES

1. George R. Bach and Peter Wyden, *The Intimate Enemy,* New York: William Morrow & Co., 1969, p. 17.

2. Rudolf Dreikurs, *The Challenge of Marriage,* New York: Duell, Sloan and Pearce, 1946, p. 109.

3. Leonard Berkowitz, "The Case for Bottling Up Rage," *Psychology Today* (July 1973), p. 30.

4. David R. Mace, Address at the national meeting of the Association of Couples for Marriage Enrichment, St. Louis, Mo., October 31, 1974.

5. David Mace and Vera Mace, *We Can Have Better Marriages If We Really Want Them,* Nashville, Tenn.: Abingdon Press, 1974, p. 90.

CHAPTER FIFTEEN

The G.R.P.R. Principle

In Chapter 14, it was noted that in our study, the couples whose marriages functioned so well excelled in their ability to meet crises and conflicts. Another notable accomplishment was the way the marriage partners met each other's needs. In Chapter 7, attention was called to the importance of what marriage can do for a person's need system. The needs of individuals vary. Some people need more freedom than others. Some are more satisfied with non-materialistic resources such as music, art, natural beauty, or literature, while others may feel they need an abundance of money, clothes, furniture, expensive cars and housing. Some have great need of reassurance and encouragement, while others appreciate being independent and self-reliant.

An important consideration in evaluating a marriage is the degree to which the partners are meeting each other's needs. To determine this, we use the "Individual Need Analysis and Compatibility Factors" inventory described in Chapter 7. We discovered in our well-functioning marriages that the needs of each partner are being satisfactorily met. The areas of special importance seemed to be those of attaining acceptance, security, sexual gratification, warmth and affection, companionship with spouse and children, personal growth and fulfillment, recreation and play, and social experience with friends and relatives.

We will examine briefly a couple in our study who were particularly sensitive to each other's needs and who made a special effort to meet them. Hal and Trudy have been married eighteen years. They have two children, Bill and Sue, ages eleven and eight, respectively. Hal is a hospital administrator, and Trudy devotes most of her time to home activities. Both evaluated their marriage on the "needs inventory" with remarkable results. Out of the forty-one needs listed there, Trudy indicated that none of her essential needs were unmet. The needs that were important to her were:

I like to be noticed and admired.

I need to have opportunities to organize, direct and influence programs and people.

I feel most secure when I am with someone who is strong in conviction and firm in decision making.

I have a desire for a considerable amount of gaiety and fun through going places and doing pleasurable things.

I put considerable emphasis on economic security.

I need better than average clothes, home, car, furniture, and money to do extra things.

I get most of my satisfactions from non-material sources: friends, music, art, beauty of nature, good literature, etc.

I have a strong sexual drive and need frequent satisfying sexual experiences.

I tend to want to be a part of group activity, organizations or clubs that provide opportunities for social experiences.

I like good food, have a healthy appetite and relish opportunities to eat with friends or family at home or in restaurants.

Talking is more important to me than listening when I am with other people.

I feel the need to be compassionate to others.

I am sensitive to criticism and need a partner who takes this into consideration.

When I have a problem, I want to get it out in the open and talk about it.

These are Trudy's basic needs as she sees them, and she feels they are more than adequately met in her marriage. Hal indicates that he believes these needs are legitimate and that he can and is meeting them.

When we examined Hal's most important needs, we found all but one satisfactorily met. This he indicated as his need to be quiet, avoid crowds, noise, and the busy world, in order to reflect and maintain emotional stability. Many men caught up in the busy, hectic world of their business life feel this need for quiet when they come home from work in the evenings, but it is not always possible to attain quiet when a wife and children are making demands upon him. The desire to have some peace and quiet is not uncommon, and the search for it will continue; for many it will be a frustrating experience.

The other needs Hal indicated were important to him were very well met:

I like to be noticed and admired.

I need to have opportunities to organize, direct and influence programs and people.

I feel most at ease when I have my affairs in order and my surroundings neat.

I have a desire for a considerable amount of gaiety and fun through going places and doing pleasurable things.

I put considerable emphasis on economic security.

I need better than average clothes, home, car, furniture, and money to do extra things.

I get most of my satisfactions from non-material sources: friends, music, art, beauty of nature, good literature, etc.

I tend to want to be a part of group activity, organizations or clubs that provide opportunities for social experiences.

I like good food, have a healthy appetite, and relish opportunities to eat with friends or family at home or in restaurants.

I receive a great deal of satisfaction in winning over others with whom I am competing.

I enjoy arguing, matching wits with another, defending my convictions.

I am sensitive to criticism and need a partner who takes this into consideration.

I find satisfaction in demonstrating my affection to people I like.

Trudy felt that Hal was justified in having these needs and that she was meeting them satisfactorily. In the taped interview I had with Hal and Trudy, this particular characteristic in their marriage was illustrated again. Hal said:

I think the most important thing in a marriage is for each person to understand and recognize the other's needs and to help the other fulfill these needs. For example, Trudy and I both have the need to succeed, so we both work hard at this. She supports me and my job, and from this I get more strength, and progress up the ladder. Now she has needs in getting out and meeting people, and I guess she would be considered the social director of our family, and I encourage her to do this. There was a time when we were getting our education. We switched back and forth working and adjusting our roles so we could both accomplish our goals. Trudy very much needed this and I think I should sacrifice so she can have her goals realized.

Trudy expressed her ideas this way:

We move a lot, so we need to be especially aware of both of our needs to help us make these adjustments. We know each other's interests get fulfilled, and so our needs get met. If we hadn't been so interested in each other, there might have been a serious void in our marriage. Hal does need more privacy than I do, and as he said, I'm the social director, but we agree on these matters and we do have a lot in common and enjoy doing many things together.

In writing about their marriage, Hal said that he believed one of the greatest contributions to the success of their marriage was in the degree each has worked to help the other fulfill his or her goals. They share the duties and responsibilities of parenthood and household chores, and they share in Hal's vocational achievements. Trudy stated that she believed the outstanding characteristics of their marriage were that they recognized each other's needs, that they complemented each other in that "my weaknesses are his strengths, and his weaknesses are my strengths." "Each of us," she wrote, "gives for the happiness and well-being of the other. This makes it unnecessary to make demands on each other. We believe we are becoming a team that can face the world together."

When one reviews the material gathered in this study concerning essentials for marital health, he finds a common thread running through all of the case histories, namely, the concern the partners have for each other and the unselfish attempt on the part of each to help the other to find meaning and fulfillment in life. In one of the tapes made by Joan and Martin, Joan said, "I think the main basis for our marriage is trust and admiration for each other, and respect for each other's feelings and a willingness to make whatever sacrifice we might feel necessary to help the other meet his goals and ideals." Martin put it this way, "Joan and I have recognized that marriage is a difficult union at best, and therefore we have tried to place the interest of the other ahead of our own. It has been a process of learning to share together rather than living individual lives."

How can we best describe this golden thread that weaves its way into the lives of these people and binds them together in such a beautiful way? I have chosen to call it the G.R.P.R. principle. This is an abbreviation for Gradual, Reciprocal, Positive, Reinforcement. This means that working slowly but surely through the marriage is a process of giving each other positive reinforcement where it is most needed. If Trudy sees that Hal is tired and full of stress when he comes home from work, she may give him a big hug and say "Why don't you stretch out for awhile on the sofa while I finish fixing you a nice dinner with the fried chicken you like so much." Hal feels better already. Here is someone who is concerned about him and wants to meet an urgent need. Hal's love feelings for Trudy are generated all over again. So he, in turn, is motivated to reciprocate. It may be as simple as his saying after dinner, "You look tired. Let me do the dishes tonight." Or, knowing how much she likes socializing, he may suggest, "How about our going to that couples' party at the church Friday night?" This reinforces Trudy positively, so she feels good about Hal and wants to do even more for him. This process goes on and on, day after day. If this continues, as it has—with some interruptions, of course—for the eighteen years Hal and Trudy have been married, it is not difficult to see why their marriage is as satisfying as it is.

Now let us look at the other side of the coin and see how a gradual, reciprocal, negative reinforcement could cause a marriage to deteriorate. Suppose Hal had come home tired and disgruntled and said, "I'm tired. Don't anyone bother me." Trudy might have replied, "You are always tired, can't you come home with a pleasant word once in your life?" Here a negative reinforcement is met with a negative reinforcement, and this causes both parties to continue the process. Hal, attempting to retaliate, says, "I don't think I'm going to be able to take you to that party Friday night." Trudy proceeds to throw the dinner together in a careless manner, and they eat together in sullen silence. If this process continues over a period of time, the relationship will deteriorate gradually but surely. Unless it is interrupted by a positive move on the part of one of them, the situation could become quite serious. We can plot graphs to show what happens to the relationship in both cases. First the gradual, reciprocal, positive reinforcement:

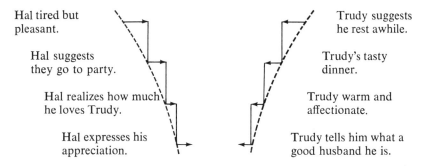

Hal tired but pleasant.

Hal suggests they go to party.

Hal realizes how much he loves Trudy.

Hal expresses his appreciation.

Trudy suggests he rest awhile.

Trudy's tasty dinner.

Trudy warm and affectionate.

Trudy tells him what a good husband he is.

The dotted line plots the growing together of the relationship. Hal's and Trudy's marriage includes much positive reinforcement each day, and it is clear that this has done a great deal to bring them closer together through the years. Being positively reinforced is a personal need that everyone has. And few there are who ever get tired of it. On the other hand, receiving negative reinforcement lowers one's self-esteem and makes one feel depressed and miserable. Examine the graph that plots this process.

The dotted line represents the growing apart as a result of the negative reinforcement reciprocally administered by both parties. If negative reinforcement becomes the style of the marriage or the dominant theme, the couple will be forced farther and farther apart over the course of time.

The couples in our model group all seem to be aware of the importance of the G.R.P.R. principle and consciously promote it in their relationship. If they slip and fall into the negative syndrome, one or the other will have the courage and the compassion to reverse the process and get it back on the positive track again. This is done by a strong determination not to allow the relationship to deteriorate, and a realization that there is too much to lose in a negatively reinforced marriage. By bringing love and rationality to the surface, one will begin the kind of communicating and reconciling process that will bring about the necessary change.

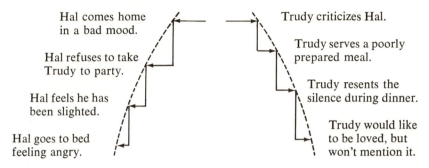

Hal comes home in a bad mood.

Hal refuses to take Trudy to party.

Hal feels he has been slighted.

Hal goes to bed feeling angry.

Trudy criticizes Hal.

Trudy serves a poorly prepared meal.

Trudy resents the silence during dinner.

Trudy would like to be loved, but won't mention it.

John Scanzoni, in his book *Sexual Bargaining,* discusses "Reciprocity and Exchange in Marriage."[1] He believes that husbands and wives are held together by a process of reciprocity. He maintains that the process of giving and receiving rewards begins in courtship and continues into the marriage. If marriage partners are deprived of the rewards, instability is the result. Why does this phenomenon work in facilitating the functioning of a marriage relationship? He states four reasons:

1. Reciprocity tends to structure roles in marriage so as to include both rights and duties. "Husbands and wives each have certain duties to perform for their spouses, and each has certain rights they expect to have fulfilled for them."

2. ". . . if a husband wants certain rewards from his wife then he must provide the rewards that she wants (conform to her reward expectations); the same is true for her."

3. This reciprocity is motivated not only for the exchange of benefits, but also from a moral obligation to benefit someone from whom you have received benefits. "It is this moral norm as well as the specific rewards that maintains the stability of any social system, including marriage." If one receives a benefit he is then obligated. He is indebted until he repays. As soon as he repays, the cycle begins again, and this may go on indefinitely.

4. There are mechanisms which cause people to remain socially indebted to each other so that complete repayment is never possible. This reciprocity sets up a "chain of enduring obligations and repayments within a system of roles in which each role contains both rights and duties."[2]

As a marriage progresses, couples consciously or unconsciously evaluate their relationship in terms of whether or not their expectations have been met, whether or not benefits have been given and received, whether or not there has been a fair exchange of positive reinforcement. If the evaluation is good, the couple will feel comfortable about the marriage. If the evaluation is a poor one, dissatisfaction will set in, and one or both will feel deprived and cheated.

If this principle seems somewhat cold and calculated, let it be known that it is much more than that. The love that marriage partners have for each other, involving unselfishness, concern, and compassion, gives it a warm and dynamic context in which to operate. Couples such as Hal and Trudy benefit from the reciprocity of gifts given and received, but their love motivates them to think more of their partner than themselves. The highest form of love we know is *agape,* and that means giving with no thought of personal gain. Although a marriage cannot exist on this giving alone, particularly if it is practiced by one partner only, no marriage can be fully functioning without it.

REFERENCES

1. John Scanzoni, *Sexual Bargaining,* Englewood Cliffs, N.J.: Prentice-Hall, 1972, pp. 62–64.

2. Also see discussion in A. W. Gouldner, "The Norm of Reciprocity: A Preliminary Statement," *American Sociological Review,* 25 (April, 1960), pp. 161–78. Scanzoni uses this material as a basis for some of his presentation.

CHAPTER SIXTEEN

The Sexually Healthy Marriage

What does it mean to have a sexually healthy marriage? What have we learned about the importance of this question in our study of couples whose marriages are considered among the best we have ever known? Let us first look at some of the results we have obtained in our study.

In our select group of eighteen couples with top-level marriages, nine husbands rated their sexual relations excellent, seven rated them fairly successful, and two rated them as a contributing factor to a lesser degree. None expressed any dissatisfaction about his marital sexual relations.

Among the wives, ten rated their sexual relations as excellent, seven rated them fairly successful, and one rated them as a contributing factor to a lesser degree. No wife was dissatisfied with the sexual relations in her marriage.

The husband who rated sexual relations as only fair and not a major factor contributing to marital happiness, did not think of this as a problem in his marriage, which he considered to be a very successful one. He did feel that couples who marry today should arrive at a common understanding about how important sexual relations need to be in their marriage. The husband who rated the sexual relations in his marriage as not a strong characteristic also stated that his sexual needs were only partially met. His wife rated sexual relations in the marriage as a contributing factor to a lesser degree, and that her sexual needs were only partially met. Yet each rated the other as warm and affectionate. An evaluation of their total relationship indicates that though their sexual life has functioned only moderately well, this couple has had many years of satisfaction and happiness in their marriage.

A review of the reasons for marital health given by all of the thirty-six people in this group indicates that although satisfactory sexual relations are important, they are not as important as other factors such as mutual respect, good communication, common goals and values, companionship, kindness, thoughtfulness, and unselfishness.

Many people today have been led to believe that sexual intercourse is the most important factor in a successful marriage, and they must measure up to certain standards set by the "experts" in the field. Lederer and Jackson discuss this in their book, *The Mirages of Marriage*.[1]

This sex act—a comparably simple matter—has become the most written about, the most talked of, and the most muddled aspect of marriage. . . .

Unsatisfactory sexual relations are a symptom of marital discord, not the cause of it. It is difficult for the victims to see this because of the mass of propaganda about sex that attacks them day and night, on the street, in the home, in the office. . . .

The reason people keep asking where sex fits into marriage is that they have been hoodwinked, bamboozled, pressured, conned, and persuaded that the sexual act is compulsory in their lives and *must be performed alike by everyone*; the "standards" are established by advertisers, publicity for sexpot motion-picture stars, literature, movies, plays, television, and so on. But these are standards of fantasy. Therefore people ask silly questions: How often should we have sex? What is the best position? How intense should it be? The questions sound like inquiries about the type of gymnastic procedures to be followed for attaining muscles like Mr. America's or a rear end or bust like Miss America's. Perhaps even worse off are the myriads of couples who don't dare ask questions and just assume they *must* be abnormal because their own practice differs from some so-called standard.

The problem is obvious. In sex, trying to keep up with the Joneses is the road to disaster. To decide where sex fits into their particular marriage, a couple must look inward at the marriage, not outward at the deceptive advice and make-believe standards set by others.

These authors apparently have very strong feelings about this matter, and to some, their statements may seem to be exaggerated; but they make a good point—sexual competence in marriage can be determined only by what the couple feels is satisfactory. If what they have experienced meets their needs and they are happy about it, then it must be judged to be functioning properly.

After carefully considering the results of the study, I conclude that where the interpersonal relationships have been functioning well in a marriage, the sexual relations are satisfactory. For where there are good interpersonal relationships, there is adequate functioning in communication, understanding, empathy, concern, companionship, and many other important factors that also influence the way sex is practiced and enjoyed. The reciprocal positive reinforcement given in such a marriage would provide an excellent context in which sexual relations could take place.

What happens in the bedroom would be a natural outcome of what has been happening in the kitchen, the living room, the nursery, and in the patio. Allan Fromme puts it this way:

It should be clear that a sexual relationship is, after all, part of a bigger relationship between human beings. There are individuals who cannot get along with themselves, let alone with others. How can we expect our sexual relationships in the long run to be any better than our general human relationships are? This means that the way we sexualize is a reflection of the way we live. In order to understand sex better, it then behooves us to study the way we live.[2]

It has been my impression from my experience as a marriage counselor that the problems people bring that seem to be sexual in nature are generally related to their inability to relate to themselves and to others. If their self-esteem is low and they have hostile feelings toward people in general, there will be problems in sexual relationships with a spouse. If a man is unable to maintain sufficient erection to have intercourse, this may be evidence that he is frustrated by personal problems, has difficulty in relating to his partner, or both. If a woman shows signs of frigidity, it may be that she lacks confidence in herself, doubts her capacity to love and be loved, or finds difficulty in relating to her partner. There are physiological difficulties, but more often they are psychological in nature. Masters and Johnson have pointed out many times that there is no such thing as the pure physiology of sexual response and no such thing as an uninvolved partner in a marital situation in which there is a sexual dysfunction.

The American Medical Association states in the book, *Human Sexuality*[3] that more than one-half of all people in this country lead sex lives that they consider unsatisfactory; that most persons experience a sexual difficulty at some point during their lives, and that physicians in their office practice discover sexual problems in roughly one patient in seven. However,

Human sexuality should not be viewed narrowly in terms of sexual response, and sexual response should not be regarded as primarily a physiologic activity. . . . Human beings function sexually as whole persons and anything which is capable of undermining them personally is capable of undermining their sexual response. A young wife may be sexually unresponsive because her husband cannot make their income cover their expenses. A wife who always tears her husband down may undercut his confidence sufficiently to create premature ejaculation or even impotence.[4]

A couple entering marriage, then, might expect the quality of their sexual relations to be directly related to the way they have learned to think, to feel, to live, and to relate. It all begins with the kind of environment into which the child is born and in which he grows up. Are the parents warm, loving, accepting? Are they able to help the child know it is loved and wanted? As the child grows, is he or she helped to accept and appreciate the fact of masculinity or femininity? Does the child achieve a healthy attitude toward its body and body functions? Is the child nurtured into a state where it likes loving and being loved? Does it come to think of sex as a healthy, natural, creative function in life?

Sherrie came into my office several months before her marriage saying she was scared to go into marriage with so much anxiety about sex. She explained that in her childhood experience at home and in school, she got the notion that sex was dirty, and that any form of it was animalistic. She never heard it mentioned except in a negative way. Her fiancé was in Europe and she couldn't talk it over with him, so she thought she should go to a marriage counselor. For a number of sessions Sherrie talked out her thoughts and feelings and compared them with the counselor's. She was also given some books to read. As the time for her marriage drew near, she said she felt much better and had confidence that with good communication she and her future husband could work it out satisfactorily. More than a year later I received this letter from her:

Remember that problem I came to you about? I thought you might like to know that we worked it out. It was really a long, tough battle but we conquered it. It took ten months! I was that scared of sex. I'm telling you because I thought it might help someone else to know my problem. I really had quite a mental block. It had become so built up in my mind that I was sure it would hurt terribly. But, you know, when we finally succeeded I could hardly believe it! It really didn't hurt at all, and as a matter of fact, at first I didn't believe we'd really done it! And, quite truthfully, now I really dig it! I can't believe I was so scared. I really have the perfect husband. Harry was so patient and understanding. I know I hurt him a lot but he handled me with kid gloves and it really showed how much he loves me. Most of this first year was really hell but we made it work for us—we're even closer now and I know we can weather anything that comes along and that's a good feeling.

The moral to this might be that it is never too late to change attitudes and overcome conditions not favorable to a healthy sex life, although they originated in one's early years.

While some women may develop a negative attitude toward sex, men often are conditioned to believe that sex is purely physical, and women are playthings to serve their need for pleasure, or objects in a game in which they must score in order to win. I have heard college women describe this game as one of offense and defense. The object of the man is to get the woman in bed as soon as possible. This is the offense. The object of the woman is to defend herself until she finds the man who really loves her or wants to marry her. This is hardly the kind of a game in which the best attitudes about love and sex can develop. A broader concept of sexuality is needed by most people, and this in itself would improve the sexual relationship in marriage. A healthy exercise in which to engage is that of reviewing some of the socially useful purposes sex may serve. Dr. Bernard H. Shulman[5] suggests there are six:

1. For reproduction. This serves a biological and psychological purpose. It reproduces the human race. People want children and this is the way to get them.

2. It is pleasurable. Sex is a time-honored way to achieve enjoyment. It is an adult form of play.

3. It brings about a feeling of belonging. "The sexual relationship can offer companionship, affection, and emotional closeness; it can produce a deep bond between the participating individuals and promote love. . . . Such a use of sex almost demands those sentiments we name *love*. To know such a relationship means that one has been touched with a new understanding of life that never quite leaves one thereafter."

4. It is a co-operative endeavor and is therefore a kind of sharing that is more than a feeling of belonging. "The amount of cooperation required in sex is probably greater than that required in most other human relationships." Anything less than undivided attention is unsatisfactory.

5. For the purpose of consolation. "When one has been hurt or humiliated, has heard bad news, or feels sad for any reason, sex can console." (I would like to add that often, caressing, short of intercourse, is more effective, because the bereaved person in this case can be the sole recipient of the affection without having to actively respond.)

6. For the purpose of self-affirmation. It helps an individual say to himself or herself, "I am really a man!" or "I am really a woman!" "I am worthwhile, competent. I can love and be loved."

Many more uses could be added to these, for example, for the purpose of comprehending the husband or the wife. The Old Testament Hebrew word for sexual intercourse is translated "to know." In Genesis 4:1, we read, "Now Adam *knew* Eve, his wife and she conceived and bore Cain. . . ." One of the problems of the human race is to get to know other people—to break through the barriers everyone consciously or unconsciously puts around himself. Sex seems to be able, under the right circumstances, to break through these barriers and bring about a greater knowledge or more complete unification of two people, physically, mentally, emotionally, and spiritually.

Other uses for sex might be: for encouragement, relaxation, release from physical and emotional tension, the giving of a gift, stimulating an individual's physical and emotional being, and even as a means of distraction from pain and discomfort. Needless to say, there are many misuses or abuses of sex. There are perversions, deviations, and variations that may be interpreted in many ways according to one's point of view. There are homosexuals, transsexualists, fetishists, voyeurs, exhibitionists, masochists, pedophiles (child molesters), sadists, transvestites, seducers, women suffering from nymphomania and men from satyriasis (exaggerated sexual desire resulting in compulsive sexual activities). The difference between sex as socially useful and sex as destructive is in terms of what it does to human lives and human relationships. In one case it is constructive: promotes social harmony, pleasure, love, closeness, and character; in the other it causes feelings of guilt, injured personalities, suffering, frustration, and damaged human relationships. No better test of the morality or value of sex can be applied than this one: what does it do to people?

What comes after you say, "I love you" by way of a sexual relationship? Basically, sexual intercourse, or coitus, seems simple—the uniting of the sexual organs of a male and female. Animals perform it quite adequately. But human beings are different. They are more complicated and sensitive, and the biological performance, including all the right moves and positions, is not enough. We are deeply indebted to contemporary women for calling attention to the fact that sex needs to be something more than genital linkage.

Are women different in their sexual natures from men? The argument about this will go on for a long time. That there is a difference in their approach to sex in most marriages is undeniable. Some endocrinologists account for this through the theory that sex hormones—female hormones, such as progesterone and various estrogens such as testosterone—influence the behavior of men and women and make them different. Anthropologist Lionel Tiger, writing in the *New York Times Magazine* of October 25, 1970, tells about the work of David Hamburg of the department of psychiatry at Stanford:

In experiments on primates, when both males and females are given extra testosterone, they show much more aggressive hyper-male activity. Humans have similar reactions under artificial manipulation of hormone levels. Among boys and girls before puberty, boys show more testosterone than girls. But at adolescence, the changes are startling: Testosterone in boys increases at least tenfold, and possibly as much as 30 times. On the other hand, girls' testosterone levels only double, from a lower base to begin with. These levels remain stable throughout the life cycle.

This is not to say that the effect of conditioning is not a great one in establishing male and female differences. Infants at an early age are in the beginning stages of "role modeling" in which they begin to search for clues to help them form a life style appropriate to their sex and culture. Little girls are taught what girls should think and be and do. And little boys are taught what boys should think and be and do. So nurture contributes its part to sex differences to add to what Nature brings to it. So what we finally are as males and females appears to be the result of a complicated interaction between nature and nurture. This difference needs to be understood by both male and female in order to appreciate and enjoy each other. A woman's sexual nature physiologically develops much more slowly than a man's. At 16 or 17 years, the male is developed sexually about as far as he ever will be, while a female does not achieve her sexual peak until about 24 years. Men and women seem to differ in terms of what stimulates them sexually. Viewing nude pictures of the opposite sex or erotic dancing might stimulate a male; this is much less likely to be true for a female. Dormitory and fraternity room walls of males are lined with pin-ups of erotic pictures of women. The walls of women's rooms are largely void of such pictures of men. Someone has oversimplified the matter by saying, "Men tend to approach sex erotically; women tend to approach sex romantically." A romantic movie or novel can be sexually stimulating to a woman. Fantasies about the opposite sex play a large part in stimulating both men and women; but the fantasies of men tend to be erotic, while the fantasies of women tend to be romantic. All of this is undergoing some changes.

Men are more aggressive in making sexual advances. There was a time when the husband almost always took the initiative in love-making. This is beginning to change. Sexual relations in the early part of marriage, in the past, have been more satisfactory to the male than to the female. One study showed that only 50 percent of wives experienced an orgasm in the first month of marriage. At the end of the first year, about 80 percent reported having had an orgasm. In my own clinical experience, I have been surprised at the number of women who have told me that, even after a number of years of marriage, they had never achieved an orgasm. Some of these women give up trying. Some become frigid as a result of developing a negative attitude toward sex. In contrast to all this, about 98 percent of all men report they had a climax right away or soon after they began married life. Also, in my experience with married couples, I find the greatest complaint about infrequency of intercourse from the husband; once in a great while this complaint will come from the female. I have noticed some change in this over the past two or three years. More women are expecting sexual satisfaction in marriage.

Not only do males and females need to understand the nature and nurture of each other, but they need to communicate on a person-to-person basis to understand each other individually. Certainly, no male or female is like any other male or female. It is by communicating about their sexual feelings and needs that two people are able to reach a satisfactory adjustment in their sexual life. By so doing, would it not be possible for the male to become more gentle and sensitive in his approach to sex, and the female to be more uninhibited in allowing herself to find greater satisfaction in sexual relations? I like what Lester Kirkendall wrote in response to an article by Gerhard Neubeck:

As women are less and less inhibited, as acceptance of their interest in sexual expression is more and more readily acknowledged, and as they can be more direct and more independent in their relationships, their sexual motivations will change also. Likewise, males need affection too, and in a world more and more dehumanized their need for intimacy and closeness grows.[6]

I appreciate the criticism that so much is being written about sex these days, and that we are bombarded from every direction by material about sex, yet it must be said that there is much to learn. We need to turn to the more intelligent and helpful sources to learn the deeper and more significant aspects of sexuality, to understand the nature of femininity and masculinity more fully, to develop more positive attitudes toward our sexual life, and to create a value system in which sex takes its proper place. We have moved from the period when sex was kept hidden behind a curtain of mystery and reticence to the present, where it is much more in the open. Perhaps we will progress to the point where we may accept it as the good thing it can be and direct our sexual desires and energies toward the production of more satisfying and invigorating married life for couples of the future.

Of all couples we have studied in our research project, none has a better sexual life than Jack and Josie, mentioned in an earlier chapter. How do they account for this happy situation? They attempt to describe how this came about in a taped interview:

J.R.H.: We have noticed that in most marriages we have studied that the sexual relationship is related to the total relationship of couples. Marriage counselors are confronted with a great many cases of sexual maladjustment in couples that come to them. What would be your feeling about this as you work on this phase of your relationship?

JACK: We really enjoy our sexual life. [Laughs] The only problem now is that we have two kids that stay up late at night. Then we have trouble finding times sometimes. But we enjoy it when we feel like it and it doesn't make any difference whether it's in the afternoon or when. Some people seem to get into the role that you have to have sex every Saturday night, or that you can only have it after you go to bed at night and that's not the way it should be. So once in awhile I'll come home and the kids are gone, and Josie will say "I've been wanting you all day," and dinner will be shoved back on the stove until we do what we feel like doing. It's a very natural thing with us.

J.R.H.: Is this something you have always agreed on, or is it something you have developed over a period of time?

JACK: We're just naturally oversexed. [Loud laughter from both]

J.R.H.: What do you have to say about that, Josie?

JOSIE: I don't know what to say to that! We do enjoy our sexual relationship but we never put a certain time on it. We take advantage of every opportunity. We just enjoy each other very much, and it really enhances our total relationship.

J.R.H.: Do you think married people need to be naturally sexually compatible? How do you see this? It has been noted in some cases that one person has a strong sexual drive and the other does not, or one has a positive attitude and the other has a negative attitude.

JOSIE: Well, we enjoy the sexual relationship. And if he seems to be unusually busy, I just say, "Can I make an appointment with you tonight? [Laugh] I just let him know when he is neglecting me. I tell him. And sometimes he does the same thing to me. You know, like, why don't you put the books away you're reading?

JACK: We can turn each other on quite easily.

J.R.H.: Yes, it seems that either of you can take the initiative at any time that you might want to.

JOSIE: Yes, that's very true.

J.R.H.: And this is a little different from the old traditional role where only the man took the initiative. Did you read books to develop your ideas?

JOSIE: We read a lot of books. We've read most of the books that are out now. I don't know whether they've helped us or given us a new perspective or—I don't really know how they have worked in our marriage, because we were never at a point sexually when we were going downhill. We have always enjoyed our sexual relationships.

JACK: We have never had any problems in this area, but we have just been interested—that's why we keep reading the books. I like to read about sex. [Laughs]

J.R.H.: Some people say they come from family backgrounds where not much was said about sex. They got the impression that sex was kind of dirty, and they carried this into marriage and they couldn't get rid of this negative way of thinking.

JOSIE: We both grew up in homes like that. But after we were married and I found out it was really something good, I started thinking for myself, you know; and I just figured my mother missed out. [Much laughter]

J.R.H.: What more than anything else is really what makes a marriage go?

JOSIE: For me, it's Jack. I just got the right guy. I just like to be with him, and he still turns me on, probably more than even when we were first married, and, I don't know, I just like the kind of person he is. He is a very good person, basically honest with lots of integrity—the kind of man I want for the father of our children. I think they will have a lot of good qualities that he brings to them. And I can see them coming out in our children now.

JACK: For some reason we both seem to think we have very rare marriage partners. I don't think that in all the sixteen years we've been married, and in all the couples we have known and been friends with, I've seen any man's wife that I thought could have been my wife. I've never met another woman I could live with as happily as I live with Josie. I'm not too easy to reason with sometimes, and she understands me.

JOSIE: But I think Jack is a cut above the average person. He has more to give than a lot of men.

J.R.H.: What do you do to encourage a good relationship to be even better?

JOSIE: When we walk down the street, Jack still takes my hand, you know, and that really means something to me. We have friends who are married, and I don't think they ever touch each other in a normal, everyday way; and Jack does these things to me. We can be in church and he'll reach over and take my hand. There are a lot of little things he does that mean so much to me. He buys me books of poetry and writes little notes in them that bring tears to my eyes. He does a lot of neat things for me.

JACK: We enjoy being alone together. Now, a lot of our friends go out to dinner always with another couple to go with them. Now we enjoy our friends, and we have them into our home, but we like to go out together to have a quiet time enjoying each other.

How well this couple illustrates the importance of a total relationship to a good sexual life. When one hears them discuss their situation with freedom, good humor, and enthusiasm, one is impressed with the fact that a good sexual adjustment is more a by-product of a couple's healthy interpersonal relationship than a sophisticated knowledge of and preoccupation with sexual techniques.

I would like to conclude this chapter by listing some of the qualities in the people in our study whose marriages exemplify a satisfying sexual life. It might be titled: The Characteristics of a Desirable Sexual Partner.

1. A person who is warm, friendly, outgoing.

2. A person who is generous, unselfish, enjoys giving other people pleasure.

3. A person who is physically and emotionally healthy: active, energetic, fun-loving, and has a good sense of humor.

4. A good communicator, skillful in settling differences. One who doesn't withdraw when arguments or conflicts arise. Doesn't harbor anger or resentment.

5. One who enjoys being himself or herself. A woman who likes her femininity, and a man who likes his masculinity. A person who has a high self-esteem and who is proud of his or her physical body.

6. One who has a positive attitude toward sex and sexual functions, and is free from negative feelings about sexual relations. One who likes closeness and physical contact.

7. One who has a high regard for sexual relations and thinks of them as a symbol of meaningful relationships and a way of expressing a physical, mental, emotional, and spiritual union.

8. A person who has the qualities of loyalty and fidelity, and can maintain a relationship over a period of time. One who has the capacity to keep a relationship alive and vigorous.

9. An altogether mentally, morally, and emotionally healthy individual.

REFERENCES

1. William J. Lederer and Don D. Jackson, *The Mirages of Marriage,* New York: W. W. Norton and Company, 1968, pp. 114, 116, 118.

2. Allan Fromme, *Understanding the Sexual Response in Humans,* New York: Simon and Schuster, 1966.

3. Committee on Human Sexuality, *Human Sexuality,* The American Medical Association, 1972.

4. *Ibid.,* p. 91.

5. Bernard H. Shulman, "The Uses and Abuses of Sex," *Medical Aspects of Human Sexuality,* Vol. 2, No. 9 (Sept. 1968), pp. 49–51.

6. Lester A. Kirkendall, quoted in "The Myriad Motives for Sex," by Gerhard Neubeck, *Sexual Behavior* (July 1972), p. 56.

CHAPTER SEVENTEEN

What Comes After? Children!

After you say, "I love you," marriage may occur, and from marriages, a great many of them, come children. And so we move from generation to generation. In this chapter we will look at our families to see how they thought about and related to their children. People who function well in their marriages might be expected to be competent parents, and this we found to be true.

All who are interested in the premarital stage of a couple's life know the importance of a careful consideration of several questions about children: Is there a mutual interest in children? Is there a common agreement on whether or not children are desired in this marriage? If there is, how many children do the couple think would be an ideal number? Is there an agreement on how children should be nurtured and developed? What sort of a division of labor and parent roles will be necessary for operating a family life effectively?

Marriage counselors know very well the importance of the answers two people contemplating marriage give to these questions. I shall never forget receiving a frantic phone call from a wife who wanted to see me as soon as possible. When she came in, she sobbed out her story. She had been married four years and she had suggested to her husband that perhaps it was time to plan to have their first child. The husband responded to her suggestion with the reply, "Oh, I wasn't planning to have any children at all!" The wife was shocked at this response. One might ask, Didn't they talk about this matter before they were married? Apparently they did not. All couples should discuss their attitudes and feelings about children before they are married, but I have discovered that many do not.

In the study of our eighteen families, we had an opportunity to observe attitudes toward children and the nature of family life-styles. Our couples were realistic about what it means to have children, but they all seemed to enjoy family life. I have attempted to summarize some of the observations we were able to make:

1. Children were liked and wanted.

2. Size of family was carefully discussed, as well as spacing.

3. Agreement was reached on the nature of discipline to be practiced with the children.

4. Couples had worked on a general concept of child rearing and development.

5. Many activities were planned for the whole family. Effort was made to obtain family unity.

6. Children were given a voice in family decision-making.

7. Vacations were planned to be an educational and recreational experience, especially for the children.

8. Although children received careful guidance, they were encouraged to be independent.

Dick and Dorene were especially happy to have a farm as the environment for child rearing. "It gives children a place to feel important and needed," Dorene reported. While this might be more difficult for city dwellers, it is one of the greatest needs of children in contemporary society, where so many feel they are of little importance and wonder if their parents really want them. The children of our families seemed to be happy, cooperative, and vigorously active. Jim and Vicki have two children, ages fourteen and nine. I asked Vicki, "Have you ever gotten tired of being a wife and mother?" She replied, "Maybe on a particularly bad day, but overall, no. I'd like to repeat some advice given me when our daughter was born. This I have tried to do. Try to think of your life as joy rather than a problem. This was easier for me because Jim always helped and took care of the children so I could have frequent breaks. Try to enjoy your children at every age and stage—they grow up so fast!" I believe this represents the general philosophy of all our families in the study.

A number of our couples had had some training in child development which proved to be very useful for them. They were impressed with the general concepts of Rudolf Dreikurs as presented in his book, *Children the Challenge.*[1] Some of Dreikur's principles of child rearing, as practiced by our couples, are summarized as follows:

1. The most important matter is the "climate" of the family. The child absorbs this unconsciously. If the parents are warm, friendly and cooperative, it is likely that the children will develop these same characteristics.

2. A great need of children is for encouragement. A misbehaving child is often a discouraged child. Provide support even when children make mistakes or do not do things perfectly.

3. Be careful about engaging in power struggles with children. Don't feel you have to win. Use other means to resolve differences.

4. Use natural and logical consequences. Allow a child to experience the consequences of his own action. If he refuses to eat, then let him be hungry. This is the best learning experience possible and is far superior to the kind of punishment which has no relation to the action.

5. Be firm, but not domineering. Children need guidance, support, and knowing what the "rules of the game" are, not bossing around.

6. Establish an "order" for the family. A consistent environment, with a certain amount of routine, is needed.

7. Make reasonable requests of children. Don't expect your children to be adults with superior minds and skills.

8. Set a good example. What you do is more convincing than what you say. Children will do as you do more than they will do as you say.

9. Have the courage to say, "No!" when you have to. Don't be afraid to set limits for the benefit of your children and the good of the family.

10. Stay out of fights. Most fights are for the benefit of the audience, and if you will reduce the audience, you will reduce the fights most of the time. Remember that at times it may be wiser to ignore bad behavior than to make a fuss over it.

11. Encourage independence. Refrain from overprotection. Give your children responsibilities that will help them grow. Don't weaken them by causing them to be overdependent on you. A time will come when they will need to be able to get along without you.

12. Include children in your family problems, decisions, and goal planning. Provide occasions for discussions, opportunities for expressing ideas and feelings. Establish a family council that meets regularly.

13. Children learn to play "games" with parents: attention getting, power struggles, revenge, helplessness, and others. Learn what the games mean and how to deal with them.

14. In and through it all, think of your children as human beings. Understand them. Have fun with them. Enjoy them. And always, think of them not as a problem, but a challenge.

Throughout the book we have described the problems our select couples had to deal with in their family life. These experiences illustrate the truth that problems do not cause marriages to fail; it is the inability of the couple to cope with the problems that causes the difficulty. In fact, many of the problems seem to have helped the marriages grow and become stronger.

One such illustration can be found in an experience in the life of Betty and Dan, one of our couples mentioned in Chapter 4. They had hoped to have three children. Kathy was born in May of 1970. Their second child, Beth, was born prematurely in January of 1975. Beth was not expected to live. During the eleven weeks she was in an intensive care unit in the hospital, the hopes of the couple for her survival periodically brightened and dimmed. Early in April the doctor permitted the couple to bring Beth home with instructions that for many weeks she was not to have contact with people outside the home in order to protect her from any possible infection. It was months before Betty and Dan were able to take her to any public function.

I visited Betty to find out what this experience had meant to their marriage. As I explained earlier, Betty and Dan had worked out problems at the beginning of their marriage that illustrated their coping power. I was anxious to find out how this coping power was applied during these trying times. I asked Betty to describe what had happened and how they reacted to it. She said it was difficult to describe, but that what had happened occurred on two levels. First was the immediate impact of the premature birth and the fear of an immediate loss of the child. The second was the long weeks of waiting, watching, and adjusting to the kind of life the situation demanded. There were daily trips to the hospital with Kathy left in the hands of a baby sitter, and evenings when Dan could go, and Betty and Kathy stayed home. Kathy, the older child, could not help feeling neglected.

Betty explained that she experienced frequent states of depression, while Dan remained steady and did not seem disturbed. Did this mean that he was not caring? Or was there something wrong with her? She wondered. The length of the stressful period was a factor. A year passed before the doctor felt it was safe for Kathy to live a normal life. It was a year full of decisions and adjustments, and needs for all the resources this family could muster. What was the final result? Betty tried to sum it up.

Dan and I realized our need for each other's support as we never had before. We grew closer together because of this experience, and it changed me. I guess my priorities are different. It isn't so important to have the house spotlessly clean. People are more important. Our marriage is stronger, and even though we know we can never have that third child, we appreciate our children more than we ever could have without this experience.

The romantic concept of married couples with neatly dressed and perfectly behaved children who never give their parents anything but happiness is not the picture we saw in the families of the couples we studied. Couples should enjoy their children, but they should be advised that this joy will be interspersed with frustration, difficult decisions, and what will seem to be endless problems of child care, nurture, and discipline. Add to this the fact that the cost of rearing a child from birth through college increases year by year. Current estimates range between $50,000 and $90,000 per child.

Couples need to consider whether or not they are capable of negotiating these matters before having children. Betty and Dan were two people who could meet the problems and come out stronger and closer. Marriage and family counselors have seen much of the other side, however. There are the couples whose lives are disrupted by children—who cannot cope with the many problems associated with their children and, as a result, harm their children as well as themselves. The reasons for having children are many, including: society expects couples to have children, parents want to have grandchildren, people think children can cure their loneliness or fulfill their desire for continuing the family line. The one and perhaps only good reason is that the couple like children and believe they can be loving and effective parents and thus provide a healthy context in which children can grow and develop.

A surprising number of young people today are interested in children and want them after marriage. In a class of 94 college students in the spring semester of 1976, 82 said they wanted children, 4 did not, and 8 were not sure. When asked how many they wanted, 5 wanted 1, 43 desired 2, 31 wanted 3, and the rest wanted 4 or more. This was not what I expected. I am convinced, however, that young people today are giving more thought to whether or not they want or should have children; and they are giving careful thought to the number of children they feel they can care for and afford.

There is good reason for a couple to wait several years before having their first child. Waiting gives them an opportunity to test the marriage for stability and permanency. Children are affected adversely by divorce; so if there are indications that the marriage might not survive, the couple should wait through this testing period before having children. Couples also need to be warned against believing that having a child will help cure an ailing marriage. Both of these points are illustrated by an interview with Glen and Tammy, who are divorced now. I wanted to find out what effect their children, Brad and Susan, had on their marriage.

GLEN: Brad was hoped to be a unifying force. It seemed to me that at that time, Tammy felt that the only reason marriage made any sense was if she got pregnant and had a baby. The pregnancy period was definitely a unifying force in our marriage. She was more at peace with herself during that time than I have ever known her to be before or since. She was filled with anticipation. Since I had never considered anything but marriage and a family, I was thankful when she became pregnant; although it happened a little sooner than I would have planned. I was ready to start raising a family anytime and that fact coupled with the marked change in my wife's attitude toward marriage and me caused the pregnancy to be a very positive force in our lives. After Brad's birth things changed somewhat, however. Although I don't feel Brad was ever a disruptive force in our marriage, we both used him in some ways to transfer our feelings—Tammy by taking her frustrations and annoyances with me through him and I by transferring the love and affection I felt would be rejected by her to him. Maybe I could say his creation was a unifying force. During his first years there was a change from increased unification to gradual decay as he was used as an outlet for both of our frustrations. This led to a situation of accelerated decay of our relationship resulting from our transference of feelings to him. Brad was a victim of circumstance in an already sick relationship rather than a disruptive force.

TAMMY: I must agree with Glen that my anticipation of having Brad was very definitely a unifying force in our marriage. I doubt that our relationship would have lasted a year had I not gotten pregnant. I had not really wanted to get married when we did (I was barely 20 years old) but Glen was so insistent (he was 27) that he wore down my defenses. After marriage I felt very hostile toward him; I felt like he had trapped me into doing something I hadn't wanted to do. When I found out I was pregnant all of my feelings changed. I truly was happy, contented, filled with purpose and love. After Brad's birth, however, I must say things changed radically. I definitely see Brad as a disruptive force in our marriage, even though we both loved and do love him dearly. Perhaps it is because of that very fact that I see him as being disruptive. I was a very anxious new mother: I wanted desperately to do everything "right." I'm sure Brad picked up on this anxiety. There were many times when we would cry and cry and nothing I could do would help. Glen would go to his aid and he would stop crying immediately. I felt rejected by this baby that I had dreamed my whole life of having. To make matters worse, Brad was accepting the very person I felt hostile toward. I guess in a sense Glen and I competed with each other for Brad's affection and love, and in that sense, Brad was disruptive to our marriage.

But the marriage plodded on. Within two years Tammy was pregnant again. She was uneasy during this pregnancy, fearing the marriage would not last. Glen thought that another child might stabilize the marriage. Susan was born, and their hopes were revived because now they had a boy and a girl. But the revival of hope was temporary, and the marriage started downhill again toward an eventual divorce. The discipline of the children was a major issue.

GLEN: Although Tammy's and my concepts of discipline aren't really so different, our means of implementation are vastly different.

TAMMY: This was the chief area of conflict between Glen and me. My perception of the situation was that Glen wanted the children to "like" him at all costs. I felt Glen constantly left all the disciplining up to me so that he could always be the "nice guy." Conversely, I always felt like the "heavy." The result was disastrous. The children figured out early that this was an area to work one parent against the other for their advantage.

Although Tammy and Glen are now divorced and no longer live together, they are good friends. Glen says, "we are more unified in divorce than we were in marriage." Tammy says that if she had been a few years older at the time of the marriage, maybe they would have made it. Yes, they told each other how strong their love was at the beginning, but what followed, including their children, did not reinforce that love. Different expectations and role concepts tore them apart.

Virginia Satir titled a book about the family, *Peoplemaking.* How expressive this title is! It is within the family that people come into being, grow, and develop.

Put together all the current existing families and you have society. It is as simple as that. Whatever kind of training took place in the individual family will be reflected in the kind of society that is created. And institutions such as schools, churches, businesses, and governments are, by and large, extensions of family forms to non-family forms.

So. Families and societies are small and large versions of one another. They are both made up of people who have to work together, whose destinies are tied up with one another. Each features the same components—relationships of leaders to the led, the young to the old, male to female; each is involved with the process of decision-making, use of authority, and the seeking of common goals.[2]

Jerome Kagan likens the development of a child to that of the leaf and the butterfly:

The phenomena of growth fall into two patterns: enlargement and change. The leaf expands as it grows, but it does not alter its essential form. The butterfly, on the other hand, passes through dramatically different stages of change en route to adulthood.[3]

The child illustrates both kinds of development. Physically, the child grows larger and stronger while maintaining its original form. But within the child develop ideas, ideals, beliefs, emotions, attitudes, and responses—all emerging and changing the caterpillar to the butterfly. Dr. Kagan believes that this emergence is affected by many sources: siblings, peers, teachers, television, books, films, etc., but the primary source is parents. This is particularly true in the first six years of the child's life. The nature of capable parents operating in a healthy environment that is the home, is the subject of many years of study and volumes of articles and books written on the topic. Parents would do well to equip themselves with the knowledge and the skill to help them in what may be the most important task of their entire lives—assisting in the development of a human life—helping to shape the destiny of the future.

What comes after you say, "I love you"? For many couples, there will be children. If you are among them, approach your responsibility with careful thought and preparation. For what you do with your children of today will determine the nature of the world of tomorrow.

REFERENCES

1. Rudolf Dreikurs, *Children the Challenge*. New York: Duell, Sloan and Pearce, 1964.

2. Virginia Satir, *Peoplemaking*. Palo Alto, Calif.: Science and Behavior Books, 1972, p. 290.

3. Jerome Kagan, *Personality Development*. New York: Harcourt Brace Jovanovich, 1971, pp. 4, 5.

CHAPTER EIGHTEEN

The Deeper Dimension
of Marital Health

This is a difficult yet important chapter to write, because it is impossible to describe certain aspects of a marriage in which two people express certain intangible qualities that words seem unable to capture. Here are Dan and Betty, Gregory and Barbara, Dick and Dorene, and other couples in our group—all inwardly beautiful people. Knowing some of them for many years and others over the past several years has presented me with a rare opportunity to see human nature at its best, and what happens when two people of such quality unite in marriage.

Paul Tillich, one of the great minds of the twentieth century, often talked about the lost dimension of contemporary culture. People today, he thought, tended to live on the surface, searching throughout their lives for superficial things, neglecting the more important. Life, to be rich and full, must be lived in the third dimension, that of depth.

Most of our life continues on the surface. We are enslaved by the routine of our daily lives, in work and pleasure, in business and recreation. We are conquered by innumerable hazards, both good and evil. We are more driven than driving. We do not stop to look at the height above us, or to the depth below us. We are always moving forward, although usually in a circle, which finally brings us back to the place from which we first moved. We are in constant motion and never stop to plunge into the depth. We talk and talk and never listen to the voices speaking to our depth and from our depth.[1]

It is easy for a family to become enslaved by the routine of daily family life. There are mouths to be fed, rooms to clean, clothes to wash, money to be earned, budgets to be balanced, bills to be paid, and all the rest. This routine with a few hours for sleep can consume most of the twenty-four hours of the day with little time to look one another in the eyes and ask the important questions: Who are we? Why are we here? Where are we going? Yet, the couples about which I have been speaking did not neglect this important dimension of their lives, and because they did not, their lives were greatly enriched, and their families benefited. Sometimes this dimension has been referred to as the "spiritual" dimension. That would be one way of describing it. Howard and Charlotte Clinebell see it this way:

> In the fullest expression of intimacy there is a vertical dimension, a sense of relatedness to the universe which both strengthens the marital relationship and is strengthened by it. Quite apart from any church or churchly considerations, the spiritual dimension of marriage is a practical source of food for marital growth and health. No single factor does more to give a marriage joy or to keep it both a venture and an adventure in mutual fulfillment than shared commitment to spiritual discovery. The life of the spirit is deeply personal, so that moments of sharing on the spiritual level are tender, precious moments in a relationship.
>
> By spiritual intimacy is meant the sense of a vital relationship with that which transcends our brief, fragile existence—a relationship with the realm of values and meanings, with the flow of history and life about us, and with that "ultimate concern" (Tillich) which we call God.[2]

It is not easy to measure the spiritual dimension of an individual, or a couple. What does one observe in order to find material that would help in such an evaluation? The value system that one holds might be a clue. We do have some statistics on our eighteen couples that indicate something about their value systems. We asked them from what source their satisfactions were obtained: was it from economic security, better-than-average clothes, home, car, furniture, and money to do extra things; or did they get most of their satisfactions from non-material sources: friends, music, art, beauty of nature, literature, etc.?

The majority agreed that their greatest satisfactions in life were derived from the non-material sources. Three husbands said this was intensely felt; eight said it was important for their well-being; four said it was a need at times but to a lesser degree; three said it was not a felt need. Among the wives, six said it was intensely felt; ten said it was important for their well-being; and two felt it was a need at times but to a lesser degree. In only two cases did couples disagree, one listing non-material sources as being most satisfactory and the other disagreeing.

When one examines the study of the interests, hobbies, and leisure-time activities of Jim and Vicki, for example, he sees a rich outlay of outdoor activities, creative work, cultural and aesthetic interests, service projects, traveling, visiting friends and relatives, and other events that cost little money yet are rewarding in helping them and their family develop socially, mentally, and spiritually. When we observed their family life at the retreat in the summer of 1972, we could see how they planned these things with their children, and how through discussion they agreed upon goals and life-styles that enriched the lives of each member of the family. Vicki said: "We are always developing new interests together as a family or as a couple, allowing individual members to pursue interests without feeling that everyone must be included." Jim said: "I had to make up my mind that the family is important enough to get a considerable portion of my time and energy." One gets a feeling that Jim and Vicki and their two children live in a dimension deeper than surface-level concerns. This can be said about all of the couples in our select group. Some may do more of it than others, but they all take time to participate in experiences that enrich the lives of each one of them in a multitude of ways.

Basic to what families do together is their attitude toward one another. Those who live in a deeper dimension think of and treat one another differently. They live together as people rather than objects. They recognize the significance of one another as individuals. Muriel James believes that the person who lives in true dialogue with others is a "spiritual" person.

Dialogic relation is possible because of the spiritual self that is inherent in all people. We are God's Thou and our spiritual self is at the deepest core of our being.

On a principle similar to that of a percolator coffee pot, the spiritual self bubbles up and transforms the personality. Because each ego state is useful and necessary, the core of being—which is the loving spiritual self—can permeate all ego states, the entire person, body, and mind.

If the spiritual self permeates a person's Child, that person will express positive childlike qualities such as affection, warmth, curiosity, and a playfulness. If the spiritual self permeates the Adult, a person will make decisions on the basis of facts, but also on the basis of other people's feelings and well-being, and with an awareness that many decisions need to be made to preserve the total environment rather than exploit it. If the spiritual self permeates the Parent, a person will express only those nurturing and positive caring qualities that can be found in parents and will not express Parent behavior that is destructive to self or others.[3]

Muriel James relates transactional analysis to Martin Buber's concept of "I-Thou" relations and gives each ego state a dynamic quality which takes into consideration a concern, a comprehension, a love for another. Whether one relates as a Parent, an Adult, or a Child, it is done so by recognizing the total significance of the other person—a "Thou." This is in contrast to thinking of others as an "It"—an object that can be dissected, analyzed, and categorized.

If I face a human being as my *Thou*, and say the primary word *I-Thou* to him, he is not a thing among things, and does not consist of things.

This human being is not *He* or *She*, bounded from every other *He* and *She*, a specific point in space and time within the net of the world; nor is he a nature able to be experienced and described, a loose bundle of named qualities. . . .

Just as the melody is not made up of notes nor the verse of words nor the statue of lines, but they must be tugged and dragged till their unity has been scattered into these many pieces, so with the man to whom I say *Thou*. I can take out from him the colour of his hair, or of his speech, or of his goodness. I must continually do this. But each time I do it he ceases to be *Thou*.[4]

To see other people, particularly members of our family, in this light would be to revolutionize family relationships, for it would mean that we were communicating, not as object to object (the material dimension), but as person to person (the spiritual dimension). How often we have seen parents screaming at their children, or ordering and pushing them around as if they were pieces of furniture to be kicked, manipulated, or arranged! How often have we seen husbands and wives lashing out at one another, or exploiting one another, or attempting to destroy one another, as if they were objects with no thoughts, feelings, dreams, or aspirations! Perhaps this lack of sensitivity to the personal and spiritual in the family has spread out to further the process of dehumanizing the community and the world where brotherhood is intended, but where people still, in primitive style, exploit, manipulate, misuse, fight, and kill.

It was Martin Buber who spoke of the spiritual life as that which participated in the "hallowing of the everyday." When one thinks of the events of the day and the people that move in and out of these events, as opportunities for dialogue, for relating, for becoming conscious of the beauty and wonder of life, then life is transformed, and drab routine is surmounted as existence becomes infused with purpose.

How were the people in our study, who illustrated this kind of attitude and relationship in their marriages and family life, helped to do so? Since the "spiritual" dimension of life is often associated with religion and religious communities, it might be expected that these people attributed much of their life-style to these sources, and this proved to be the case. A survey of their attitudes and activities indicated that four husbands were deeply religious and had a need for God, worship, meditation, and exercising faith; eight husbands felt religion was important to their lives; four felt so to a lesser degree; and two felt no particular need, but did participate with their wives, who thought religion was important. Among the wives, six expressed a great need for religion; ten felt it was important; and two felt so to a lesser degree. In regard to attending church services, eight husbands thought it was very important; eight felt it was helpful and enjoyable; one hadn't participated; and one didn't feel it was necessary for him personally. As to the wives: twelve thought it was very important; three felt it was helpful and enjoyable; four didn't find church services helpful. In the cases where husbands or wives did not feel that attending church was particularly helpful, they did participate in some phase of the life of the church, such as a discussion group or a project related to the community. Most of the thirty-six people had some type of religious nurture as children, which, for the most part, had a positive effect on their lives, though a few desired a different kind of church and religious point of view from those of their childhood.

Carrie explained that both she and Joe came from "church-going" families, and think "it is necessary for both parents to participate in order for children to gain a feel for religion." Joe added: "I think our adjustment in marriage was due in part to our similar religious backgrounds. Together we have made substantial contributions to our church in terms of service." Carrie: "I teach Sunday school; we belong to choir and a number of our church organizations. It has affected our whole value system; and since we are such busy people, going to church is one of the few things we do together as a family." Joe: "Religion has affected my life a great deal. I have a lot of time to think about it while riding on my tractor. Farmers feel close to God, working on the land."

Dick and Dorene met while singing in the same choir in their college church, which gives them warm feelings about their church experience. Currently, Dorene helps in the music program of their church, and Dick is a church officer. They feel that their religion has contributed to creating a sound basis for their marriage.

Jim and Vicki said they felt very close because they share their religious beliefs and values, although this is "not always through a conscious effort to do so." Jim: "We're both church members. I was active at first then got busy and fell away; now I am more active again in the outreach program of our church. Religion has probably greatly affected our value system over the years. As a result we have common goals, as Vicki said, without any really conscious effort." Vicki: "We have made a great many contacts through our religious activities; some of our closest friends have come out of our study groups. Most of our social activities are church oriented. Religious training in our family really shows up in your children. We notice it particularly in our daughter who is now in high school."

In a tape made more than a year ago with Henry and Doris, who have been married the longest of any of our couples, Henry was asked: "Since you and Doris have been married for over forty-seven years, have you any thought as to why your marriage has been successful and has lasted as long as it has?" Henry: "Yes, I think fundamentally for two reasons: one is that we were both brought up in families that were quite religious in their thinking. Secondly, I think the influence of the church has meant a lot in our marriage. While there are a lot of people who say they can get along without church, hardly any of us would be content to live in a town or city without churches."

Are religion and religious institutions having a positive effect on individual persons and the institution of marriage and the family? Many writers in this field believe they are. Robert Williamson reviews some of the statistics on the number of people affected:

The United States is regarded as a religious nation, however secularized it has become. In the 1957 census of individuals fourteen years or older, there were 78 million Protestants, Roman Catholics numbered 30 million, and Jews, 4 million. Other types of Catholics possibly constitute 2 million. There are perhaps 20 million Americans who have given religious preference, largely Protestant, but who are not active members, in addition to some millions who have no religious preference. . . . In a number of respects the church influences family behavior. . . . Religion does offer a rationalizing and ritualistic sanction to marriage and family functioning. The belief in religious concepts is one means of providing the individual with a sense of purpose in his life, and his identification with religious groups offers a medium of socialization within the community. Worship and the festivities in connection with religious holidays, such as Christmas, Easter, Hanukkah, and Yom Kippur, are interrelated with family solidarity.[5]

James Peterson thinks that religion affects almost everyone in our culture, although some may not realize that it does:

More than ninety million persons in the United States belong to religious organizations. An additional large group of individuals do not hold church membership but participate to some degree in religious activities. A third group of adults no longer participate, but as children were associated with a church and received some degree of religious education. Beyond this, all of us live in a democratic society whose laws, spirit, and mores are largely an outgrowth of the close relationship of religion to life during the most formative decades of the nation's history. The influence of the Hebraic-Christian tradition is so pervasive in our national laws, ideals, and customs that even the agnostic is largely the product of a religious background.

It is reasonable to think that an institution with such a wide and historic function in all human culture and in our own civilization has many influences upon the family.

Religion is a way of bringing some organization and meaning to the infinite number of experiences which happen to us in life. Religious values absorbed in the home give the individual a philosophy or a system of values which enables him to look at life with serenity and confidence.[6]

Bossard and Boll believe that religion should be viewed as something more than worshipping in a church or temple. It operates as a culture influencing people in a number of ways:

1. A system of beliefs about God, life, and man.
2. Established forms of worship.
3. A set of observances in the lives of its followers.
4. A number of attitudes, life values, and behavior judgments.
5. A conception of life, now and in the hereafter; the relative impor-

tance of the now and the hereafter; the purpose of life; and the role of unseen forces and factors in life.[7]

Gerhard Lenski's comprehensive study of the effect of religion on family life was published in a book titled, *The Religious Factor*.[8] His conclusions were that, depending on the particular socio-religious group to which a person belonged, there would be a marked difference in his attitude toward his job, his buying habits, the goals of his nation, his politics, his sociological views, his attitudes toward race, family values, education, and many other areas. Robert Kelley sums up what he believes religion does for a marriage and recommends that all newly married couples should seek out a church or synagogue that will help them achieve marital health and family stability.

> Religion makes a number of positive contributions to family life. It gives men and women a high ideal of marriage and of the value of human personality. It is linked with the stability of the established patterns and dominant values of our society. It gives practical encouragement to the family for daily living, particularly in the education and guidance of children. It may be linked to certain factors that favor success in social and economic life.
> The choice of a church or synagogue is an important one for a newly married couple. The couple may continue as they are; or they may choose to make a change, following his religion, or turning to her faith, or seeking a new adherence.[9]

At this point, it is necessary to say that religions vary considerably. Some are conservative, some are liberal, many are in the middle of the road theologically and in regard to attitude toward social issues. Some religious groups are narrow, some broad, some foster prejudice, some are exclusive, some widely ecumenical. Some encourage personal piety, while others put stress on social action. So, according to one's choice, the final effect on him and his children will be very different. It must be said that people who marry with compatible religious backgrounds are more apt to find a satisfactory adjustment and stability than those who marry from very different backgrounds. Of the eighteen husbands in our study of successful marriages, fifteen indicated that their religious compatibility with their spouses was either outstanding or fairly successful. Only three reported that it was not a substantial contribution. Of the eighteen wives, sixteen thought their religious compatibility with their husbands was outstanding or fairly successful. Only two felt that it was otherwise. We were able to test fifteen of our couples to see how much agreement there was on sixty-five statements of faith covering such subjects as God, Prayer, Church, Society, the Religious Life, and Life After Death. One couple had but three disagreements. One had twenty-five. Only two couples had more than fourteen disagreements. The average number of disagreements was 11.4, or 17½ %. That religious compatibility had much to do with the marital adjustment and life of our couples, there is no doubt.

After reviewing studies of the way people function in marriage and family life, and as a result of our own study with our select group of eighteen couples and a host of others with whom we have made comparisons, we would have to conclude that religion and communities of faith have a decided influence upon marital health and how people function in marriage. There are all kinds of "religious" people, and one can find some horrible examples among them, but by and large, the majority of them are better for their religious experience and activity and are enriched by an additional dimension to their lives, the spiritual dimension. One of the best discussions of this dimension is that of Howard and Charlotte Clinebell in the book referred to earlier in this chapter. In the chapter entitled "The Spiritual Dimension of Marriage," they call our attention to a person's need for spiritual relatedness in the face of what is called his "existential anxiety." We are finite and stand in a "fragile position in the face of sickness, nature, fate and ultimately, death."[10]

Earlier in the book we noted the ability to face a crisis as one of the most important elements in the stable marriage. The knowledge that such crises will come from time to time is the cause of our existential anxiety.

The impact of existential anxiety has had many effects in the life of mankind, including his long pilgrimage in every known culture toward understanding the nature of existence. This pilgrimage is man's religion. Existential anxiety drives man to seek a relationship beyond the limitations of human ties. Unlike neurotic anxiety, there is no psychotherapeutic answer to existential anxiety. It is existential in that it is an inescapable part of existence—a normal response to man's awareness of his own mortality. *But,* the way a man handles his existential anxiety makes it either a stimulus to creativity or a paralyzing force which dulls his vitality and self-awareness.[11]

The courage to face it in a positive way can "come only from *facing existential anxiety within a relationship of trust and a philosophy of life which gives meaning to existence.*"[12]

Because all married couples go through crisis experiences during their married lifetime, they need to have a faith, hope, and trust that will take them victoriously through their journey. We had known for some time that a couple who were neighbors of ours for many years in another city were going through a difficult period in their lives. Bernt, the husband and father, was dying of cancer. The family was prepared. On December 18, 1974, just before Christmas, he died. This was the letter we received from his wife:

Our beloved Bernt's suffering ended last night. He was at home and in my arms, and all of his boys and grandchildren were with him his last three days on earth. Now we'll be looking up. A memorial service will be at our church this Saturday at 2:00 p.m. Friends are invited to greet the family at home tomorrow, and again, in the church parlor after the service.

Family and friends and neighbors and colleagues have all been so wonderfully wonderful! (Doctors and nurses, too!) The intangible good vibrations are the best of all. We haven't even written to express our gratitude, but please know that though life is terribly complex for each individual—it is truly beautiful—and you are helping make it so.

Oh! we are so very blessed to have God's love and Bernt's. We'll sing "Joy to the World" at his service and know you'll be singing with us.

Please—no flowers; just your love.

MARGIE

The spirit of this letter speaks for itself. It is truly a product of a deeper dimension of life!

What about the future? I have read several thousand autobiographies of college students during the past seven years. There is a chapter in each autobiography on the religious attitudes and practices of the student. Rarely do I ever read one in which a young person declares himself or herself to be irreligious. Most of them begin with a statement like: "I consider myself to be a very religious person." Many of them, at least for the present time, seem alienated from the church or synagogue. A portion of them are devoutly dedicated to small sects or movements that gather informally to pray and study the Bible. Many state that they cannot see the value of "going to church." Some view "church-goers" as those who are just going through motions or are hypocritical.

On the other hand, churches are changing to meet the times. Many are trying to put more meaning into the service of worship. Some are using contemporary music and art forms. There is a genuine effort in many of the churches to become inclusive rather than exclusive, to be racially integrated and ecumenical. Most of the churches today are trying to relate faith and belief to the current needs of people and society. Henry Bowman thinks many of our young people will eventually return to their church homes.

College students often abandon religion and the church temporarily, only to return to them later in life, when the responsibilities of marriage and parenthood awaken them to a new sense of religious values. When this occurs, early training often reasserts itself. The apple seldom falls far from the tree.[13]

Will the spiritual dimension of life be preserved for the future? I think it will. It is too much a part of man's quest for meaning. In 1974, *Psychology Today* magazine made a survey of the religious beliefs, ideas, and practices of its readers. The results were surprising in terms of the numbers who replied and what they had to say. Apparently, the survey did hit an "exposed nerve." The questionnaire motivated 40,000 readers to reply, of which the researchers drew 2,000 for analysis. Readers of *Psychology Today* are less likely than most Americans to identify with conventional religious bodies (53 percent did so). This, they concluded, was not a consequence of the fact that many of their sample were from the younger generation, since a recent Gallup poll found that three-fourths of all Americans between eighteen and twenty-four belong to one of the three main religions.

What were the conclusions of the analysts? Here are some of their observations:

More and more Americans have come to regard formal religion with skepticism or disinterest. . . . Those who went weekly now go a few times a year. Those who went to church occasionally now never do.

The logical assumption was that if the church is crumbling, religion must be crumbling, too. If people aren't praying at fixed times in sacred places, they obviously aren't praying.

Our research shows this assumption is not true. Religious sentiment is everywhere. People still seek answers to the great religious questions that human beings have addressed themselves to for centuries, and they still ache to believe that someone is minding the store, that there is something beyond our personal and collective reach. "There must be something more," wrote one reader. "I'd hate to think that we humans are the most superior."[14]

Perhaps there is a restlessness in the hearts of humanity to find the lost dimension that Dr. Tillich felt is most important. If this be true, then people who marry and establish families will recover a sense of the significance of life which will enrich their relationships, promote marital health, and help the family to be what it always needs to be, the basis for a sound society in the days to come.

REFERENCES

1. Paul Tillich, *The Shaking of the Foundations.* New York: Charles Scribner's Sons, 1948, pp. 55, 56.

2. Howard J. Clinebell and Charlotte H. Clinebell, *The Intimate Marriage.* New York: Harper and Row, 1970, pp. 179, 180.

3. Muriel M. James, *Born to Love.* Reading, Mass.: Addison-Wesley Publishing Co., 1973, pp. 197, 198.

4. Martin Buber, *I and Thou.* New York: Charles Scribner's Sons, 1958, pp. 8, 9.

5. Robert C. Williamson, *Marriage and Family Relations.* New York: John Wiley and Sons, 1972, pp. 44, 45.

6. James A. Peterson, *Education for Marriage.* New York: Charles Scribner's Sons, 1964, p. 435.

7. James H. Bossard and Eleanor Boll, *One Marriage—Two Faiths.* New York: Ronald Press, 1959, pp. 48, 49.

8. Gerhard Lenski, *The Religious Factor.* New York: Doubleday and Co., 1961.

9. Robert K. Kelley, *Courtship, Marriage, and the Family.* New York: Harcourt, Brace and World, 1969, pp. 437–438.

10. Howard J. Clinebell and Charlotte H. Clinebell, *The Intimate Marriage.* New York: Harper and Row, 1970, p. 188.

11. *Ibid.,* pp. 188, 189.

12. *Ibid.,* pp. 189.

13. Henry A. Bowman, *Marriage for Moderns.* New York: McGraw-Hill Book Co., 1974, p. 163.

14. Robert Wuthnow and Charles Y. Glock, "The Shifting Focus of Faith: A Survey Report. God in the Gut," *Psychology Today,* Vol. 8, No. 6 (November 1974), p. 136.

CHAPTER NINETEEN

The Long-Distance Runners

Throughout this book we have talked about the "sprinters" and the "long-distance runners" in married life. The "sprinters," of course, are those who start out strong and fast, but fall by the wayside after a few years. They do not seem to have the qualities of endurance and durability. But the "long-distance runners" just keep going year after year. If we could learn more about how they do it, we might be more able to keep marriages healthy over a longer period of time and stop the accelerating divorce rate.

Henry and Doris have been married the longest of any couple in our group—forty-seven years. We have already quoted Doris as saying that she attributed their long happy marriage to the fact that she liked Henry before she married him, and she still likes him. Apparently, they have been able to continue to meet each other's expectations through the various changes of the years. They also mention the quality of "give and take" which is very much in evidence in their marriage. They communicate well and exhibit considerable skill in working out their problems and resolving their conflicts.

Bill and Beth, the couple married next to longest in our group—forty-five years—are highly companionable. They like to be together and do things together. Within the past few years, Beth has taken courses in a university. Bill reads widely and keeps up on current affairs. They like to discuss whatever happens to be of current interest to them. Along with these characteristics, both have an earnest desire to improve their marriage even after all these years. For forty-five years they have worked with unceasing determination to make their marriage function. Beth said, "Both Bill and I are from families that have stayed together (I can think of no divorce among our forebears), so that we entered marriage expecting it to be a commitment for life." This expectation and commitment have given birth to rewarding experiences and pleasant memories.

Fred and Claudia have been married twenty-eight years. They, too, attribute their lengthy success to the fact they have developed the capacity to "give and take." One notices the regard they have for each other and the kind and understanding manner they exhibit in each other's presence. Claudia says, "Through the years we have learned to really communicate our feelings, needs, and ideas to each other. This wasn't easy at first." But it seems easy to them now, for it is an established habit of interacting. They are honest, frank, but always discuss or argue with understanding and good humor.

Oliver and Alice have been married twenty-five years. A study of the history of their married life indicates two people who have worked to make their marriage function. Their conscious effort to make their marriage work has carried them through good times and bad. They believe that a couple should start from the very beginning with the conviction that they can make it work. As they put it, "We really did not know that the marriage would be successful. We were both convinced we would do everything to make it work." And that is what they have done.

Russell and Andrea have been married twenty-three years. They stress the fact that their marriage has been outstanding in that they have managed to be companions enjoying common interests, meeting each other's needs, and communicating in ways that lead to understanding and problem solving. They stress that they like each other and how much this has helped them to have so many pleasant experiences together.

We have already written a great deal about Jack and Josie. They have been married nineteen years. Here are two people who feel they were most fortunate to have found each other. They do seem to be temperamentally suited to each other. They like each other and are proud of each other's accomplishments. They give each other a considerable amount of positive reinforcement, which keeps them going. They stress the fact that they have the same goals and value system and that this keeps them growing together.

Ann Roberts, one of my former graduate students, has completed a thesis on couples that have been married more than fifty years.[1] Participating with her in the project was her husband, William L. Roberts, Director of the Family Practice Center at the University of Arizona College of Medicine. Their research gives us some interesting material to consider. In stating her purpose, Ann Roberts writes: "Perhaps this opportunity to study marriages which have lasted over fifty years will bring to light some happily married couples who have built up patterns of mutual encouragement and appreciation over the years."

One of her general conclusions is:

The older couples in the study sample appeared to be no less happy than young couples. The majority of the older couples in the study sample are happily married and have a favorable view of life, as seen in their morale scores. For them, marriage is a source of comfort and support. Their continuous relationship over the years has taught them to cope with crisis and change. Their early commitment to each other may have been tested many times over the years, but they had "staying power." This sense of commitment and mutual support challenges the myth of progressive disenchantment in the later years of marriage. Many of the older couples are experiencing an increasing closeness as they depend less on their families and social institutions. The sharing and caring for each other in these later years give them a sense of purpose and usefulness.

The mean age of the husbands studied was 80.40, while the mean age of the wives was 77.94. Twenty-seven couples had been married between 50 and 54 years. Nine couples had been married between 55 and 59 years. Fourteen couples had been married between 60 and 65 years. The mean age at the time of their marriage for the men was 24.08; for the women, it was 21.64. In my opinion, this would still stand today as sound ages at which to begin a marriage.

When asked if they would marry the same person if they had it to do all over again, 93 percent said, "Yes." Four said they would marry a different person, and three said they would not marry at all. When asked if they had ever considered a divorce, only two persons said they had. Several laughed and replied, "Divorce—no, but murder—yes."

To have a well-functioning marriage fifty or more years after having said, "I love you," is not an easy accomplishment, and many find it impossible. There are some "sprinters" who have high expectations at the start but last no longer than one or two years. There are also many couples who stay together as long as they both live, yet who do not feel that marriage in the later years is a very happy state. A number of researchers such as Peter Pineo[2] conclude that there is a gradual change from a state of satisfaction in the early years to one of disenchantment in the later years. He discovered in couples twenty years after the engagement period, a decline in marital satisfaction, a loss of intimacy, and a slowing down of certain activities, mostly sexual relations. Other studies show that there are fluctuations rather than declines and that while there may be a loss in one area, there may be a gain in another. In an earlier chapter I reflected on the married life of my own parents, who lived together satisfactorily for sixty-nine years, until my father's death at the age of ninety-six. The last thirty-five years of their married life were much happier than their middle years. These very satisfactory years occurred after my father's retirement. This may be due in part to the fact that my father's work was in the nature of routine drudgery, and financial problems were ever present until the children left home and became independent. After retirement, money was not a great problem, and many of the hassles of earlier years were resolved. My father was a man who enjoyed domestic activities and thoroughly enjoyed working around the home, gardening, repairing, and even doing housework. Aaron Lipman illustrates this in his study showing that many married couples find life as satisfactory, or even more satisfactory in their later years, than they did in earlier ones.[3]

One can readily understand that older couples have a number of new problems to negotiate which require certain attitudes and skills. The husband needs to find meaning in life after he has retired from a job that has occupied his time and attention for many years. He must find a way through social security, pension, and perhaps part-time employment to provide an income sufficient for the needs of himself and his wife. Both husband and wife need to maintain their physical health the best they can. The wife may feel that in addition to being physically healthy, she must remain as attractive as possible. Both must shift from instrumental roles formerly performed in job tasks and child rearing to expressive roles, where they need to support each other emotionally. New interests and sometimes new friends must be found to keep life worthwhile. In the group married more than fifty years, mobility became a problem. Some were physically unable to get to the places to which they wanted to go. Others found difficulty in obtaining transportation. But many older couples are able to negotiate these difficulties and live contented lives to the end.

Herbert Otto feels that the failure of many people and their marriages is the result of a lack of well-formulated life goals.

Very few people have ever taken the time to formulate clearly their life goals— what they wish to accomplish during their all too brief sojourn on earth. Much of human life seems to be pervaded by an aimlessness, a drifting with the currents and tides of happenstance. Human aimlessness is responsible for considerable unhappiness as well as much anger and hostility.[4]

People, he believes, become trapped into the narrow confines of dealing in short-time goals earlier in life and therefore neglect that which could help them realize their potential later in life. This is in line with what Albert Ellis has said many times—that marriages fail, for the most part, because of "goofing" or "drifting." Couples who plan ahead early in their married life, reap benefits later. James Peterson, an authority on married life in the middle years, emphasizes this need of getting ready early for the later years.

How men and women resolve the crisis of middle age is in a sense an indication of how they will live in retirement. If they do not perfect the use of leisure at this time, they will hardly be ready for a total life of leisure at fifty-five, sixty, or sixty-five. Middle age is a school for retirement, and new activities developed then bloom fully in later years. Thus the positive adoption of new patterns in the middle years not only enriches those months, but also prepares the person for the last part of the cycle. There are other aspects of this preparation that must occupy the attention of men and women at the prime of life, such as careful economic planning for the years ahead and conservation of health so that there will be some reserves to help enjoy retirement. When the problems of middle age are solved, it is hoped that in the solution will be a promise for a many-faceted life of satisfaction during the sunset years.[5]

We should add to this by stating that a successful marriage in the last stage begins in the first stage, and that marriages that are functioning satisfactorily in the early stages are more apt to function satisfactorily in the later stages. What are the areas that need to be looked after from the beginning? I have examined the case histories of the couples in our study who have been married more than fifteen years, the fifty couples married more than fifty years in the study of Ann Roberts, and the long married life of my own parents, and have attempted to list what the important areas are. These are the areas in which these people, the long-distance runners, have excelled.

1. A positive, decisive attitude toward marital success. Many of these people stated that from the start they believed it would work and they intended to make it work. They entered into marriage, liking it, anticipating it, determined to take care of all circumstances as they arose. They had the courage to face hazardous situations, and they felt confident and capable in the face of the future, come wind, come weather.

2. The ability to adapt and adjust to changing circumstances. The various stages of marriage through the years are very different and require resilience and flexibility in the persons involved, if they are to be met successfully. There are the early years when two people are first married; the child-bearing years; the child-rearing years; the child-leaving years; the empty nest; middle age; retirement; finding a new kind of relationship with children living elsewhere; the joy of grandchildren; the challenge of finding meaning in the later years. There will be good days and bad days, times of economic hardship and days of affluence, sickness and health, joy and sorrow. The couples we have studied seem to be able to adapt and adjust to all of these changing scenes of married life.

Lest anyone get a false impression that these older couples had an easier time than most throughout their married lives, let it be known that they had their share of troubles through it all. Among the fifty couples in the Roberts study, one had thirteen children, one had ten, two had nine, one had eight, one had seven, one had six, and two had five. No one who has had children would imagine that all of these children could have been reared without some difficulty. Many of the couples reported the death of young children and the loss of sons in the Second World War. There were many accounts of sudden illnesses followed by death that might have been prevented with modern-day medicine. All married couples have problems. These problems are different for different couples, but no marriage escapes problems. The problems do not destroy the marriage, but the lack of ability to meet the problems has a disastrous effect. The older couples seemed to have developed the capacity to meet and negotiate their problems.

3. A gradual growing together. The opposite of this is seen in couples that grow apart as they develop different interests and move toward different goals. All people will change, but this change can be a productive factor in marriage if the couple understands the changes that are taking place and adjusts to them. New interests in common can be developed. Ideas and knowledge can be shared. The sharing of long-range, important life goals naturally brings a couple closer together as time passes. Communication plays an important role in making this possible. Companionship is the reward.

4. The development and exercise of personality characteristics that act as a lubricant to the relationship and keep the parts functioning smoothly. Marriages deteriorate when the people in them are critical, complaining, pessimistic, moody, short-tempered, caustic, and tense. Marriages tend to operate smoothly when spouses display characteristics of tolerance, understanding, good humor, forgiveness, warmth, optimism, and encouragement. The people who had made it successfully over a long period of time seemed to mellow with age and were comfortable to live with.

5. Characteristics that make for durability. We were not sure how to describe this quality in our couples, but we knew it was there. Of course, there were physical stamina and good health, which contributed to the durable quality of the relationship. The average number of years a couple can expect to be together is from forty to forty-five. Most of these couples had exceeded that by a number of years. In addition to this, we noticed an emotional stability consisting of patience, tolerance, evenness, the ability to take things in stride, and a general tendency to be happy with whatever came. As Ann Roberts viewed the situation with the couples married more than fifty years: "The general picture of high satisfaction with life in older married persons which has been reported in many previous studies was substantiated by the study sample." The diet and exercise that were practiced in their physical program were matched by their practice

of keeping mentally and emotionally healthy. The combination made them "durable" people. As to those married the longest, it would seem that the Fates did indeed conspire to weave those staminiferous threads in mind and body to give strength and length of life, and long and enduring marriages.

6. The learned art of reciprocal, positive reinforcement that builds morale. As people grow older, they need increasing amounts of encouragement and reinforcement. The tendency to become depressed and lose the desire to meet each new day with enthusiasm and expectation is ever present. The couples we observed helped each other overcome this tendency. People who live alone cannot have this opportunity to the degree that married couples can. Ann Roberts concluded that "marriage appears to contribute to the morale of older persons," and in her study of the literature on the subject over the past twenty years found most researchers reaching the same conclusion. In most of the older couples, we noticed an attentiveness to each other's needs and a daily desire to serve the best interests of each other. Through companionship they shared pleasantries and sadness as they came into their lives; thus the joys were doubled, and the sorrows were halved.

7. The development of skills in handling conflict and disagreements. In the study of the couples married more than fifty years, Ann Roberts reported: "When the subjects were asked how the couple handled disagreements, 63 percent said that matters were handled by 'give and take', 19 percent indicated that the wives give in. 85 percent indicated that they participate as a team in outside activities, and 99 percent reported that they confide in their spouse in most everything. These findings tend to indicate that there is little struggle for dominance and point in the direction of a companionship relationship between husband and wife." In the matter of family finances, there was an 84 percent agreement; recreation—81; choice of friends—84; matters relating to affection—89; philosophy of life—78; and basic belief in proper conduct—79. In testing their decision-making by suggesting fantasy situations, she observed "no conclusive pattern of male dominance or female aggressiveness."

8. The ability to adapt to changing expectations. Naturally the expectations entertained by a couple in the first ten years of marriage are going to be quite different from the expectations of that same couple in their fortieth or fiftieth year of marriage. Satisfactions that were more romantic in nature in early years need to be translated into satisfactions that are more comfort- and security-oriented later. We felt that the older couples, for the most part, had made this transition satisfactorily. Ann Roberts tested the couples married more than fifty years with the *Life*

Satisfaction Index-Z developed by Neugarten, Havighurst, and Tobin.[6] This instrument tested in five categories considered important for older people: 1. Zest—showing zest in several areas of life, liking to do things, and being enthusiastic. 2. Resolution and fortitude, not giving up, accepting the good with the bad and making the best of it, and accepting responsibility for one's own personal life. 3. Agreement between desired and achieved goals—the feeling of having accomplished what one set out to do. 4. Positive self-concept—feeling one is worthwhile. 5. A general mood tone—indicating a general state of happiness, optimism, and pleasant reaction in life situations.

Twenty-six couples out of the fifty scored high satisfaction with life. Only in the case of eight couples did both husband and wife score below the mean, rating a low satisfaction with life. Most of them indicated a high or above-average satisfaction with life. Forty-two out of the fifty couples had incomes under $10,000 a year, but this did not seem to create an undue amount of anxiety for them. The couples interviewed seemed content with what they found in life at their age and had few regrets or disappointments to mention. Life seemed as rewarding currently as it had been in their early years. They had made a satisfactory reconciliation between expectations and reality.

9. Reliance on religious resources as a source of well-being. All the couples in my study were related to a church and participated fairly regularly. Ninety-nine persons in the study of Ann Roberts had a religious preference. Only fourteen were not members of a church or synagogue. Sixty-one percent said that religion was very important or the most important factor in their lives. Only two persons said religion had no importance, while thirteen said that it was not very important to them. Fifty-three percent were very active and participated in a religious service at least once a week. Some of the people shared all their social life with church friends. Many said that they could face death more easily because of their religious faith. There is no doubt from the subjects we studied in these two groups that religion was an important factor in giving the couples faith, hope, stability, and meaning.

We quoted earlier in the book from Dr. Hobart Mowrer, who said to a group of young would-be counselors, "If you want to learn how to get some place, talk to someone who has been there." How well this wisdom applies here. If people would like to know something about the matrimonial journey that wends its way far into the future, let them stop for awhile and talk to those who have made this journey, and made it successfully. Perhaps they can tell us what we need to be thinking about and doing to prepare for a similar journey, which most of us would like to take, particularly so, if it can be as rich and rewarding for us as for the long-distance runners we have just met. In the words of the poet, they say to us:

> Grow old along with me!
> The best is yet to be,
> The last of life, for which the first was made:
> Our times are in his hand
> Who saith, "A whole I planned,
> Youth shows but half; trust God: see all,
> nor be afraid!"[7]

REFERENCES

1. Ann Roberts, *Factors in Lifestyle of Couples Married Fifty Years or More in Tucson, Arizona, 1975.* (Unpublished thesis, used by permission)

2. Peter C. Pineo, "Disenchantment in the Later Years of Marriage," *Marriage and Family Living,* Vol. 23 (1961), pp. 3–11.

3. Aaron Lipman, "Role Conceptions and Morale of Couples in Retirement," *Journal of Gerontology,* Vol. 16 (1961), pp. 267–71.

4. Herbert A. Otto, *More Joy in Your Marriage.* New York: Hawthorn Books, 1969, p. 149.

5. James A. Peterson, *Married Love in the Middle Years.* New York: Association Press, 1968, p. 26.

6. Bernice Neugarten, Robert Havighurst, and Sheldon Tobin, "The Measurement of Life Satisfaction," *Journal of Gerontology,* Vol. 16 (1961), pp. 134–43.

7. Robert Browning, *Rabbi Ben Ezra.*

CHAPTER TWENTY

The Marital Health Checkup

It is natural that the final chapter in this book should be on the subject of how to keep a marriage healthy. What comes after you say, "I love you"? A great amount of thought, effort, experimentation, and hard work. The couples in our select group who have experienced so much fulfillment in their married lives, reveal a practice that cannot be overlooked. They continue to work to improve their marriages day after day, week after week, year after year. They take advantage of numerous opportunities to enrich their relationships and their family life. They are conscious of the need of a periodic marital health check-up. This is a daily matter, of course, but many of us have come to believe that something additional is necessary. David and Vera Mace point this out very effectively in a book written to stress the importance of becoming involved with others to keep one's marriage rich and growing:

> We have become deeply convinced that the real agents of change in our lives are *other people with whom we become involved*. Just as the achievement of a truly satisfying marriage comes from the deepening of mutual involvement between the partners, so the motivation to work at enriching a marriage comes from involvement with people who can guide and support our efforts (like marriage counselors) and people who can join with us in the same kind of endeavor (like other couples in a group). Reading about marriage enrichment or hearing about it can be a very significant first step in giving us the idea, in telling us what is possible. But nothing significant is going to happen for most of us until we take the decisive step of linking up with other people who can work with us and hold us to achieve our purpose.[1]

Marriage is no different from many things we all do in life: if we do not work to improve ourselves, we deteriorate. This is true in matters of health—physical, mental, and emotional. Without proper habits of diet, exercise, right thinking and acting, we will lose our vitality and capability to function in all of these areas. As Albert Ellis has said, we will "goof" or "drift." I am reminded of the person who begins to play golf without instruction, and continues to play without practice or getting help from those better players who may be his golfing companions. He not only fails to improve his game, but also acquires bad habits and poor techniques which become habitual and self-defeating as time goes on. After a number of years the situation becomes almost hopeless, even though he may go for help at that time. His manner of playing has become so deeply ingrained that change is almost impossible.

This same thing is true in the lives of married couples. Often they begin without instruction and training in how to be married, how to organize family life, and how to enrich this important experience through the years. Mistakes are made, misunderstandings arise, differences are noted, and bad habits of living and relating make themselves felt. If allowed to continue without developing methods and attitudes to take care of them, these habits will begin to cause erosion in the relationship between husband and wife, and disorganization in the family. Every marriage counselor knows the sadness of the occasion when a couple comes in after many years with a multitude of problems and asks for help. They sometimes are beyond the point where help can be given effectively. Many times the couple does not go for help until they are considering a divorce, and want the marriage counselor to have a chance to help save the marriage before the divorce is final.

We are urged to get annual check-ups from our dentists and medical doctors. We are told repeatedly not to wait until we have a serious health problem before we go to a doctor. Preventive medicine is recognized as the best channel to good health. Why should it not also be the best channel to good marital health? The answer: it most certainly is! Almost every marriage counselor I know would like to participate in a program in which people are *kept* healthy in their marriages, and it is a very real possibility if married people would seek it urgently.

One might try to predict what would happen if all couples at the end of the first six months of married life, or on their first wedding anniversary, would come to a marriage counselor, trained clergyman, or social worker, for a discussion of how they are progressing in this new and important endeavor of their lives. It is during the first year or two that trouble begins to show in the marital relationship. Two people are trying to learn to live together, and adapt and adjust to a whole new way of life. Of course, they are going to make mistakes, discover different ways of thinking and doing, argue and disagree, and become upset and frustrated. These things happen to all married couples, and it is not that they happen, but how the couple reacts to them and meets them that is important. It is here that they could use a helper. Just as the athlete needs a coach, a trainer, or a "pro," so does the young married couple need someone to help them evaluate their progress and encourage them in positive ways to meet their problems.

In the chapter, "Don't Say Goodbye to Love Too Soon," we tried to explain what a marriage counselor tries to do to help a couple who comes to him for help. Marriage counselors are trained and experienced in helping people improve their marriages. They would be delighted to have couples come with no particular serious problem to learn more about how to keep their marriages healthy. If this were common practice, marriages would improve in quality, the divorce rate would drop sharply, and family life would improve to the extent that both parents and children would find a great deal more happiness and fulfillment.

How many marriages ever attain their full potential? The answer most surely must be: Not many. Most of us as individuals operate on a mere fraction of our potential, probably not more than 10 percent. If that be the case, then marriages must operate on a fraction of what they might be in terms of their ultimate capacity and capability. To develop potential, individually or in a group, there must be help from the outside. We must join with others to receive the knowledge and the motivation to grow. In no place does the truth of this apply more than to the growth and development of marriages.

In 1947 in Bethel, Maine, a very interesting movement got started in this country. Kurt Lewin, a social psychologist working at the Massachusetts Institute of Technology with his staff and students, had suggested earlier that training in the skill of relating to others was essential but often neglected in our society. Shortly after Lewin's death, the Bethel meeting was held and became the first T Group (T stands for training) in this country. Lewin's colleagues continued to promote and facilitate the movement, and an organization, the National Training Laboratories, was formed. In the years following, the movement spread and took many forms called by different names: encounter groups, T groups, sensitivity training groups, creativity workshops, Gestalt groups, etc. Not all groups have been of equal value. Some have helped individuals and marriages develop and grow. Others have had little effect or have been harmful. Results have been directly proportional to the quality of the leadership and the people who come into the group.

In the late 1950's, the Marriage Encounter[2] program was developed in Spain by a Roman Catholic priest named Father Gabriel Calvo. It was influenced by another program known as the Spanish Christian Family

Movement. The Marriage Encounter idea spread to Latin America, and in 1967, Father Calvo came to the United States with fifty Mexican and Spanish "team couples" and started encounter weekends in Spanish-speaking American communities.

The first Marriage Encounter in English sponsored by the Roman Catholic church was held at Notre Dame University in August of 1967. Since that time, more than 100,000 couples have participated in this particular program, and the movement has spread to more than a dozen countries of the world.

David and Vera Mace conducted their first retreat for couples desiring marriage enrichment at Kirkridge in Pennsylvania in October, 1962. Later they conducted training sessions for Quaker couples selected by their Yearly Meetings from all over the United States and brought to Pendle Hill near Philadelphia. Here they were prepared to go back to lead retreats set up for them in their own regions.[3]

The United Methodist Church has a program for an area or a church with at least ten couples who would like to participate in a marriage enrichment weekend. The local area selects a dean to handle arrangements and organize publicity, after which the Director of Marriage Enrichment Programming[4] is contacted to establish a date and arrange for the necessary leadership couples. The Board provides brochures that contain a description of the weekend and logistical details.

I have had a number of experiences with training groups for people about to enter marriage, and with groups seeking to improve their marriages. My wife and I, along with another couple, recently helped organize and facilitate a marriage enrichment group following a pattern described later in this chapter. All of these projects seem to us to be highly productive in the lives of those who participated. The experience was positive for the groups, both as individuals and as couples. Why is this group experience needed and appreciated? Carl Rogers explains it this way:

I believe the soil out of which this demand grows has two elements. The first is the increasing dehumanization of our culture, where the person does not count—only his IBM card or Social Security number. This impersonal quality runs through all the institutions in our land. The second element is that we are sufficiently affluent to pay attention to our psychological wants. . . . But what is the psychological need that draws people into encounter groups? I believe it is a hunger for something the person does not find in his work environment, in his church, certainly not in his school or college, and sadly enough, not even in modern family life. It is a hunger for relationships which are close and real; in which feelings and emotions can be spontaneously expressed without first being carefully censored or bottled up; where deep experiences—disappointments and joys—can be shared; where new ways of behaving can be risked and tried out, where, in a word, he approaches the state where all is known and all accepted, and thus further growth becomes possible.[5]

Many of the goals and accomplishments of this group experience can be helpful to married couples who need them to revitalize their own marriages. Couples here may sense the importance of trust, the reduction of rigidity and defensiveness, freedom of communication, better listening habits, and the expression of true feelings. The experiences that have been learned and felt in the group may spill over into the marriage relationship and family life of the couple. It is possible that married couples who are not accustomed to sharing the nature of their marital relationships with others can find a new freedom and openness with others, and get the kind of help they need by so doing.

Couples who have not had the experience of being in a marriage enrichment group are curious to know what happens in a typical group, and some are a bit apprehensive. At the beginning of one of our sessions, one couple asked: "Do we have to touch one another?" There are other fears, such as that of telling intimate matters concerning their marriage. These people are reassured by being told that they do not have to share at all, if they do not wish to do so.

Our most recent group had a very simple format. We met on two successive Friday evenings with no time limit on the sessions. The first objective was to let the couples get to know one another to feel comfortable. Then each married couple was asked to get together and draw a picture of their married life or symbolize their marriage in a drawing. When all had completed their drawings, each couple was given the opportunity to explain the meaning of their joint artistic endeavor. A discussion followed in which the entire group raised matters about which they wished to know more. We hadn't expected that this would take so long and would be so productive. But at the end of the two long sessions, all present felt that they had been greatly helped through the experience and that each had grown closer to his spouse and to others in the group.

David and Vera Mace have written in their book, referred to earlier, about what happens in their groups.[6] I will attempt to summarize the general structure of their retreats, feeling it might be helpful in understanding the nature of their work in this area as it has developed through the years.

1. Getting acquainted. This occupies the first evening, which is generally Friday. Each couple takes turns at being questioned about themselves by the whole group. This avoids the traditional and less effective method of "going around the circle," each telling about himself or herself. Everyone is called by his first name throughout the sessions. This

getting acquainted period is essential to all that follows, and that is the reason the entire evening is given to it.

2. Next morning (Saturday) the group assembles for a three-hour session. At the beginning of each of the remaining sessions everyone present is given the opportunity to express "concerns"—a chance to express negative feelings, ask questions, or suggest changes. After this the group is asked where they want to begin to look at their marriages and consider how to enrich them. The suggestions are written into an agenda, and later a decision is made as to which item should be dealt with first. It is desirable to bring the discussion from an intellectual level to one of sharing personal experiences. This is kept on a voluntary basis, and no one is pressured to share. A couple who are telling about their particular experience may be asked to face each other and engage in a dialogue on the matter being discussed.

3. The couples are free after lunch to do whatever they wish—rest, walk, drive—but they also have some work that must be done. At the end of the morning session, each person is asked to write down five things he likes about his marriage, five things he would like to see improved in the marriage, and five things he could do himself to improve the marriage relationship. When the couples are alone together in the afternoon, they are asked to share these items with each other in any manner they wish. The group reassembles in the late afternoon, and couples who are willing are given an opportunity to tell the group what was accomplished in their encounter earlier.

4. On the following morning (Sunday), there is a three-hour session which concludes the retreat. During this time the couples are asked, after a period of consultation with each other, to report on any new ideas or insights they may have gotten so far and what they might be planning to do to help their marriages grow in the days to come.

The Maces believe that marriage enrichment programs commonly have four results:

1. *A new awareness of growth potential in marriage.* A static concept of marriage is replaced with a dynamic one.

2. *The discovery that few couples have unique difficulties.* It does not take long for a couple in the group to discover that other couples are experiencing much of the same circumstances as they are.

3. *The clearing away of some obstacles to growth.* Often a marriage fails to grow because of some unresolved conflict or a block to communication. A marriage enrichment experience can provide help and motivation to make it possible to start growing.

4. *A sense of vocation to help others.* A couple having a good experi-

ence in the group will be moved to share what they gained from it with other couples. Couples who have found a way to enrich their marriages are the logical ones to help others who could also benefit from a similar experience. Out of this conviction has come the idea for ACME (Association of Couples for Marriage Enrichment),[7] a nationwide movement to organize married couples into groups for the purpose of experiencing the benefits of marriage enrichment, and aid in establishing additional chapters in as many places as possible. State and local chairmen help promote the organization. Training groups are set up for couples who wish to be leaders of enrichment groups at a future time. To be a "lead couple," they must have been through an enrichment group as participants and have completed a training program.

Church denominations, the YMCA, and other movements have organized programs to encourage the spread of marriage enrichment groups, couples communication seminars, family "Understand-ins," marriage encounter groups, etc. All of these movements emphasize the importance of growth in marriage and family life as it can take place in a group experience. This cannot be overemphasized. Lectures on the subject of improving marriages, discussion groups, classes, and individual reading will help, but the group experience is unique in providing the help and motivation so greatly needed in contemporary marriages.

REFERENCES

1. David Mace and Vera Mace, *We Can Have Better Marriages If We Really Want Them.* Nashville, Tenn.: Abingdon Press, 1974, p. 117.
2. Antoinette Bosco, *Marriage Encounter: The Rediscovery of Love.* St. Meinrad, Ind.: Abbey Press, 1972.
3. David Mace and Vera Mace, *Marriage Enrichment Retreats: Story of a Quaker Project.* Philadelphia: Friends General Conference.
4. Director of Marriage Enrichment Programming, United Methodist Board of Discipleship, Box 840, Nashville, Tenn., 37202.
5. Carl R. Rogers, *Carl Rogers on Encounter Groups.* New York: Harper and Row, 1970, pp. 10, 11.
6. David Mace and Vera Mace, *We Can Have Better Marriages,* Ch. 18.
7. Information and membership forms may be obtained by writing to ACME, P.O. Box 10596, Winston-Salem, N.C. 27108.

Bibliography

Adler, Alfred. *The Science of Living*. Garden City, N.Y.: Doubleday and Co., 1969.

Albee, Edward. *Who's Afraid of Virginia Woolf?* New York: Simon and Schuster, 1962.

Alexander, Paul W. "The Follies of Divorce—A Therapeutic Approach to the Problem," *University of Illinois Law Forum*, Vol. 1949 (Winter Number).

Allport, G. W., Vernon, P. E., Lindzey, G. *Study of Values*. 3rd ed. Boston, Mass.: Houghton Mifflin Co., 1960.

American Medical Association, Committee on Human Sexuality, 1973.

Arieti, Silvano, & Arieti, James. *Love Can Be Found*. New York: Harcourt Brace Jovanovich, 1977.

Bach, George R., and Wyden, Peter. *The Intimate Enemy*. New York: William Morrow & Co., 1969.

Bell, Robert R. *Marriage and Family Interaction*. Homewood, Ill.: The Dorsey Press, 1967.

Bennis, W. G., Schein, E. H., Steele, F. I., and Berlew, D. E. *Interpersonal Dynamics*. Homewood, Ill.: The Dorsey Press, 1968.

Berkowitz, Leonard. "The Case for Bottling Up Rage," *Psychology Today* (July 1973).

Bestor, Arthur. *Backwoods Utopias*. Philadelphia: University of Pennsylvania Press, 1950.

Blood, Robert O., Jr., and Wolfe, Donald M. *Husbands and Wives: The Dynamics of Married Living*. Glencoe, Ill.: The Free Press, 1960.

Bohannan, Paul. *Divorce and After*. New York: Doubleday and Co., 1970.

Bosco, Antoinette. *Marriage Encounter: The Rediscovery of Love*. St. Meinrad, Ind.: Abbey Press, 1972.

Bossard, James, and Boll, Eleanor. *One Marriage—Two Faiths*. New York: Ronald Press, 1959.

Bowman, Henry A. *Marriage for Moderns*. New York: McGraw-Hill Book Co., 1974.

Broderick, Carlfred B., and Fowler, Stanley E. "New Patterns of Relationships Between the Sexes Among Preadolescents," *Marriage and Family Living* (February 1961).

Bronfenbrenner, Urie. "Nobody Home: The Erosion of the American Family," *Psychology Today* (May 1977).

Buber, Martin. *I and Thou.* New York: Charles Scribner's Sons, 1958.

Burchinal, Lee G. "The Premarital Dyad and Love Involvement," in Harold Christensen (Ed.), *Handbook of Marriage and the Family.* Chicago: Rand McNally & Co., 1964.

Burgess, Ernest. *Marriage Prediction Schedule.* Saluda, N.C.: Family Life Publications.

Cadwallader, Mervyn. "Changing Social Mores," *Current* (February 1967).

Chess, Stella, Thomas, Alexander, and Birch, Herbert. *Your Child Is a Person.* New York: Viking Press, 1965.

Clinebell, Howard J., and Clinebell, Charlotte H. *The Intimate Marriage.* New York: Harper & Row, 1970.

Cox, Frank D. *Human Intimacy: Marriage, the Family and Its Meaning.* St. Paul: West Publishing Co., 1978.

Dreikurs, Rudolf. *Children the Challenge.* New York: Duell, Sloan and Pearce, 1964.

_____. *The Challenge of Marriage.* New York: Duell, Sloan and Pearce, 1946.

Ellis, Albert. "Group Marriage: A Possible Alternative," in Herbert A. Otto (Ed.), *The Family in Search of a Future.* New York: Appleton-Century-Crofts, 1970.

Frankl, Viktor E. *The Unheard Cry for Meaning.* New York: Simon and Schuster, 1978.

Fromme, Allan. *The Ability to Love.* New York: Simon and Schuster (Pocket Books), 1966. (Originally published by Farrar, Straus, & Giroux, New York, 1963, 1965.)

_____. *Understanding the Sexual Response in Humans.* New York: Simon and Schuster, 1966.

Gagnon, John H., & Greenblat, Cathy E. *Designs: Individuals, Marriages, and Families.* Glenview, Ill.: Scott, Foresman and Co., 1978.

Gouldner, A. W. "The Norm of Reciprocity: A Preliminary Statement," *American Sociological Review,* 25 (April 1960).

Hicks, Mary W., and Platt, Marilyn. "Marital Happiness and Stability: A Review of the Research in the Sixties," *Journal of Marriage and the Family* (November 1970).

Hine, James R. *Come Prepared to Stay Forever.* Danville, Ill.: Interstate Printers and Publishers, 1966.

_____. *Marriage Counseling Kit.* Danville, Ill.: Interstate Printers and Publishers, 1970.

_____. *Religious Beliefs Inventory Kit.* Danville, Ill.: Interstate Printers and Publishers, 1970.

_____. *Grounds for Marriage.* Danville, Ill.: Interstate Printers and Publishers, 1971.

_____. *Your Marriage: Analysis and Renewal.* Danville, Ill.: Interstate Printers and Publishers, 1976.

_____. *Will You Make a Wise Marriage Choice?* Danville, Ill.: Interstate Printers and Publishers, 1978.

_____. *Will We Meet Each Other's Needs?* Danville, Ill.: Interstate Printers and Publishers, 1979.

Hodge, Marshall Bryant. *Your Fear of Love.* Garden City, N.Y.: Doubleday and Co., 1967.

James, Muriel H. *Born to Love.* Reading, Mass.: Addison-Wesley Publishing Co., 1973.

————, and Jongeward, Dorothy. *Born to Win: Transactional Analysis with Gestalt Experiments.* Menlo Park, Calif.: Addison-Wesley Publishing Co., 1971.

Kagan, Jerome. *Personality Development.* New York: Harcourt Brace Jovanovich, 1971.

Kaplan, Helen Singer. *The New Sex Therapy.* New York: Brunner/Mazel, 1974.

Kelley, Robert K. *Courtship, Marriage and the Family.* New York: Harcourt Brace Jovanovich, 1974.

Kinsey, Alfred C., Pomeroy, Wardell B., Martin, Clyde E., and Gebhard, Paul H. *Sexual Behavior in the Human Female.* Philadelphia: W. B. Saunders Co., 1953.

Kirkendall, Lester A., in Gertrude Neubeck, "The Myriad Motives for Sex," *Sexual Behavior* (July 1972).

Klemer, Richard H. *Marriage and Family Relationships.* New York: Harper & Row, 1970.

Knox, David. *Exploring Marriage and the Family.* Glenview, Ill.: Scott Foresman and Co., 1979.

Landis, Judson T., and Landis, Mary G. *Building a Successful Marriage.* Englewood Cliffs, N.J.: Prentice-Hall, 1963.

Lederer, William J., and Jackson, Don B. *The Mirages of Marriage.* New York: W. W. Norton & Company, 1968.

Lenski, Gerhard. *The Religious Factor.* New York: Doubleday and Co., 1961.

Levinger, George. "Task and Social Behavior in Marriage," *Sociometry,* Vol. 27 (1964), 433–48.

Lewis, Oscar. *Five Families.* New York: New American Library, 1959.

Lipman, Aaron. "Role Conceptions and Morale of Couples in Retirement," *Journal of Gerontology,* Vol. 16 (1961).

Lyness, Judith L., Lipetz, Milton E., and Davis, Keith E. "Living Together: An Alternative to Marriage," *Journal of Marriage and the Family,* Vol. 34, No. 3 (May 1972).

Mace, David. "Marital Intimacy and the Deadly Love-Anger Cycle." Address at national meeting of Association of Couples for Marriage Enrichment, St. Louis, Mo., October 31, 1974.

————, and Mace, Vera. *Marriage Enrichment Retreats: Story of a Quaker Project.* Philadelphia: Friends General Conference.

————. *We Can Have Better Marriages If We Really Want Them.* Nashville, Tenn.: Abingdon Press, 1974.

May, Rollo. *Love and Will.* New York: Dell Publishing Co. 1973.

McHugh, Gelolo. *Sex Knowledge Inventory.* Saluda, N.C.: Family Life Publications, 1967.

Mead, Margaret. "Marriage in Two Steps," *Redbook Magazine,* Vol. 27 (July 1966). Copyright 1966 by McCall Corporation.

Miller, Sherod, Nunnally, Elam, and Wackman, Daniel. *Alive and Aware.* Minneapolis, Minn.: Interpersonal Communication Programs, Inc.

Montagu, Ashley. *Touching.* New York: Columbia University Press, 1971.

Neugarten, Bernice, Havighurst, Robert, and Tobin, Sheldon. "The Measurement of Satisfaction," *Journal of Gerontology,* Vol. 16 (1961).

Otto, Herbert A. *More Joy in Your Marriage.* New York: Hawthorn Books, 1969.

Peele, Stanton, with Brodsky, Archie. *Love and Addiction.* New York: New American Library, 1976. (Originally published by Taplinger Publishing Company, New York, 1975.)

Perry, John, and Perry, Erna. *Pairing and Parenthood.* San Francisco: Canfield Press, 1977.

Peterman, Dan J., Ridley, Carl A., and Anderson, Scott M. "A Comparison of Cohabiting and Noncohabiting College Students," *Journal of Marriage and the Family,* Vol. 36, No. 2 (May 1974).

Peterson, James A. *Education for Marriage.* New York: Charles Scribner's Sons, 1964.

————. *Married Love in the Middle Years.* New York: Association Press, 1968.

Pineo, Peter C. "Disenchantment in the Later Years of Marriage," *Marriage and Family Living,* Vol. 23 (1961).

Powers, Edward, and Lees, Mary. *Encounter with Family Realities.* New York: West Publishing Co., 1977.

Ramey, James W. "Emerging Patterns of Behavior in Marriage: Deviations or Innovations?" *Journal of Sexual Research,* Vol. 8, No. 1.

Reiss, Ira L. "Toward a Sociology of the Heterosexual Love Relationship," *Marriage and Family Living,* Vol. 22, No. 1 (February 1960).

————. *Family Systems in America.* Hinsdale, Ill.: Dryden Press, 1976.

Roberts, Ann. "Factors in Lifestyle of Couples Married Fifty Years or More in Tucson, Arizona." (Unpublished master's dissertation, University of Arizona, 1975.)

Rogers, Carl. *Carl Rogers on Encounter Groups.* New York: Harper & Row, 1970.

Rubin, Zick. *Liking and Loving: An Invitation to Social Psychology.* New York: Holt, Rinehart and Winston, 1973.

Sager, Clifford J. *Marriage Contracts and Couple Therapy.* New York: Brunner/Mazel, 1976.

Satir, Virginia. "Marriage as a Human-Actualizing Contract," in Herbert Otto (Ed.), *The Family in Search of a Future.* New York: Appleton-Century-Crofts, 1970.

————. *Peoplemarking.* Palo Alto, Calif.: Science and Behavior Books, 1972.

Saxton, Lloyd. *The Individual, Marriage, and the Family.* Belmont, Calif.: Wadsworth Publishing Co., 1977.

Scanzoni, John. *Sexual Bargaining.* Englewood Cliffs, N.J.: Prentice-Hall, 1972.

————, and Scanzoni, Letha. *Men, Women, and Change.* New York: McGraw-Hill Book Co., 1976.

Shulman, Bernard H. "The Uses and Abuses of Sex," *Medical Aspects of Human Sexuality,* Vol. 2, No. 9 (September 1968).

Sullivan, Harry Stack. *Conceptions of Modern Psychiatry.* New York: W. W. Norton and Co., 1946.

Symonds, Percival M. *The Dynamics of Human Adjustment.* New York: D. Appleton-Century Co., 1946.

Terman, Lewis M. *Psychological Factors in Marital Happiness.* New York: McGraw-Hill Book Co., 1938.

Thomas, Alexander, and Chess, Stella. *Temperament and Development.* New York: Brunner/Mazel, 1977.

Tillich, Paul. *The Shaking of the Foundations.* New York: Charles Scribner's Sons, 1948.

————. *Love, Power and Justice.* New York: Oxford University Press, 1960.

Udry, J. Richard. *The Social Context of Marriage.* Philadelphia: J. B. Lippincott Company, 1971.

U.S. Department of Health, Education and Welfare. *Vital Statistics of the United States,* 1968, Vol. III, Marriage and Divorce.

Williamson, Robert C. *Marriage and Family Relations.* New York: John Wiley and Sons, 1972.